AF114515

THE PUBLISHERS' ADVERTISEMENT.

WE present this book to students, teachers, and the literary public generally, as one which, for both its subject-matter and its style of composition, will be found to be full of enchanting interest. As for our part, we have spared no expense in respect to typography, paper, and mechanical execution, to make it in appearance equal to its own inward merits in fact. While it abounds in learning, it is also written in a spirited *con amore* style. It is the result of the author's enthusiastic devotion for years, to a new and great science, which one of the first linguists of the country has justly said, "may almost be called *the science of the age*." It has been prepared on the basis of several articles published at different times in The Bibliotheca Sacra, at Andover, and The New Englander, at New Haven; which have since been re-written and greatly enlarged and improved, and are accompanied with philological maps and tabular views of great interest. In their original although abbreviated form they attracted great attention in many directions, not only for the scholarship and research displayed in them, but also for the beauty of their style of composition, which has been lavishly commended by many of our best scholars and writers as "clear and vigorous," "earnest and spirited," "beautiful," "attractive," "elegant," "fascinating," and "brilliant," and placing Mr. Dwight, in the language of still another, "among the most eminent writers of the day."

We believe that no book has appeared from the press in our country for a long time that will command in itself a larger and more eager reception than this. It supplies a great desideratum to the students of language among us, young and old; as, with the other works that are to follow it from the author's pen, it will make the study of the science of Philology not only feasible but also delightful to scholars; and will give to multitudes of our literary men especially, who know enough of the discoveries of modern Philology to desire to know more, the opportunity to gratify that desire upon a scale that they will greatly value.

The book is likewise fitted not only for general reading, but also for study and recitation, in schools and colleges, like any of our best school histories, and will be held in high account for historical, philosophical, linguistic and even rhetorical purposes alike, wherever it is so used. Its preparation has been hailed, and indeed solicited in advance by several leading teachers in different States, from the felt want of such a help to a higher style of linguistic study, than hitherto.

We subjoin a few of the notices taken of the original articles as they appeared from time to time, which have incidentally come to hand.

" We have read Mr. Dwight's essay on ' The Indo-European Languages,' in the Bibliotheca Sacra, with great pleasure : the style giving attractiveness to the instruction of a subject removed from the ordinary line of thought. We commend it not only to classical scholars, who will hail new light in comparative grammar, lexicography, and ethnology, but to ministers generally and the still larger community of general scholars who abound in our country."—*Independent.*

" This is an article (the same) of great value, showing careful and scholarly investigation."—*Evangelist.*

" This is an able and instructive discussion."—*The Intelligencer.*

" This admirable essay ('The Science of Etymology') is to appear, as we understand, together with other kindred articles written by Mr. Dwight for the Bibliotheca Sacra, in a published volume ; and we believe we speak the sentiments of those who are conversant with this important but recondite subject, when we say that the *forthcoming book will be a valuable and honorable addition to American literature.*"—*New York Observer.* (By Dr. John J. Owen, *Professor in the Free Academy.*)

"*The History of Modern Philology.*—The science of philology is assuming so much importance in its relations to historical questions and to the great problem of the unity of the race, that the general scholar must at least comprehend its principles, and keep pace with its results. The sketch of the history of Philology in the New Englander, from the competent and practised hand of Mr. Dwight, will be of much service to readers not versed in the science itself."—*Independent.*

"I have read with much pleasure Mr. Dwight's articles in the Bibliotheca Sacra. I am also informed that he has a work in preparation on philology. If suited to my purposes I would be glad to use it as a text-book in my higher classes."—C. W. Smythe, *Catawba College, North Carolina.*

"I have examined with great interest Mr. Dwight's essays on Philology, in reference to using them in our seminary; and I am convinced that they will be invaluable to our students, not only for their views of the historical unity and principles of climatic change in language, but for their philosophic generalizations. I therefore earnestly hope that they will be published in a form adapted to our classes."—Mrs. Sarah L. Willard, *Principal of the Troy Female Seminary.*

"Mr. Dwight's views show such rare and extensive research, the results of such discrimination and analysis, of such historical, ethnological, and philosophical acquaintance with words, languages, roots, branches, themes and their logical and comprehensive classifications, ancient, very ancient, and modern, European and Asiatic, that we have been feasted as well as strengthened and enlightened with their consecutive display, and congratulate the public as well as ourselves, in prospect of their gathered riches being permanently communicated from the press, in a practical form for general use, in all our learned institutions."—Rev. Dr. Samuel H. Cox, *Ingham University.*

"I did not know who in this country could have written the article in the New Englander, on Modern Philology, without hashing it up from other authors. It would seem to be quite within the range of Mr. Dwight. How he can do so much an invalid like me can hardly see."—Professor Francis A. March, *Lafayette College, Penn.*

"I am delighted to learn that Mr. Dwight intends to bring out all his articles on philology together in one work. I shall look for it with great eagerness."—Edward P. Crowell, Professor of Latin, *Amherst College.*

'I have read several articles in the Bibliotheca Sacra, by Mr. Dwight, and am greatly pleased with the earnest and spirited manner in which they are written, as well as with the thorough research which they display. He owes it to the cause of education to collect and enlarge them somewhat, and prepare them for publication in a book. They would form, I think, a text-book in many schools, and be welcomed by hundreds of private readers and learners. *Such a work would really supply a desideratum.* I feel exceedingly gratified that he has turned his attention and devoted so much labor to this important branch of science, which indeed may be almost regarded as the science of the age. He must let the world have the benefit of his labors."—Asahel C. Kendrick, D. D., Professor of Greek, *Rochester University.*

"The articles published by Mr. Dwight, I have enjoyed much. They show a wide range of study, and a fine appreciation of the great laws and principles of language. The republication of them in a separate form will be a valuable service to the cause of philology."—Samuel H. Taylor, LL. D., Principal of Phillips' Academy, *Andover, Mass.*

A. S. BARNES & BURR,

51 & 53 JOHN STREET, NEW YORK.

DWIGHT'S

MODERN PHILOLOGY.

MODERN PHILOLOGY:

Its Discoveries

HISTORY AND INFLUENCE,

WITH

MAPS, TABULAR VIEWS, AND AN INDEX.

BY

BENJAMIN W. DWIGHT,
AUTHOR OF "THE HIGHER CHRISTIAN EDUCATION."

NEW YORK:
A. S. BARNES & BURR, 51 & 53 JOHN STREET.
1859.

Entered, according to Act of Congress, in the year 1859, by
A. S. BARNES & BURR,
In the Clerk's Office of the District Court of the United States for the Southern District of New York.

TABLE OF CONTENTS.

I.

HISTORICAL SKETCH OF THE INDO-EUROPEAN LANGUAGES.

	PAGE.
Introduction, with List of Authors consulted	5–10
Philosophic Divisions of Languages	14
Peculiarities of Chinese Languages	15
The Agglutinative Languages	16–180
The Inflected Languages	18–190
Other Possible Classifications	19–20
The Semitic Languages	20–28
Connection of Hebrew and Phœnician Languages	20–22
Contrasts of the Semitic and Indo-European	22–25
Influence of Judaism on Indo-Europeanism	25–27
Climatic Influences	27
Area of Indo-European Development	28
Classification of Indo-European Languages	29
I. The Arian Family-pair	29–48
Arian Migrations	31
Arian Climatology	32
1st. The Indian Family	32–45
(1) The Sanskrit	32–42
Vêdic Sanskrit and Vêdas	33–40
Devanagari Alphabet	36–40
Pali and Pråkrit Dialects	41–43
(2) The Gypsy Language	43–45
Gypsy Correspondences	44
2d. The Iranian Family	45
(1) Zend, Zend Avesta, &c.	45–47
(2) Old Persian, (3) Pehlevi, (4) Pazend, (5) New Persian	47
3d. The Ossetian; 4th. The Armenian	48

CONTENTS.

	PAGE.
II. Græco-Italic Family-pair	48–112
1st. The Greek Family	49–68
False Theory of Connections of Greek and Latin	49
Dialectic Developments of the Greek	50
Greek and Latin Correspondences	52
The Pelasgic or Pioneer Period	53–54
The Hellenic or Classic Period	54–6
Value of an Early History of Asia Minor	56
Language as a Mass of Ethnologic Records	57
Zend, Welsh, and Greek Correspondences	58
Area of Greek Development	60
Philological Value of Homeric Poems	61
Giese's Sketch of Pre-Hellenic Period	62–63
The Romaic or Modern Greek	64
The Albanian Language	65
Albanian Correspondences	66
Schleicher's Historical Epochs of the Greek	67
Greek Climatology	68
2d. The Italic Family	70–112
(1) Iapygians, (2) Etruscans	70–74
(3) Italians	74–97
Italic Home-growth	74–75
(a) Umbro-Samnite Dialects	75–79
(b) Latin	79–112
Latin Climatology	80–82
Peculiarities of Roman Mind	82
§ 1. Historical View of Latin Language and Literature	83–96
Classical Latin	83–85
Middle Latin	85–87
Romanic Dialects	87–112
Germanic Influences on Romanic Languages	83–93
Specimens of Ante-Mediæval Latin	94
Do. Græco-Romanic Elements	95
Do. Germano-Romanic do.	95
§ 2. The Romanic Languages	97–112
(1) The Italian and its Literature	97–99
(2) The Wallachian do.	99–100
(3) The Spanish do.	100–105
(4) The Portuguese do.	105–107
(5) The Provençal do.	107–108
(6) The French do.	108–111
Correspondences in Romanic Languages.	112

CONTENTS. iii

	PAGE.
III. The Lettic Family	113–117
1st. The Lithuanian and its Peculiarities	113–115
2d. The Old Prussian	116
3d. The Lettish	116
IV. The Slavic Family	117–130
Historical Eras of this Family	117
Their Internal Connections	118
Their Different Alphabets: Cyrillic, Roman, Hieronymic	119
First. South-Eastern Slavic	120
1st. The Russian and its Literature	121–3
2d. The Bulgarian do.	123–4
3d. The Servian do.	125
Second. Western Slavic	126–130
Slavonic Correspondences	126
1st. The Lechish: Poland and the Polish	127–128
2d. The Tschechish, 3d. the Sorbish, 4th. the Polabish	128
The Area of Slavism and its Neighborhood	129
V. The Gothic or Germanic Family	130–150
The First Historical Appearance of the Goths	130–131
1st. The Low German	132–145
(1) The Norse Languages, Old and New	132–133
(2) The Anglo-Saxon	133–143
History of the Anglo-Saxons	134
Elements of the English Language	134–138
Its Greatest of Authors: Shakspeare	136
Its Comparison with German	137
Its Correspondences with Sanskrit	138–9
Its Orthoepical and Orthographical Peculiarities	140
American Provincialisms	140–3
(3) The Frisic, (4) the Low Dutch	144–146
2d. The High German	145–151
Etymology of the Word German	146
Peculiarities of the German	147
Different Eras of its Development	147
Luther's Influence upon it	148
Its Comparison with the English	149
VI. The Celtic	
Prichard's, Jones', and Bunsen's Views	151
Early Westward Movements of the Celts	152
Celtic Poetry: Ossian, &c.	153

iv CONTENTS.

	PAGE.
Present Remains of Celtic	154
Present Geographical Position of Celts	155
Celtic Correspondences	156
1st. The Kymric Languages	156-158
2d. The Gadhelic do.	157-159
Comparison of Welsh and Irish Numerals	159
Celtic and Sanskrit Correspondences	160
Inferences: 1st. Unity of the Race	161
2d. Power of Physical Influences	163
3d. Smallness of Man's Inventiveness	164-176
Origin of Language as Divine	168
Development-Theory of Word-germs	168-174
Max Müller's Theory of its Human Origin	173-175
Bunsen's Theory of Millennial Periods	176
4th. Each Language to be Studied in its Connections	177-179
Value of Scientific Etymology	177
Sanskrit Philology in the University-Course	178
Tabular Views	181-190

II.

HISTORY OF MODERN PHILOLOGY.

Philology: its Meaning and Different Phases	192
Grammar and the Alexandrian Grammarians	194
Influence of the Reformation on Modern Scholarship	195
State of Linguistic Culture in the 18th Century	197
Infidel Attempts to Pervert Philology	198
Leibnitz the Early Prophet of Philology	199
Efforts of Catharine II. of Russia	199
Formation of Asiatic Society	200
Adelung's Mithridates	200
Indo-Europeanism *versus* Indo-Germanism	201
Sanskrit Literature: its Character, &c.	202
East India Company: Halhed, Jones	203
First English Translations of Sanskrit	204
Colebrooke, H. H. Wilson	205
Frederic Schlegel: the Man and his Services	206-9
Augustus W. Schlegel, his Brother	210-2
Bopp's First Philological Work	212
Rask: his Travels and Researches	212-215
Jacob Grimm's Teutonic Grammar	215
His Scale of Correspondences	216-218

CONTENTS. v
                                                                                PAGE.

His Present Labors.................................... 218–219
Francis Bopp: his Great Learning and Great Deeds. 219–225
A. F. Pott, as a Philologist..... 225
William Humboldt......................... 226
Burnouf and Eichhoff in France, 1836).... 227–230
Albert Giese's Æolischer Dialekt.... 230
Benary and Höfer................. 231–232
Ahrens on the Conjugation in—μι. 233
Düntzer and Kaltschmidt.. 234
Diefenbach and Schleicher............................. 235
George Curtius and Diez.............................. 236–237
Diez's View of Philology............................... 238
Present Condition of Philology in Germany................ 239
Ernst Curtius and Theodore Mommsen.................. 240
Zeitschrift für Vergleich. Sprachforschung................ 241
Aufrecht, Kirchhoff, and Benfey......................... 241
Heyse, Kuhn, and Weber.............................. 242–243
Rapp's Grammar and Phonography...................... 244–5
Rapp and Diez Compared.... 246
Fritsch on Particles.................................... 247
Sanskrit Philology in England.......................... 248
Prichard and Rosen.................................... 249
Donaldson: his Learning, Labors, and Vanity 250–2
Winning's Comparative Philology....................... 252–4
Richard Garnett's Articles.... 255
Max Müller's Survey of Languages...................... 255
Bunsen's Phil. Universal History....................... 256
English Writers on Teutonic Elements in English.......... 256–257
State of Philology in America.......................... 257
Philological Authors Compared together................. 258
Philology Arranged according to Subjects................ 258–259
Relative State of Philology in Different Countries of Europe 260
Classical Philology, as such............................ 260–263
Heyne, Buttmann, Döderlein............................ 261–262
Inferences: 1st. The Charms of Linguistic Study.......... 264
        2d. Resolution of Grammatical Difficulties........ 266–268
        3d. The Relative Imperishableness of Language... 268
        4th. The Scope of Analogy in Language 269
        5th. The Mutual Connection of Languages......... 269
        6th The Light Shed by Philology on Ethnography 270
Weber's Sketch of Primeval Arian History................ 272–274

III.

SCIENCE OF ETYMOLOGY.

	PAGE.
I. The General Proportions and Relations of the Subject	278–287
English Etymology Dependent on Classical	278
The Real Connections of all Languages	279–281
The Peculiar Philological Relations of the Latin	282
The Great Breadth of English Etymology	284
Our Present Languages but Linguistic Herbariums	285
II. The History of Etymology	287–311
1st. Its Popular Empirical Treatment	287–289
Ancient Legends and Mythology	288
False Etymologies of a Recent Sort	289
2d. Its Literary Empirical Treatment	290–306
The Theory of the Derivation of Latin from Greek	291
L. Ross's Recent Attempts to Revive it	292
History of Lexicography, (Latin, Greek, and English)	292–311
Freund's Latin Dictionary	293–297
Schwenck's and Valpy's Dictionary	297
Jäkel and Nork's Ideas of Latin, &c.	297
Klotz's New Latin Dictionary	299
Passow, Pape, and Kaltschmidt in Greek Lexicography	300–301
Webster's English Dictionary	302–306
3d. Its Exact Scientific Treatment	306–311
The Grimms' Great German Dictionary	306–308
Indo-Europeanism Essential to all Etymology	309
Etymology an Inductive Science	311
III. The Constituent Elements of Etymology as a Science	311–331
1st. Those of Comparative Etymology	312–327
(1) Comparative Phonology	312–322
(2) Comparative Lexicography	322–325
(3) Comparative Grammar	325–327
Criteria of Relative Antiquity of Languages	326–327
2d. Those of Specific Etymology	328–331
(1) The Originals of Words	328
(2) Comparative Forms	328
(3) Derived Forms	329
(4) Interior Logical Etymology	329

CONTENTS.

	PAGE.
IV. Determinate Tests of Etymology	331–337
1st. Of Comparative Etymology	332–333
(1) Correspondence in Base or Theme	332
(2) Minute Mutual Resemblances	332
(3) Euphonic Laws of Definite Scope	332
(4) Certain Specific Axioms	333
2d. Of Specific Etymology	333–337
(1) The Genius of the Language	333–334
(2) Naturalness of Derivation	335
(3) Determinate Archaic Forms	335
(4) Double Forms	335–336
(5) Dialectic Changes and Differences	337
V. Advantages of the Study of Etymology	337–347
1st. The High Pleasure of it	338–341
2d. Its Advancement of the Higher Mental Discipline	341–344
3d. Its Value in Acquiring Power of Speech	344–347

INTRODUCTION.

It has been the Author's pastime for several years, to employ himself in the study of Comparative Philology. When wearied by the many toils of his profession, as a teacher, he has found constant refreshment or exhilaration rather, day by day, in devoting his attention to the history, literature, researches and results of this new Science. No study is more pleasing or profitable to a classical scholar, or even to a general student of an earnest type, than that of Modern Philology : so multiform are its relations, so surprising its discoveries, and so splendid the train of its attending influences. The excitement of perpetual effort to find its hidden wonders, keeps ever growing unto the end.

The Author has written what he has, because he

must: necessity has been upon him: the fire kindled within his heart has found its own vent: he could not keep to himself the pleasure that he constantly experienced, in his pathway of investigation. And if his papers had all perished by accident, after the careful preparation of years, the pleasure of the ever-present intention cherished and executed with patient, hopeful, happy toil so long, to participate with as many as possible the bliss that had welled-up, all the time, in his own silent heart unknown to others, would have still glowed on undimmed, as a great permanent fact to him in his life-work: illuminating not only the whole conscious past, as it was transpiring, but also the memory of it when gone forever from the view. He would have still testified to his own ear, if not to others, that verily it is more blessed to give than to receive. If the student finds but a moiety of the gratification, in the results here reached or announced, which the author himself has experienced; and surely it can be but a moiety of his, in either time or degree: he will enjoy still another pleasure in his philological labors, which will crown all those received before with its own added light and beauty.

No one, who has not undertaken such a work, can have any just conception of the amount of thought and time, requisite to pass in thorough critical review the great number of facts, principles and relations, pertaining to the many topics connected with the science of comparative philology; and the processes of close, severe analysis, discrimination, comparison and judgment, to be repeated over and over again, from every possible angle of observation, in order to come to a clear and stable decision of matters having so many elements of separate and connected interest. But the joy has all the time more than equalled the toil.

Should any think, that the rhetorical element is allowed, perchance, too free play to any degree in affairs of such high science, the plea is offered in self-defence, that, whatever there may be of it, came spontaneously from the depths of the subject itself; which is full to the brim of its own lively appeals both to the reason and the imagination. Nor does the Author think, in introducing this new study, so favorite in Germany, to the regards of the great community of general scholars here, who are just beginning to open their eyes upon its charms, that he should ruthlessly strip it of all its blossoming fulness of beauty, in order to show in more sharp and unclothed outline, to eyes that relish dissected rather than living forms, the mere unadorned framework of its branches. Nor could he think of inviting, exclusively, mere technical scholars in philology to the literary banquet which he would fain provide for them: fit audience, indeed, if small; because of the very limited number who have as yet acquired, in this country, any complete special knowledge of its facts and principles. His purpose has been, on the contrary, to do what he could to attract the greatest possible number of eyes to the glory of the New Philology.

The articles composing the present volume were published: the first and third, at different times, in the Bibliotheca Sacra, and the second in the New Englander; and were much compressed in their details, in order to adapt their length to the limits of those valuable Quarterlies. They have been all since carefully rewritten and enlarged, and particularly the first, which is now of more than twice its previous dimensions and value. The maps and tabular views of the different languages and index of contents will aid much, it is believed, in the comprehension of the whole subject.

The Author loves to look hopefully, upon the sure and speedy progress of American scholarship to heights of attainment almost unthought of now. We are not to be always spoken of lightly as mere borrowers of others, and as accomplishing at the best only superficial results. There is, in the qualities of activity, enter-

INTRODUCTION. 9

prise, ingenuity and endurance, that distinguish us as a people, a substantial preparation for the highest scientific and artistic development of the American mind and character, in all the varied departments of scholarly acquisition. So many of our finest minds are ere long not to be led, as now, like oxen garlanded for sacrifice, to the altars of Mammon; and American scholarship, like American literature, which has hitherto surpassed it in the signals of its growth and greatness that it has waved exulting before the nations, is to stand up in the highest proportions, attained among any people, for breadth and strength and beauty of aspect, in the sight of an admiring world.

If this humble effort may suffice to kindle any new enthusiasm among the younger scholars of the land, who are just lighting their torches at the fires, which other hands, now growing feeble from age, have kindled: to God alone, who has given all the strength, resources and opportunities for doing so, be the glory and the praise.

Dwight's Rural High School,
Clinton, Oneida Co., N. Y., July 1, 1859.

AMONG the Authors consulted in the preparation of the first article, are the following:—

Grote's History of Greece; Smith's do.; Niebuhr's History of Rome; Niebuhr's Lectures on Ancient History; Brown's History of Greek Classical Literature; Brown's Roman Classical Literature; Donaldson's New Cratylus; Donaldson's Varronianus; Taylor's Ancient History; Bunsen's Philosophy of Universal History; Bopp's Comparative Grammar, by Eastwick; Bopp's Vergleichende Grammatik (Neue Auflage); Rapp's do.; Eichhoff's Vergleichung der Sprachen; Grimm's Geschichte der Deutschen Sprache; Diefenbach's Gothisches Wörterbuch; Giese's Aeolischer Dialekt; Mommsen's Römische Geschichte; Schleicher's Geschichte der Sprachen Europa's; Heyse's System der Sprachwissenschaft; Diez' Grammatik der Roman. Sprachen; Ahrens' De Linguæ Græcæ Dialectis; Aufrecht's Umbrischen Sprachdenkmäler; Lersch's Sprachphilosophie; Winning's Comparative Philology; Garnett's Philological Essays; Monier Williams' Sanskrit Grammar; Kuhn's Beiträge zur Sprachforschung; Gesenii Monumenta; Max Müller's Survey of Languages; Asiatic Researches; Frederic Schlegel's Æsthetical Works; Prichard's Natural History of Man; Prichard's Eastern Origin of the Celtic Nations; Journal of American Oriental Society; Du Cange's Glossarium; Gibbon's Decline and Fall of the Roman Empire; Gieseler's Ch. Hist.; Buckle's Hist. of Civilization in England; Blair's Chronology; etc., etc.

I.

AN HISTORICAL SKETCH OF THE INDO-EUROPEAN LANGUAGES.

MODERN PHILOLOGY.

I.

AN HISTORICAL SKETCH OF THE INDO-EUROPEAN LANGUAGES.

THE design of the following essay, is not to enter into the details of ethnography, as such, except so far as they may subserve directly the one object, of better unfolding the connection and growth of different languages; or, to give any distinct history of the literature of each language, but to adhere closely to the text furnished in its title. For the same reason, neither chronology nor geography occupy any very conspicuous position. While it has required, at times, as much effort in the selection of materials, to determine what to reject as what to employ; it will be found, it is hoped, that the golden mean has been attained, between too great diffuseness on the one hand and too much condensation on the other.

It is not an easy task for curious minds to learn, to leave dark what is dark, and to state supposed facts with no more assurance, than the actual evidence of their existence, according to the most careful measurement of its dimensions, justifies. Almost all earnest writers, accordingly, on the early history of nations and of languages, have undertaken to be luminous amid obscure data, and to interpret the past in the same style of self-confident certainty, in which the interpreters of prophecy usually open the scroll of revelation for the future. The great Niebuhr, and more recently the lesser Donaldson, strikingly exemplify this tendency.

But it is still more difficult for a generous mind, to conceal within itself some new light that serves greatly to illuminate and cheer its own vision; and from weak, unmanly over-caution, to understate truths that deserve a large and bold utterance.

The terms of comparison between different languages are limited, of course, to that mere moiety of words which is preserved to us in books. Could that other large portion of each language, when in its fullest state of expansion, which is now lost to us, be recovered, many of the results that are gained by philological analysis would receive an assurance and an amplification, which would be grand in both their proportions and their benefits.

The different languages of the world may be arranged philosophically, in three great classes:

1. Those, consisting of mere separate, unvaried monosyllables, like the Chinese. There are no lan-

THE INDO-EUROPEAN LANGUAGES. 15

guages of this kind, but the Chinese and a few Indo-Chinese languages in its neighborhood, as the Brahman, Siamese, &c., which were originally without doubt identical with it. In exact antipodes to the monosyllabism of this class of languages, stands the polysyllabism of the North American languages, with their wonderful tendencies to concatenated formations: for which reason they have sometimes been called the polysynthetic languages; and yet, in their interior grammatical constitution, both of these classes of languages are of the same general grade of character. The words composing the Chinese language are all so many distinct monads unrelated to each other, and without any organization that adapts them for mutual affiliation. There is, accordingly, an utter absence of all scientific forms and principles of grammar, in a language thus composed of a mere congeries of separate units. Each word therefore exists, in a close, sharply defined, permanent status of its own; and that play of light and shade, which words, containing each so many different senses, possess in other languages, is here lost. Some fifty thousand characters are accordingly employed in the Chinese tongue, to express the wants of speech. These are some of them simply pictorial still; while others are idiographic now in their form, although many, if not most, of this class are probably but abbreviations of original pictorial representations of the object described. That class of theorists, who account for the origin of language, as others do of nature, by what is termed the development-theory, love to represent language as having been at the first in the same crude inorganic state, in which we now find the Chinese: conceiving of it, as they do, as a mere human invention or rather incident, a sort of wild indigenous product of the social state. Language as such, on the contrary is, it is believed, a beautiful piece of Divine mechanism: contrived by Him who made man, and who made him to speak both to Himself and to his fellows; and therefore the nearer to its first beginnings that we ascend in our investigations, the more full and complete we find it in its forms.

2. Those formed by agglutination. This is an advance on the preceding in style of construction, as here words do show some appetency and affinity for each other, although in the simplest of all modes of combination: mere cohesion. Such are the Tatar, Finnish, Lappish, Hungarian and Caucasian languages: sometimes called the Nomadic or Turanian languages. Words in these languages combine, without any elective affinity, in but a mere mechanical way. They have not toward each other, either any of the active, or any of the sensitive receptive, capabilities of living organisms. Prepositions are joined in them to substantives, and pronouns to verbs, as if flexion-endings; but never so as to make a new form of the original word, as in the inflective languages. The words thus placed in

THE INDO-EUROPEAN LANGUAGES. 17

juxtaposition, still retain each of them their own personal identity unimpaired. These languages are thus classified in one group, almost exclusively on the ground of correspondence in their grammatical structure, rather than of any additional lexical agreement. Rask, Castren and Gabelentz, the great investigators of the Turanian languages, all unite in testifying that they are bound together by ties of far less strength than the Indo-European; while they also maintain with equal firmness, that they all belong fundamentally to one race. This race has, from the first, occupied more of the surface of the earth, than either of the others; as, in nature hitherto, the aggregate extent of wilderness has always been greater than that of the gardens of the world. Like the Chinese language, the Tatar family of languages reigns over an immense territory in Asia; and covers with its folds the Mantchoos, Mongols, and the whole wide-spread Turkish race in the east, and in the west the Finnish, Lappish and Magyar tribes of men: stretching westward, from the shores of the Japan Sea to the neighborhood of Vienna; and southward, from the northern Arctic Ocean to Affghanistan and the southern coasts of Asia Minor. The Caucasian languages lie spread out between the Black and Caspian seas; and are historically too insignificant to deserve much attention. One of these, the Abchasic, is said to be the lowest of all this class of languages, in its grammatical constitution : having no flexion of the noun, and no distinction of number or person in the verb.

The agglutinative languages have some special peculiarities that are quite remarkable. One, is the arrangement of governed words before those governing them ; so that even prepositions are placed after, instead of before, the nouns in regimen with them, and are properly therefore postpositional in their character. Another, is the law of vowel-harmony, by which added syllables are made to correspond, as being hard, middle or soft, with the vowels of the radical syllables.

3. The inflected languages. These are all of a complete interior organization : complicated with many mutual relations and adaptations, and thoroughly systematized in all their parts. There is all the difference between this class and the monosyllabic, that there is between organic and inorganic forms of matter ; as also the difference between them and the agglutinative languages is like that in nature between mineral accretions and vegetable growths. In their history lies embosomed that of the civilized portions of the world. The boundaries of this class of languages are the boundaries of cultivated humanity. The languages of Africa, which have been but recently revealed to European eyes by missionary zeal, are, especially the Congo and Bechuana families of them, deserving to a considerable degree of the title of inflected languages, but only in limited forms and directions. Words are linked together in

THE INDO-EUROPEAN LANGUAGES. 19

continued discourse by a few prefixes, suffixes and inserted syllables of a simple sort: the same suffix being duplicated on the connecting as well as on the connected word; so that the style of inflection is one which would seem to a cultivated, logical, artistic grammarian of the Grecian and Latin school, to be in many cases but a piece of tawdry syntactical patchwork.

The classification which we have presented of the various languages of the world, is based on their outward differences of form. In reference to their inward structural differences, they might be divided into two great families: 1. The ungrammatical, as the Chinese and North American. 2. The grammatical or organic languages, namely, the Semitic, the Indo-European and the Turanian. The great basis of identity in each of these classes of languages lies in the fact, that they are inflected in the same way respectively, or, which is the same thing, that the grammar of each class is identical in all the families of the class. In respect to their phenomenal or historical differences, they are capable of still another arrangement: 1. Those which have utterly perished, and they must have been many. 2. Those called "dead;" or those that, like the Sanskrit, Hebrew, Greek, Latin and Gothic, are no more used in the daily commerce of men's thoughts and wants, but are yet preserved in books in all their ancient strength and beauty. 3. The living languages of the world.

Two great races, speaking inflected languages, have

shared between them the peopling of the historic portions of the earth : the Semitic and the Indo-European. On this account their languages have sometimes been called the political or state-languages of the world, in contrast with the appellation of the Turanian as Nomadic. In each of the three great classes of languages : the monosyllabic, the agglutinated and the inflected, there may be found isolated instances of forms that occur in characteristic abundance in the others. Thus, both monosyllabic and agglutinated forms occur in the inflected languages; and yet the distinctions described separate the different classes, in the mass, quite absolutely from each other.

The Semitic family of languages consists of three principal divisions : the Hebrew, the Aramæan and the Arabic.* With the Hebrew, the leading ancient language of the Semitic family, the Canaanitish or Phœnician language stands in the most intimate relation. Canaan was the primitive home of the Hebrew tongue. It was a spoken language in Judea from the days of Moses (B. C. 1500) to those of Nehemiah (B. C. 450). It was essentially the language of the Phœnician race, by whom Palestine was inhabited before

* To the Arabic belongs also the Ethiopic, as a branch of the Southern Arabic. The Aramæan is called Syriac in the form in which it appears in the Christian Aramæan literature; but Chaldee, as it exists in the Aramæan writings of the Jews; and this is still spoken by some tribes near Damascus and by the Nestorian Koords. To the Chaldee is closely allied the Samaritan.

the immigration of Abraham's posterity. It became the adopted language of his descendants, and was transferred with them to Egypt and brought back to Canaan. Whatever variations there may have been in the speech of those dwelling in Tyre and Sidon, compared with that of the inhabitants of Jerusalem, they were very slight. Even the language of Numidia is supposed by Gesenius, to have been pure, or nearly pure Hebrew.* The remaining fragments, accordingly, of the Phœnician and Punic languages agree with the Hebrew. The Semitic languages were native in the countries lying between the Mediterranean, the Armenian mountains, the Tigris and the southern coast of Arabia; or, in other words, in South-western Asia. The Arabic is the only present living language, of any great importance, belonging to this family. Since the conquest of Syria and Palestine, in the middle of the seventh century, it has swept from its presence, as with a

---

* Augustine, himself a native Carthaginian, said in his day, that "the Hebrew and Carthaginian languages differ but little. The Hebrew, Carthaginian and Phœnician languages, are of one origin and character." So Hieronymus: "The Carthaginian language is, to a great extent, allied with the Hebrew; and is said, indeed, to flow forth from the fountains of the Hebrew." Gesenius himself adds, that "this is to be thoroughly maintained, that the Phœnician language, in the main, and indeed as to almost every thing, agrees with the Hebrew, whether you consider their roots or the mode of forming and inflecting their words: a point which it is superfluous to illustrate with examples." Gesenii Monumenta, § 3. Chap. " Linguæ Phœniciæ indoles et cum Hebræa necessitudo."

breath of flame, the Hebrew and the Syriac in their own native dwelling-place. This language now covers, with its mantle of Oriental beauty, a large part of Western Asia and Northern Africa. It exhibits also in the Maltese, which is but a dialect of the Arabic, a solitary representative of itself in Europe. Like the German in the western world in so many other respects, this Eastern language is like it also in this, that it has diffused its elements wonderfully among the constituents of many surrounding languages: as the Turkish, the New Persian and Syriac; while, in Europe also, it has left its impress ineffaceably on the Spanish language, upon whose features, as well as upon the face of whose literature, the Moorish tint is unmistakable. In its grammatical system or inward constitution, it affords, at the same time, both the most normal and the most improved style of structure of all the Semitic languages. The Hebrew, when compared with it in respect to either its grammar or its lexical resources, is decidedly inferior.

The Semitic languages differ widely from the Indo-European, in reference to their grammar, vocabulary and idioms. The consonantal system, for example, of all the Semitic languages is singular in the fact, that every root consists of three letters; while, in the other great families of languages, they may be of one, two, or three, and are indeed seldom of three. And yet, although the Semitic and Indo-European families do not stand in any close relationship to each other, a remote connection between them cannot be denied. So far as yet traced, the Semitic seems to be the elder family of the two, but its limits and its functions have ever been of a far narrower range. The old Egyptian, one of this family, is the most ancient language now known. It was a form of speech that seems to have had force enough in itself, to rise, like the sun emerging from a bank of mist, just out of a state of mere monosyllabic development. Every thing, indeed, Egyptian was from the first strangely unique, and was petrified by physical or moral causes, when but half complete, beyond the power of further change. We have been also recently informed of other ante-historical branches of the Semitic family, beside the old Egyptian, as of the old Assyrian and Babylonian. Clay tablets have been found by thousands at Nineveh, containing treatises on almost every subject, and also grammars, dictionaries, histories and works on geography, astronomy and painting: "presenting," as Rawlinson, one of its explorers, remarks, "a perfect cyclopædia of Assyrian science." So also the characters found on the bricks in the disentombed palaces at Babylon have been clearly proved to be Semitic. These antique languages lived and died, in the darkness of an otherwise utterly unmemorialized past.

Indo-European literature, although not of so high antiquity as the Semitic, far surpasses it in variety, flexibility, beauty, strength and luxuriance. The ultimate roots of the Semitic tongues are few in number; and the formation of words by prefixes and affixes is simple, and in most cases similar; while, in the Indo-European, we have a range and style of words and inflections adapted to the truest and finest possible expression of thought of whatever height or depth, or of whatever scope or bearing.

The Semitic languages might justly be called, on a general scale of comparison, the metaphorical languages, on account of the great preponderance in them of the pictorial element; and the Indo-European, the philosophical languages, as descriptive of the prevailing style of their higher literature. The two living languages of these two great families that most resemble each other, in combining, to a high degree, both the philosophical and pictorial element in their natural constitution and literature, are the Arabic and the German. The Semitic nations have had either a stronger love of place and of home than the Indo-European, or a greater aversion to effort and adventure; since, with the exception of the Arabians, whose spirit of conquest, like that of the Turks of the Turanian family, must be ascribed to the fierce propagandist influence of Mohammedism, they have ever dwelt within close narrow bounds, while in them, however, they have often manifested intense energy. In hieroglyphs, the Semitic mind first recorded its thoughts and wants and achievements, in ancient Egypt; and afterwards another branch of the same family, the Phœnicians, foremost in their day in commerce and the arts, invented alphabetic letters of which all the world has since made use. The Semitic nations also first ripened in arts and arms; but, like precocious children, early failed to yield the fruit that they had promised. The Semitic and Indo-European families are complementary to each other in their characteristics; and almost as strongly so as are the masculine and feminine constitution of mind, respectively, to each other.

What influence the Semitic family, especially the religionized Judaic portion of it, has had directly or indirectly on the development of any or all of the Indo-European family, it would be a matter of capital interest, were there sufficient data for such an examination, to investigate and decide. There are a few streaks of light, at any rate, upon this subject, visible in the horizon of history. Babylonia was greatly influenced by Judaic commerce, religion and literature, as early as the days of Solomon (B. C. 1000). Phœnicia also, over which reigned contemporaneously with him King Hiram, the grandfather of Dido, who founded Carthage, was, both by its proximity and the sameness of its language, brought powerfully under Hebrew influence. Persia was filled with Jews, as we know, in the days of Daniel, Ezra, Nehemiah and Queen Esther, in the fourth, fifth and sixth centuries before Christ. What quickening influences and what new ideas were thus set in motion, throughout these various countries, and indeed throughout also India in the East, Egypt and Arabia on the South, and even Greece in the West, who can say? They must, indeed, have been many and great. Judea was designed, like all the rest of God's works, to have the chief ends and uses of her existence outside of herself. While Judaism was not essentially, like Christianity, a Missionary Institute, but, owing to the stern necessities of the times, was built for defensive rather than offensive operations; still, it was thus fenced in with privileges and illuminated with light from above, that it might be seen over all the earth, that God who made the earth and heavens, He is Lord; and that blessed is that people whose God is the Lord. The Holy Land was made the garden of the Lord, that the leaves of its trees might be for the healing of the nations. Phœnicia and Egypt were the countries that were specially brought into full and long contact with the truths and influences, that made Jerusalem glorious for beauty. The Phœnicians and Hebrews were as intimate for that day in commerce and friendship, as the English and Americans in our times. And, as for the Egyptians, not only were the Israelites tabernacled by God among them for more than four hundred years; but ever afterwards they were held together by ties of intercourse and commerce more or less firm: as, Solomon married his wife in Egypt, and thither, a thousand

THE INDO-EUROPEAN LANGUAGES. 27

years afterward, Joseph and Mary fled with the infant Jesus from the face of Herod. But Phœnicia and Egypt exerted, in their turn, a very great influence on the early progress of the European world. From Phœnicia came the alphabet to Greece; and from them both came stores of wisdom and influences intellectual and moral, which, by their very essential invisibility, hid themselves, even in the time of their greatest power, from observation. Is it not pleasant to think that the Jewish theocracy, erected like a tower of light by our great Father above among the people of the old world, was set up in love, not only for those who dwelt under its immediate effulgence, but also for the other nations that looked on it from afar, for whose good his heart yearned as tenderly as it does for that of all men now.

The Semitic nations have lived with remarkable uniformity on vast open plains; or wandered over wide and dreary deserts, by which the negative side of their character has been more cultivated than the positive. The lot, on the contrary, of the Indo-European nations, has been ever, with as remarkable uniformity, cast by a favoring Providence amid rivers, mountains, vales and gorges; where they might gaze upon an ever-changing sky, and breathe a vigorous ever-changing air; and where they would be required to accoutre themselves, continually, for new enterprises and endeavors.

The Indo-European nations and languages have

spread themselves, in the eastern hemisphere, over the vast area from the mouth of the Ganges, to the British Islands and the northern extremities of Scandinavia. They comprise the Sanskrit, Zend, Old Persian, Greek, Latin, Lettic, Slavonic, German and Celtic families of tongues; and these languages compare quite as closely, one with another, in both their lexical and grammatical elements, as do the Romanic languages: the Italian, Wallachian, Spanish, Portuguese and French, with each other. As we go eastward geographically and backward historically, we find, as a general fact, a greater and greater approximation constantly to the pure Indo-European types of words, as found in the Sanskrit; and, as we go westward, less and less; until, in the Celtic, the most western European language, we find the fewest traces left of the common original mother-tongue. It is indeed but a recent discovery, made by the late distinguished Prichard, that the Celtic actually belongs to the same great parent stock of languages. Still more recently, by the discovery of the Old Egyptian language and the comparison of the Celtic languages with it, the conviction is reached, as Bunsen claims, that the original Celtic is more ancient, not only than the Teutonic branch of languages, but even than the Sanskrit itself: forming a sort of connecting link between the Old Egyptian and the Sanskrit, in the stages of lingual development. If this view of the Celtic shall be, at any time hereafter, really substantiated, then to the Celtic must be conceded the honor, now given to the Sanskrit and otherwise to be given to it still, of retaining in itself more fully than any other one of the sister-languages still preserved to us, that ancient mother-tongue, now lost in its pure primal form from the eyes of men; from which yet all the subsequent languages of the civilized world have been derived. The real connection also of the Celtic and the Sanskrit, as belonging to the same family, will remain unchanged; while the order of sequence between the two will be directly alternated.

The most ancient languages of the Indo-European stock may be grouped in two family-pairs: the Arian family-pair and the Græco-Italic or Pelasgian family-pair. The whole series of families is as follows:

    I. The Arian family-pair.
   II. The Græco-Italic, or Pelasgic family-pair.
  III. The Lettic family.
  IV. The Slavic family.
   V. The Gothic family.
  VI. The Celtic family.

The Celtic is placed last, because it is yet least explored, and its full definite relations have been least ascertained.

I. The Arian family-pair. This comprises, as the title indicates, two leading families:

    1st. The Indian family.
    2d. The Iranian family

The word Arian (Sanskrit Arya, Zend Airya) signifies noble, well-born: a name applied by the Ancient Hindûs to themselves, in contradistinction to the rest of the world, whom they considered base-born and contemptible. This is the oldest known name of the entire Indo-European family. With this name all chance to trace the pedigree of the family back to the early dawn of time ends. From what circumstances of social contrast in their favor, they came to apply this self-flattering title to themselves it is impossible to say. As the words "Slavonic" and "Irish" (from Airya) contain the same utterance of national pride in them, the name is probably but another evidence of mens' disposition in all ages, not to esteem others as themselves. So the Greeks called the rest of the world "barbarians;" and the Jews termed the Gentiles "dogs." Arii was the ancient name of the Medes: a name afterward preserved in the Aria and Ariana of the Greek geographers. Aryavarta, the country lying between the Himalaya and the Vindhya mountains, the primeval abode of their fathers, is now regarded as their "holy land" by the Brahmins. There, in that high table-land of central Asia, two thousand years and more before Christ, our Hindû ancestors had their early national home. So also to Bactria near the Indus, the earliest traditions of the Persians point as the ancient and romantic seat of their race. Iran then, a country bounded on the north by the Caspian, on the south by the Indian Ocean, on the east by the Indus, and on the west by the Euphrates, is the spot to which all the languages of the civilized world, ancient and modern, now unite in pointing as the place of their origin.

The absolutely primeval home of the original Arians cannot now be determined. In tracing any of the great currents of Arian migration back from whatever direction to their central source, we soon find ourselves, here as on every other topic of ultimate inquiry, groping in irremediable darkness. There have been historically two great streams of Arian overflow : the one southern, including the Brahmanic Arians of India and the Persian followers of Zarathustra (Zoroaster) : the other northern at the outset but western in the end, embracing the great families of nations in north-western Asia and in Europe. But for this great western Arian manifestation of intellect, enterprise and character, the history of the world hitherto would have had but little significance : as, all of the present and most of the past civilized nations of the world belong to this branch of humanity; and as, for some reason or for many, all the early Semitic tendencies to high and broad enlargement were of very short duration and circumscribed influence. Like trees, at first loaded with blossoms but subsequently shorn of their riches by killing frosts, they gave a larger promise than they afterward realized in the result. The southern Arian migrations stagnated in the valleys which they occupied ; as in them they were walled in from all danger of invasion from the restless nations in the west, by the snow-towers of the Himalaya on the north, the expanse of the Indian Ocean on the south and the deserts of Bactria on the west. There, in the rich valleys of the Indus and its many streams, with no motive to labor from poverty of soil and no need of self-protection against aggressive assaults upon their life of ease, the common mass sank, like the other nations of the earth that have not been constantly goaded by the sharp spur of necessity, into a life of base inglorious inactivity. The more studious and thoughtful, the natural quality of whose minds forbade voluntary torpidity of intellect, wasted their powers in roaming about aimlessly in the regions of dreamy mystic subjectivity. The western nations have been forced by circumstances into a more objective life; and, under the stimulus of physical influences better fitted to test and temper the character and by constant friction one upon the other, have been brought into a state of individual and social activity and progress; the products of which seem as marvellous to an Oriental mind, as can any of the gorgeous fancies of eastern fable to a youthful reader among us.

1. The Indian family.

Of this the Sanskrit is the most remarkable: standing farthest east and at the farthest distance of time, full-orbed in its brightness, casting splendor on every language around it and on every language to be found in the long procession of different tongues related

THE INDO-EUROPEAN LANGUAGES. 33

to it from that day to this. In the Vêdas, it has come down to us from the borders of the primitive world, on the margin of which the Genius of history never planted its foot. The Vêdic Sanskrit was a spoken language in India, as late probably as 1500 years before Christ, or five hundred years before the days of Homer and Solomon, who were contemporaries. The original Vêda the Hindûs believe to have been revealed by Brahma; and to have been preserved by tradition, until it was arranged in its present order by a sage, who thence obtained the name of Vyasa or Vedavyasa or compiler of the Vêdas. These Indian Scriptures, which are all lyrical in their form, he divided into four parts, named Rich, Yajush, Saman and Atharvarna: each with the common denomination Vêda,* which means primarily knowledge or science, and is now used to denote the whole mass of Hindû sacred literature. The fourth of these Vêdas is undoubtedly more modern than the first three, and like in this respect the Itihasa and Puranas, which together constitute a fifth and still more recent Vêda. In the Vêdas themselves they have a fabulous origin ascribed to them: "the Rigveda from fire,† the Yajurveda from air, and the Samaveda from the sun." Some Indian commentators ascribe the

* Lat. video, Gr. οἶδα for Ϝοῖδα: Germ. Wissen: Eng. wit, wist, viz.:—vide, vision, etc.
† Asiatic Researches. Art. by H. T. Colebrooke, vol. viii. (year 1808.)

fable to the fact that the Rigveda opens with a hymn to fire, and the Yajurveda with one in which air is mentioned; but others see in it a transcendental philosophy of the primeval order of things in the universe. The Vêdas are properly a compilation of prayers, called Mantras when spoken of by themselves, and Brahmanas or precepts and maxims. In the three principal Vêdas,* prayers employed at solemn public rites, called Yajnyas, are found: those in metre being called Rich, those in prose Yajush, and those designed to be chanted Saman. The prayers of the fourth or Atharvarna Vêda, were used on different occasions and for different purposes from the preceding; as for imprecations on enemies. And, as in all other parts of the world where thinking men have lived, as in the different schools of philosophy in Greece and Rome, the different sects of Christendom and even the different monastic orders of popery; which yet makes boast of possessing a permanent leaden uniformity of character, as if it were meritorious to be in a state of utter metaphysical and moral stagnation: so in India, the minds of men have separated and scattered the pure white light, as they deemed it, received from their Vêdas, into many distinct sects and schools of theology, of every varied hue of thought.

* In former days learned priests took their titles from the number of Vêdas with which they were conversant. Thus, one who had studied two Vêdas was called Dwivedi: one, who had studied three, Trivedi and one who had studied four, Chaturvedi.

It has been stated that each Vêda consists of two parts: the Mantras or prayers and the Brahmanas or precepts, under which term are included also explanatory maxims and theological arguments. The Rigveda* means literally the Vêda of verses, from rich, to praise; and consists of somewhat more than a thousand hymns of praise, called Sûktas, to the Deity, of various length from one to fifty verses. The religious literature of the Hindûs consists of such works, beside the Vêdas themselves, as the Upanishads, which are theological tracts containing the argumentative portion called Vedanta, of the Indian Scriptures, and also some detached essays of a kindred sort, but of what origin is not known. On the Upanishads the whole of their

* In the study of the Vêdas, which is enjoined upon all priests, the student is always required to note distinctly the author, subject, metre, and purpose of each prayer, more than to understand the prayer itself; and thus most of what is taught in the Vêdas has now become obsolete. So strong is the tendency everywhere in human nature to put the gloss of mere formal respect on every thing ancient, and to satisfy its religious instincts, by carefully preserving religious truths and principles, as if a mere cabinet of elegant curiosities. The Vêda is accordingly the Hindû's book of education for his child, whom he requires to learn it at an early age: as a precious mass of holy words, without any thought or care about its holy sense. And, as the Tatars, according to Huc, construct multitudes of little water-mills covered with scraps of prayers, and set them along the courses of their streams, that, by their revolution day and night they may keep up a constant round of prayer for them, whether awake or asleep; so the superstitious Indians abound in vain repetitions of chance-portions of the Vêdas, repeating them forwards and backwards, backwards and forwards, in idle emptiness of thought, in order to benefit their souls, if possible, in some way by such foolish mummery.

theology is professedly founded. Their remaining literature which is abundant, spreads over the varied fields of grammar, accentuation, prosody, interpretation, lexicography, language, logic, philosophy, ethics, astronomy, &c.

The dialect of the Vêdas, especially of the first three, is very ancient and very difficult; but, as the earlier form of the polished Sanskrit, it possesses great interest, as it does also even still more from the fact of the resemblance of the Graeco-Latin stock of words very largely to its primeval forms, rather than to those of the proper Sanskrit itself; much of which seems to have been developed, as a distinct home-growth by itself, after the departure of the Pelasgian emigration from its borders.

The Sanskrit is then the learned language of the Hindûs: sustaining the same relation to their present dialects, that the Latin sustains to the modern Romanic tongues. While it is written in various Indian characters, it has an alphabet peculiarly its own, called the Deva-nagari, literally "that of the divine or royal city." The remotest date to which its existence çan be traced, is the third century before Christ; but at this period, its forms had only the rudimentary features of the shape, which they have since come to possess in all Sanskrit writings, and which, for convenience sake, are called modern in distinction from the original imperfect alphabet of symbols which preceded it. The "modern" Devanagari is the most complete and philosophical in its construction, of all known alphabets. The "ancient" occurs only in antique inscriptions, found on pillars and high rock-walls throughout India; and the dialect in which these characters appear, is not the Sanskrit or "classical" language of the literary class; but the Prâkrit, a "natural" or "uncultivated" idiom of it, adopted in accommodation to the people, for whose eyes they were thus carved in imperishable stone: since they prove to be but royal commands to them, to obey the priests and to practise various social virtues. There are good historical data for referring them to the time immediately succeeding Alexander's invasion of the East. The true or "modern" Devanagari was, like the literature enclosed as in a casket in it, kept out of sight from the people by the proud Brahmins of ancient times as now, who delighted in fencing off others from their selfish seclusion of false dignity, by withholding from them as many privileges as possible. The word Sanskrit or "classical" had an icy coldness of meaning in it, even then, to those shut out from its favored pale: as, occasionally in modern times, some standing under the very canopy of divine revelation affect to make it, and together with it all the beauty of mental and moral culture denoted by it, appear to imply to the uninitiated. Indeed, as Milton's Eve, when bending over the river's bank in Eden saw as in a mirror her own image and was astonished; so, we may gaze from the verge of the present upon the wondrous stream of the past, in the ancient Indian home of our race, and see with amazement not only our own outward selves all imaged there, but also the most inward and subtle features of our hearts. In the sixth century before Christ, when Buddhism, well styled the ancient Protestant religion of India, rose into full view, the Sanskrit was no longer a spoken language. As the most ancient of all literary documents of the Arian race upon the earth, the Rig-Vedas possess quite a special interest of their own. They were all probably written before the days of Solomon. The grammar and lexicography of the Vêdas are now being laboriously studied in Germany and Russia and by Prof. Whitney in this country; and much progress has been made in the great work of accurately deciphering their contents.

The relation of the Vêdic dialect to the classical Sanskrit is peculiar. "Phonetically they are almost exactly the same:* grammatically they are nearly the same; while lexically they are very different." There are grammatical treatises in manuscript appended to the different Vêdas called Prâtisâkhyas. In these the science of phonetics, called Sikshâ, is reduced to a very perfect system: far more so than in any other language since; and yet these grammars date back as far as to the fifth century before Christ. They have not yet been

* Prof. W. D. Whitney, of Yale.

published, but philologists now are returning to the same classification of vowels and consonants that occurs in them, as the result of their own independent research. The Sanskrit is both read and written by the learned in India, up to the present day; but, since the days of Pânini, their great grammarian, who lived in the fourth century before Christ, the Sanskrit has remained in a state of cold and glazed unchangeableness; like some of the fossil elephants found nowadays in the icy realms of Siberia, as perfect even to the short thin hair of their hides, as when they walked in pomp upon the Pre-Adamic earth. Beside the Vêdas and Upanishads, two great epic poems called the Mahâbâratah and Râmâyana are very celebrated, as also the so-called laws of Menu. These were probably written in the fourth century before Christ.

It was in the Vêdic period of Sanskrit literature that the Southern Arian mind, or what became afterward the proper Hindû mind, was at its highest point of culmination: exhibiting the most and the strongest signs of its original individuality. After that period it seems to have lost its first vigor; although ever worshipping, under the name of Brahma, Force or Propulsive Will as the all-presiding Deity of the Universe.

Between the Vêdic dialect and the Zend striking resemblances are found to exist.

"The Sanskrit is," in the language of Eichhoff, "the richest of all languages in the world, in its combinations. Its words melt and run continually together, in harmony of sound* and sense; and their full splendor is but faintly imaged to the view even by the beautiful and pictorial language of Greece; while the coarser and sterner Latin represents in its features still less of this high characteristic of its elder sister, the Sanskrit.

* The words of Lepsius also are worth quoting here (Standard Alphabet, p. 15):—"No language has a system of sounds more rich and regularly developed than the Sanskrit, or expresses them so perfectly by its alphabet. The old grammarians of India did not indeed invent the Devnagari characters; but they brought them to that state of perfection which they now possess. With an acumen worthy of all admiration, with physiological and linguistic views more accurate than those of any other people, these grammarians penetrated so deeply into the relations of sounds in their own language, that we at this day may gain instruction from them, for the better understanding of the sounds of our own languages. On this account no language and no alphabet are better suited to serve, not indeed as an absolute rule but as a starting-point, for the construction of an universal linguistic alphabet, than that of ancient India. Hence it is that the late progress in the solution of the alphabet problem has been associated in Europe, as formerly in India, with Sanskrit studies." "The alphabet problem" of which he speaks, is that of establishing an uniform orthography for writing foreign languages in European characters, or a standard alphabet for all unwritten languages and foreign graphic systems.

The Devanagari is adapted to the expression of almost every known gradation of sound; and every letter has a fixed and invariable pronunciation. There are fourteen vowels and thirty-three simple consonants: to which may be added the nasal symbol called Anuswara and the symbol for a final aspirate called Visarga. The vowels are a, á, i, í, u, ú, ri, rí, lri, lrí, e, ai, o, au. The consonants are: the gutturals k, kh, g, gh, n : the palatals ch, chh, j, jh, n: the cerebrals ṭ, ṭh, ḍ, ḍh, ṇ: the dentals t, th, d, dh, n : the labials p, ph, b, bh, m : the semi-vowels y, r, l, v: the sibilants ś, sh, s; and the aspirate h. The compound or conjunct consonants may be multiplied, to the extent of four or five hundred.

It must however be remembered, in connection with this statement, that in respect to the artistic elaboration of language, in variety and exactness of form, as well as in outward phonetic beauty and effect, the Greek far surpassed not only the Sanskrit, but also every other language ancient or modern. Of the Sanskrit also it must be said, that in many particulars it has experienced, in the type in which it has reached our eyes, alterations of its original elements and characteristics: so much so, that not unfrequently some of the other families of languages present to us the primal theme of a word, in a much purer form than even the Sanskrit itself, as is often especially true of the Lithuanian. No one of the sister languages of the Indo-European family has as clear and transparent a style of flexional organism as the Sanskrit.

In remote times other languages as dialects sprang up from the Sanskrit, which ere long supplanted it on its own soil: leaving it to maintain its existence at last, only as the language of the sacred books of India and of its learned men. These dialects are denominated the Pali and the Prâkrit, and are now found as dead languages, by the side of their Sanskrit mother in northern Hindûstan. Dialects are the result of mixtures of the stable element of the original tongue in which they occur, with a new variable element introduced from without, sometimes by conquest, and sometimes by commerce or other modes of social contact and influence. The Pali grew up, as the offspring of the Sanskrit, in the province of Bahar, and is to this day the sacred language of all the nations that cherish Buddhism in Ceylon and farther India; since, among those that speak this dialect, that singular democratic form of heathenism originated. The Prâkrit languages (for they are many: the idea is plural) include numerous low depraved dialects, which grew up as parasites on the decaying trunk of the original Sanskrit tree. The word Sanskrit is derived from the preposition sam, with (Gr. συν, Latin cum) and krita, made; and like the Lat. confectus means "carefully constructed," "complete," "classical:" that of Prâkrit is "natural," "uncultivated;" while Pali means "ancient." The Pali and Prâkrit dialects represent the middle age of the Sanskrit. The Pali was at the height of its excellence full 500 years before Christ; while the Prâkrit was not fully developed until one or two centuries later. The present languages of Hindûstan, some twenty or thirty in all, represent the Sanskrit in its most degenerate state: having swerved very greatly from their original model. Most of the languages now spoken in Upper India are immediately derived from the Prâkrit.

Distinctions of caste have long prevailed in India and are founded, there as everywhere, in the distinction of conquering and conquered races: this being hitherto the history of the treatment that inferior races have always received from superior when in mutual contact.

THE INDO-EUROPEAN LANGUAGES. 43

Hindû nationality is therefore now, partly of Arian origin and partly of either Semitic or Turanian, probably the latter: one language in its various dialects embracing them all, but not one wide fraternal spirit.

Beside the Sanskrit, there is also another member of the Indian family, a vagrant language, whose geographical home like that of those who speak it is everywhere. Only two people, while preserving their national distinctness in all times and places, have spread themselves as such over all the earth : one belonging to the Semitic family, the Jews ; and the other to the Indo-European, the Gypsies. Their law of extension from age to age has not been orbital but cometary. They claim the wide world as their domain. The Jew preserves his language as a sacred relic, and prizes it for the fathers' sake. It contains in it a Divine deposit, the law and the testimony ; and is beautiful for its antiquity and the honor that it has received from above ; but it is a living language no more and has lost all function in the present. But how different is it with the Gypsy ! His language is everywhere the same intact cherished old mother-tongue : as distinct and separate from the other languages among which it is found, as are the people from those over whose territories they wander. Their language and their roving habits of life are all that constitute their national identity. Their names are quite various : as Gypsy* from

* The Finns, like the English, give them a name of their own devising, and call them Mustalainen or dark people.

their supposed home in Egypt: Zigeuner, their name in Germany, a word of doubtful meaning: Sinte, the name by which they call themselves, perhaps from Saindhawa, "inhabitants of Sindhu or the Indus;" and also Roem meaning man and Kala "of dark skin" from Sanskrit Kala "dark." They first appeared in Europe in the beginning of the fifteenth century.

Their language,* in its great and manifold resemblances to the Sanskrit, nullifies absolutely before the court of classical and historical criticism the so common conception of their Egyptian origin; and shows that

* CORRESPONDENCES OF THE GYPSY LANGUAGE.

Sanskrit.	Greek.	Latin.	Gypsy.	Lithuan.	Various Languages.	German.	English.
1. aksha (s) the eye	ὄκος	oculus	ak yakcha yak	akis	(Russian) oko	auge	eye
2. agni (s) fire angâra, a coal	(perhaps) αἴγλη	ignis	yâk fire angar a coal	ugnis	(Old Slavonic.) ogny		
3. nava (s) new	νέος for νεϝος	novus	nevo	naujas	(Illyrian) nov	neu	new
4. vid, to see: vind to discover. vedaya (causative) to teach	εἴδειν for ϝείδειν ἴσημι	videre visere	bedar to teach		(Zend) vid causative vedemi I teach	wissen to know weisen to show	wit wise viz -vide -vise
5. bhratar brother	φρατήρ	frater	brâl	brolis	(Lettish) brâlis	bruder	brother

they came from Northern India. This however is not the first or greatest ethnological fallacy, that has originated in a popular empirical style of etymological guessing. The ancients especially were very fond of weaving legendary history, out of such dubious materials.

2. The Iranian family.

The name Iran is derived from Arya; and includes those people, whose languages were originally allied closely with those of the Indian family, but yet by certain definite laws of sound separated from them, such as these: (1.) The change of a dental into s before t, as in Zend basta from Sanskrit baddha, bound. (2.) The Sanskrit sv changed into a guttural, as in Sansk. svasr, sister: New Persian châher. (3.) A radical s changed into h, as in Sansk. saptan, Zend hapta and Sansk. sam, with: Old Persian ham. (4.) The frequent substitution of the dental sibilant z for the guttural aspirate h, as in Sansk. aham, I, and mih,* to urinate: Zend azem and miz. The two chief languages of this class are the Zend and the Old Persian. The Zend is the language of the most ancient cuneiform inscriptions, made in the 6th century before Christ, which are Persian inscriptions carved in the Assyrian character; and also of the holy books of the Parsees, the Zend Avesta. The Avesta is a collection of sacred books, containing their early traditions and the religious and

* Gr. ὀμίχειν: Lat. mingere and meiere.

ethical system of Zarathustra, commonly called Zoroaster, their great legislator; as well as a liturgy which is used to this day by some of the modern Persians in the oasis of Yezd, who still worship the element of fire. It seems to have been preserved in the world for many centuries, like the Iliad which may almost be called the Bible of the early Greeks, by mere oral transmission. It can be traced back in written records, and no farther in such a form, than, to the dynasty of the Sassanides (A. D. 226.) The Zend was the original vernacular of the Medes and Bactrians. So closely does it resemble the Sanskrit, that in very many words, by merely changing the Zend letters into their Sanskrit equivalents, you obtain at once precisely the same identical word. Very striking also in particular is the correspondence between Persia and India, in the elements of their religion and mythology. It is not indeed too much to say, that all the Indo-European nations have a common fundamental basis for their mythology, in their common sense of natural phenomena: with such variations in the myths, contrived by their sensuous imaginations for the ideal embodiment of their conceptions among different nations, as the greater or less luxuriance of the poetic faculty in different climates sufficed to suggest. Still there were gods worshipped under the same names in Sanskrit and Zend, of which the other Indo-European nations seem to have had no idea. In many points the Zend compares with the

Vêdic or primitive natural Sanskrit, better than with the subsequent cultivated or classical Sanskrit. It is a fact also worthy of remembrance in this connection, that the Zend is found to be throughout wonderfully congruous and correlated with the German languages. The Old Persian is the language of many, now perfectly deciphered, arrow-headed inscriptions of the Achæmenidian kings. The intermediate forms of the Persian were the Pehlevi, the language of the Sassanians (A. D. 226–651); and the Pazend, the mother of the new Persian, with which also the Pushtu spoken in Affghanistan is connected. The Pehlevi, which was the language of western Persia, had in it a strong admixture of Aramaic words; while the Pazend, that of eastern Persia, was but the Old Persian greatly commingled with Arabic. The New Persian also has been much altered in flowing down from its original sources by the influence of the Arabic, through the long reign of Mohammedism over that region of the world. The greatest literary work in the New Persian is an immense epic poem, called the Shah Nameh or Book of Kings, written by Ferdousi, about the middle of the 10th century. It is a traditionary history so mingled with fiction and metamorphosed by it, as to be rather an Oriental Romance than a splendid structure of real and connected facts. This was the classic age of the New Persian.

But there are other languages of this stock, of

much smaller philological value than those already mentioned: the Ossetian and Armenian. In the midst of the Caucasus, alone by itself though surrounded by men of other tongues, like the solitary nest of a wild bird in the mountains, is the home of the Ossetian* tongue. The people still call themselves by the old family name, Iron. They are but rude highlanders, without a literature or a history. The Armenian language, on the contrary, has a rich historical literature, but of no older date than the 4th century of our era. The alphabet is peculiar, being immediately modelled after the Greek. Although the language is of an original Iranian constitution, its form and features have been much altered by contact with surrounding languages, especially the Turkish. The Ancient Armenian was a living language down to the 12th century; since which time the present dialect has grown up into full individual stature. The skirts of the Armenian language, and of the busy trafficking people that speak it, are found now resting, in Europe, in Southern Russia around the Sea of Azof, and in Turkey, Galicia and Hungary.

II. The Græco-Italic or Pelasgic family-pair.

But a little while ago Latin etymology was univer-

* Correspondences of the Ossetian Language:

Sanskrit.	Ossetian.	Gothic.	Latin.
pitar, father	fid	fadar	pater
panchan, five	fonz	fimf	quinque
paśu(s), a flock	fos	faihu	pecu
kas, who	kha	hvas	quis

sally constructed: as it still is by many who are entirely ignorant of its true foundations, although fancying themselves to be on the pathway of high classical scholarship: on altogether a Greek basis. The Latin such writers have derived immediately from the Greek: accounting for the differences of form and structure, by all sorts of empirical explanations; whose chief merit has consisted in their being an ingenious dodge of difficulties, that could not be solved. Such works as Valpy's Etymol. Latin Dictionary, Mair's Tyro, Döderlein's various works, and Schwenck's Etymologisches Wörterbuch, illustrate this era and style of Latin etymology. These works still have a value, and that often considerable, in exhibiting correspondences in the two languages and suggesting hints for farther research. But they are no guide-books, as they profess to be, in either philological or historical research. The fundamental conception which they undertake to unfold is false and ridiculous.

In very remote ages there existed evidently a Græco-Italic race, to which the progenitors of both the Latin and Greek nations, as they came afterwards to be and to be called, belonged in common; and from which they afterwards branched off into a separate manifestation. The time, when they thus parted into two distinct individualities, was many centuries before either Romulus lived or Homer sang.

1st. The Greek race, remaining nearer geographically

and in closer contact, commercially and socially, with that Oriental world, amid whose abounding and inspiring luxuriance God Himself prepared the first home of the human family, came in every respect to a higher and nobler style of growth and greatness, than the Latin. The people and their language spread out themselves, in different periods and localities, into a vigorous fourfold demonstration: as expressed in the Æolic, Doric, Ionic and Attic dialects; which mark indeed but so many stages or epochs of the same language. The Doric is but a variety of the Æolic; and these two dialects may, without impropriety, be said to mark the earlier and later aspects of the Pelasgic period. The Ionic, as a subsequent development of the same language, took on its separate form, under the influence of national progress, as a distinct home-product; and, "so far," as K. O. Müller well observes, "as it differs in any word, in respect to either its vowels or its consonants, from the Æolic; it differs also from the original type of the word."

The Italic race parted from the common Græco-Italic stock, by a more western migration; where, in another climate and under other influences, they matured into a well-defined development of their own. They ere long separated into an eastern and western branch; and the eastern subsequently divided itself into the Umbrian and Oscan. The causes, times and modes of these different migrations and separations lie out of the field of exact historic vision. As agriculture is the basis of all stable social organization, we are compelled to believe that the original Græco-Italic race were given to the culture of grain, oil and wine; instead of leading that wandering shepherd-life, to which Orientals have ever been so much addicted, and which was undoubtedly therefore a leading feature at the first of Indo-European life in the East. The very names given to the first inhabitants of Italy declare this historic fact; as Œnotria (from οἶνος wine) from which the title Œnotrians; and so Opsci and Osci, laborers (ops) and Siculi and Sicani (secare to cut), reapers.

The Greek and Latin languages have then a common origin, and possess a common substantive being. The mould and model of the Latin are the more antique in their forms of the two. In the Æolic dialect, in which we have the remains, in general, of the Greek as it was in its primeval state, it resembles the Latin much more than in its later dialects. In this dialect, the Græco-Italic or Pelasgic element that forms the common stock of the Greek and Latin languages is found most abundantly, and with the fewest adulterations and additions. The words most distinctly common to the Greek and Latin, are those that thereby show themselves to characterize that period, in which they had a blended life in one common stock. These words relate to the domestic animals, the soil, the phenomena of nature, objects of worship, articles of subsistence and implements of industry; or, in other words, to the elements and experiences * of every-day life. In the Attic

* Specimens of the correspondence alluded to in the Greek and Latin as well as in Sanskrit.

Sanskrit.	Latin.	Greek.	Their sense in English.
gaus	bos	βοῦς	ox
avis	ovis	ὄϊς	sheep
hansas	anser	χήν	goose
aśvas	equus	ἵππος Æol. ἵκκος	horse
paśu	pecu	πῶυ	flock
sthûras	taurus	ταῦρος	bull
akshas	axis	ἄξων	axis
a wheel		ἄμ-αξα	axle
saras	sal	ἅλς	salt
varahas	porcus verres	πόρκος	pig
sûkaras	sus	σῦς and ὗς	sow
śvan	canis	κύων	dog
mûsh	mus	μῦς	mouse
âtis	anas	νῆσσα for ἀνησσα	duck
rajata	argentum	ἀργύριον	silver
arbhas	orbus	ὀρφανός	orphan
damas	domus	δόμος	house
dêvas	deus	θεός	God
ajra, from aj	ager	ἀγρός	field
arv, to divide or break up	arare aratrum	ἀροῦν ἄροτρον	to plough a plough
garhan	hortus	χόρτος	garden
—	vinum	οἶνος	wine
lî, to melt	oliva	ἐλαία	olive
	oleum	ἔλαιον	oil
—	lancea	λόγχη	lance
nâus (gen. navas)	navis	ναῦς	ship
	remus	ἔρετμος	oar

dialect, or classic Greek, it departs farthest from the original elements of its common parentage and character. It is in the Greek that we find most of the altered and secondary sounds and forms; while in the Latin they maintain more generally their primitive aspect. At the remotest period, of which we have any historical records concerning the Greek, it had already undergone great changes from its primitive state. In that dark unwritten era, as in "the womb of the morning," the Greek* and Latin dwelt together in their

Sanskrit.	Latin.	Greek.	English.
pû, to purify	poena	ποίνη	punishment
(tam, to divide prob. root.)	templum	τέμενος from τέμνω	temple
tam-âlas, a knife.			
—	puls	πόλτος	pulse
pish, to bruise	pinso	πτίσσω	to bruise or grind
mal, to break in pieces	mola	μύλη	mill
kókilas	cuculus	κόκκυξ	cuckoo
kâravas	corvus	κορώνη	crow
ahis	anguis	ἔχις	snake
śarabhas	carabus	κάραβος	crab
makshikâs	musca	μυῖα	gnat
—	grus	γέρανος	crane
—	vespa	σφήξ	wasp
—	fera	θήρ	a wild animal
karkaṭas	cancer	καρκίνος	crab
—	aranea	ἀράχνη	spider

* The name Greece was given by the Romans: the vernacular name for the country being Hellas and for the people Hellenes. So the Germans, as we call them, are named by the French Les Allemands and by themselves Deutsch. The old Etrusci or Tusci, as they were called by the Romans, denominated themselves Rasena and the Wallachians call themselves Români: while the Gypsies' name for themselves is

embryo state, yet to be developed into a separate life and activity. This is its Græco-Latin, Pelasgic, or Archaic period. So much of that great common primitive Græco-Italic race, as, in overflowing the plains of Greece rested permanently upon them as its abode, soon came, under local influences, to assume a corresponding definite character: determined by their climate, sky, landscape and soil and the habits of life that these necessitated and suggested.

The next period of Grecian development was the Hellenic or Classic: covering all the more enlarged and cultivated conditions of Grecian character and society. As the terms, Pelasgic and Hellenic, are commonly used to denote different elementary races; it must be ever borne in mind, that, contrarily, they are used here, to denote only different eras of historic development in the same identical race. The term Pelasgic accordingly determines the epoch of the first Græco-Italic emigrations into Greece, and, so, that of its first permanent settlement and of the establishment of its primitive institutions. The term Hellenic separates from this first epoch that subsequent era marked, on the one hand, by the later emigrations of the same Græco-Italic race from their trans-Ægean homes in Western Asia, when in a more cultivated condition; and also especially by a

---

Sinte. So in southern Africa, as Livingstone informs us, "most of the tribes are known by names applied to them by strangers only, as the Caffres, Hottentots and Bushmen."

THE INDO-EUROPEAN LANGUAGES. 55

fuller and higher home-development, on the other hand, within the bounds of Hellas itself. By these agencies combined, and by the latter more than the former, the original institutions, habits, ideas and language of primitive Greece were greatly modified and improved.

In this second and advanced period of the Greeks, they came to possess a much higher cast of character and style of speech, than ever before. The four dialects, the Æolic, Doric, Ionic and Attic, like the four moons revolving in the sky of Jupiter, appeared also, at this time, in full view together above the horizon of Greek literature. The Æolic * and Doric dialects, which are essentially identical, had their distinct sphere of manifestation in the Pelasgic period; while the Ionic and Attic, which are also identical in nature, and but different stages and phases of the same improved state of the original Greek language, found their proper native element in the Hellenic period. In the Æolic and Doric dialects, accordingly, the Greek appears in a more plain and homely garb; while in the Ionic and Attic it comes forth in full costume, wearing a robe wrought by many hands into its most artistic and perfect shape. By its own finished excellence the Attic came in the end to be admired, throughout all Greece, as "the perfection of beauty," and to become dominant in the

* The Æolic and Doric were far purer in their forms, in the Pelasgic period, when no Grecian literature existed, than found now to be, in the remains left of them in the Greek writers; all of whom lived in the Hellenic period.

whole domain of speech, whether uttered or written. By this dialect, as a standard, the deviations of the other dialects, as such, were measured. While the Ionians did not dislike a concurrence of vowels, they rejected the harsh consonantal combinations abounding in the early types of the language ; and the Athenians carried the improvement of original forms still farther, by contracting all proximate vowels which would produce an hiatus into one.

Could the early history of Asia Minor, in its westernmost borders, be fully written, especially that of Phrygia, Caria and Lydia; we should doubtless find there, in great abundance, the first swelling buds of Grecian growth and greatness. Cyrus found at Sardis (B. C. 550) Crœsus dwelling in great magnificence and in all the luxury of a court, whose power had already culminated after ages of slow national growth, and was indeed beginning to yield to that inevitable law of decay, which all things human, when having reached the acme of their elevation, have hitherto obeyed : the law of inward dissolution : thereby preparing the elements of its own strength to be incorporated anew into the frame of a more vigorous and useful successor. In the Græco-Italic period of European history, the character and condition of those, who, as the primitive inhabitants of Europe, planted the germs of all its subsequent enlargement, are revealed to us. In them and in the armies of Teutonic emigrants that followed them. of the same blood and of the same primeval language, we behold our own early ancestors when first entering on the great world-stage of life. For, thanks to philology, we can not only trace our ancestors to England, Germany, France and Rome, but, beyond the boundaries of man's recorded memory where the torch of history fails to cast its light, throughout the long wastes of space and time that stretch through Asia, to their first homes in Media and India. Their social life and spirit, their migrations, their victories and defeats are all drawn in living lines and painted in imperishable colors, on the tablets of their different languages. These even Time's effacing fingers have spared to modern eyes. Nowhere are "stubborn facts" more stubborn, than in the department of linguistic ethnography. The Indo-European nations generally are, indeed, but a series of colonies of the Arian race, which, in an age long preceding any known dates, spread out itself from its common centre, north and west. The colonies, which formed the northern nations of Europe, probably traversed the regions lying northward of the Caspian; while the nations of southern Europe went through Asia Minor and across the Hellespont or the Bosphorus. Emigration and colonization have ever been marked peculiarities, in the history of this family of nations: emigration in masses from a period beyond the reach of documentary history, down to the present hour. Westward, ever westward for thousands of years, has flowed the living tide. In the Hellenic period, whatever the actual amount of immigration was, the tide of colonization set immediately from Ionia in Asia Minor, and, if swelled perhaps to some extent at the same time, incidentally, by kindred elements from Persia, those elements were certainly few and small; while, in the earlier Pelasgic period, the overflow seems to have spread directly from the regions of Media. The only plausible argument, in favor of the supposed influence of Persian elements directly or indirectly, on the form and features of the Hellenic period, is found in the fact of the special resemblance of the classic Greek, in some things, to the Persian both ancient and modern: a resemblance, which its Latin sister, of a more homogeneous Pelasgic constitution, does not at all possess. The resemblances between the Persian and Greek are owing, probably, to phonetic principles common to them both, under similar climatic influences. The Welsh, although a Celtic language, agrees with the Persian phonetically, as much or nearly so at least as does the classic Greek. How often is what is plausible proved to have been only so by wider research. The chief point of correspondence between the Persian and Greek, as also the Welsh, is the general substitution of * h, for s in the Sanskrit,

Sanscrit.	Zend.	Greek.	Welsh.
sâ, she	hâ	ἡ	hi
saptan, seven	hapta	ἑπτα	
sara, salt		ἅλς	halen
svar, the sun	hvare	ἥλιος	heol
sam, with	ham	ἅμα	evo

especially in initial syllables. The induction therefore of facts, in this direction, is not yet sufficiently wide and clear, to make a proper foundation for the statement, that there is any absolute connection between them. On any supposition, the Hellenic development must have been, in all its higher aspects, a matter of home-growth. Its characteristics are all indigenous. Persia had not, until the time of Cyrus (B. C. 560), any high or even distinct character of its own. Under him the Persians came, by contact with the cultivated nations that he conquered and with the men and institutions of Judea, to receive impressions that awakened in them the consciousness of new wants and the impulse to new activity and enterprise. Donaldson therefore and some few others speak too decisively, of Persian influence upon Grecian progress. As the present German, technically called the New High German, was gradually advanced under the slow action of centuries, by Luther's time, from the original Gothic, as found existing in Ulfilas' translation of the Scriptures (A. D. 380); and is so different from its first beginnings, that a native himself cannot unravel them, without as much close study as if upon a foreign tongue: so, Hellenic Greek was slowly moulded, under the pressure of individual energy, character and experience, by many hands in successive ages, into the grand and elegant proportions, in which it has ever since stood high and firm, as the most finished artistic structure of the elements of language, that the world has ever seen. Says Niebuhr: "The Hellenes and Pelasgians were kindred nations; identity of religion and similarity of language connected them with each other. Here we find a fundamental difference and a fundamental relationship, bound together by an inexplicable law." On his theory of a difference of races, the combination is an enigma; but not at all on our theory, that the difference between them was merely a difference in the stages of growth of the same race. Let it then be remembered carefully that the terms Pelasgic and Hellenic simply describe different historic eras of the same people, and not differences at all of national origin.

The domain of the Greek language was coextensive with the colonies and conquests of that ever-busy moving people. The term Græcia was applied in fact to two countries: Græcia Antiqua or Greece Proper, and Græcia Magna or the south-eastern portion of Italy. For, at a very early day, colonies from Greece crossed the Adriatic, and spread themselves over Lucania, Apulia and Calabria, and covered up ere long in their overflow all traces of the original population and the dialects that they had spoken. But, while the colonists of Magna Græcia contributed largely to the development of Greek literature, the mother-country always wore the crown of intellectual supremacy. Her colonies filled the islands of the Ægean Sea and belted its shores, on both the European and Asiatic coasts, and

THE INDO-EUROPEAN LANGUAGES. 61

spread even northwards, around the upper and under sides of the Baltic. By the victorious arms also of Alexander, Greek ideas, influences, institutions and minds were planted .over all the East, from Macedonia to the Indus and around about the coast of the Mediterranean to Alexandria in Egypt. To the Greeks the world is indebted for literature, grammar, philosophy and art, beyond any other nation. With the abounding information of scholars concerning Greek literature, and the facile helps at hand everywhere for obtaining it; it is not necessary, of course, to mention in detail the splendid structures of thought, that, with such amazing skill and zeal, they reared for the advantage and admiration alike of all ages. In the Pelasgic period, the Greeks, as was natural in their weakness and amid the rude beginnings of pioneer life, when every thing lay new and unclaimed by others before them, were peaceful and laborious; but, in the Hellenic or more cultivated period, the arts of war sprang up, and commerce and conquest extended the power of Greece in all directions. In the Homeric poems, the oldest monument of the Greek tongue, we see the three leading dialects, the Æolic, Ionic and Attic, all variously appearing together on the stage. The language was then still, to a great degree, in a transition-state, casting off its old skin and taking on a new one. Homer is as dear to the philologist, as to the poet, presenting a rich array of curiosities and treasures to his delighted gaze; and, all the more, as his two great poems stand, not only nearest the first beginnings of Greek nationality, but also by themselves, in solitary sublime splendor in that far-off position. Nor are they ruins: every column of these magnificent structures remains in its place, as when set up by his hands, and every line of grace and beauty is as freshly carved and as distinct, as if the artist's spirit were still lingering, responsive to our gaze, within his work.

Giese, in his Æolische Dialekt, draws incidentally a picture of the pre-Hellenic period, in somewhat the same spirit, or style at least, in which geologists describe the pre-Adamite earth, too graphic and interesting to be lost. In that archaic unhistoric period he says, for substance: "No opposition had grown up, as afterwards, against the consonant F or Digamma, imported from Phœnicia, and the Sibilant S. The half vowel y (Latin i), afterwards wanting, was then in vogue. The vowel-hues of words were not multiplied, as afterwards. The vowel a was the common vowel-sound, as in Sanskrit, used in the utterance of all consonantal sounds; which afterward scame to be changed, in so many cases, into its weaker or stronger cognates ε, η, o; and the diphthongs $\alpha\iota, \varepsilon\iota, o\iota$, were but of infrequent occurrence. Consonantal changes were few. The aspirate was not in existence or, if so, only as a consonant. Euphonic mutations were few, being guided by only simple natural principles, of convenience or pleasure; and not, as afterwards, brought to a state of scientific and artistic elaboration. The rejection of consonants, when final, had not yet grown into extensive use; nor had the principle of assimilation yet become strong. The aspirating influence of a σ or π on a smooth mute preceding or following it had hardly yet shown itself. So also vowel-contractions, the result of active business-habits of life and speech and so an after-growth, had not yet occurred to any great extent. The whole subject of case-development was still, in a simple uncomplicated state. Prepositions had not yet come into much use, as helps and additions to case-endings; and, when used, were employed to a great extent adverbially. The demonstrative pronoun had not yet taken on also the aspect of the definite article. The signification of words in this primitive state of the language was, in reference to some classes of them, more specific and, in reference to others, more general than afterwards, when, by the increase of ideas and the multiplication of wants, the same words came to have many more shades of meaning." Secondary meanings and multiform senses of the same words keep ever growing up in any living language, however stable, as the people, who use them as the medium of exchange in the world of thought, expand perpetually over a wider area of activity and enlargement. In the description furnished above, of the contrasts that existed in the Pelasgic and Hellenic periods, though general and brief, the student will find an accurate outline of the style of changes wrought in the Greek language, as it became more and more moulded into its final classic form.

The Modern living representative of the Greek is the Romaic or Modern Greek, into which the Ancient Greek has at last dropped, from its Byzantine corruptions; but which much more resembles its progenitor, than the Romanic languages do the Latin. The Modern Greek reigns over substantially the same region, as did the Ancient. It has however so changed from its first form and features, while still remaining as a Guardian Angel in the home of its early splendor, watching the precious relics of the past: that, could the men of elder times rise from the dust to gaze upon its face and figure, they would stand wondering long at its strange appearance. And yet its changes are chiefly those in its mere outward aspect. The old visage soon reveals itself again, to an eye that keeps looking inquiringly after it. It is Greek still, that the dwellers of the Peloponnesus and Hellas and Epirus and Thessaly and Macedonia and Thrace, although called now by other names, yet speak. The peculiarities of Modern Greek are various. The tendency of the ancient Greek, to exalt the deep u-sound of other languages to the high i-sound, as in the French u and German ue, has not only been kept in Modern Greek, but extended also to other vowels as η, $\varepsilon\iota$, and $o\iota$: β is pronounced nearly as our v and γ like y, except before α and o where it is sounded as gh, and before $αι$, $ε$ and $ι$ where it is pronounced as y: $δ$ is sounded nearly like dh and $ζ$ like our z.

In the Albanian, the probable representative of a more primitive Illyrian, spoken along the eastern coast of the Adriatic, we have a language, which seems to resemble both it and the Latin in combination, and to have grown up, as a seedling, in that primitive Graeco-Italic period, in which neither the Greek nor Latin had any distinct, separate existence: a living specimen of the primeval language of Southern Europe, retaining still its first identity unimpaired. It resembles of course the Latin much more than the Hellenic Greek. It contains also a few Gothic words, as a memorial of the incursions made upon their fathers by that fierce tribe of warriors, who, under Alaric, swooped down in the fifth century upon them from the North, and devoured them and all their resources throughout northern Epirus. And, so, also in succeeding centuries (the seventh, eighth and ninth), Slavonian tribes, the Bulgarians and Servians, made irruptions upon them: as human wolves have, in all ages, delighted to prey upon weak defenceless lambs; and they have left many proofs, in the names of places as well as in the ordinary staple elements of the language itself, that they came not in vain out of their forest-lairs: while yet the evidence is equally clear, in the relatively small impression that they made upon the language, as a whole, that they found the Epirotes a brave people, who knew well how to cover, by their arms, their altars and their fires from the approach of invaders. So, also, while the Albanian tongue contains in itself many signs of commercial contact, at different times and to different degrees, with various people, as the Germans, Swedes, Danes, English, Turks and others, yet, in respect to this class of disturbing influences, the great staple substratum of its words remains still homogeneous and unique. The Albanians* call themselves Skipetars, or mountaineers. There are different dialects of the Albanian, which is also called the Arnautic; as of every other language that has stretched over much space or over much time: the two principal ones, the Geghian or Northern and the Toskian or Southern, prevailing, the former in the regions of northern Illyria, and the latter in Epirus. Every thing new pertaining to the Albanians, as to the Celts, is hailed with special delight by philologists, on account of their connection, genetically, with the old Illyrian stock of the earliest settlers of Greece.

* A view of some Albanian correspondences with the Greek:

Albanian.	Greek.	Albanian.	Greek.
1. νιὲ	1. εἶς for ἕνς	1. πάρε	πρῶτος
2. δὶ	2. δύο	2. δίτε	δεύτερος
3. τρὶ	3. τρεῖς	3. τρέτε	τρίτος
4. κάτερ	4. τέρραρες	4. κάτερτε	τέτταρτος
5. πεσε	5. πέντε	5. πέσετε	πέμπτος

So compare also

Albanian,		Greek.	Latin.
σίπερ,	over.	ὑπέρ,	super.
κίντ,	a hundred.	ἑκατόν,	centum.
πας,	afterwards.	ὄπισθε,	post.

THE INDO-EUROPEAN LANGUAGES. 67

Schleicher's fivefold division of the historical epochs of the Greek language, deserves a record and notice here:

I. The Classic period; and this in two portions.

1st. That of the contemporaneous flowering forth of the different dialects in full vigor: from Homer to Pindar.

2d. That of the Attic dialect, when fully triumphant.

II. The Alexandrine period, in which "the Common Greek" became evolved out of the Attic.

III. The Roman period.

IV. The Byzantine, after the removal of the seat of empire to Constantinople, at which time its forms were much bruised and broken. As Byzantium was called New Rome, the New Greek came to be denominated the Romaic, as it is often termed now.

V. The strictly and fully New Greek period since 1453.

The primitive ancestors of the Indo-European nations, whether in their original eastern home or their subsequent western one, were evidently but little advanced in the arts of life. They were probably, as says Prichard, "ignorant of the use of iron and other metals, since the terms used to denote them are fundamentally different in their various languages; and must therefore, it would seem, have been adopted subsequently to the era of the individual languages derived from the parent stock. What could be more unlike, than χρυσός, aurum and gold or σίδηρος, ferrum and iron." The use of letters was also entirely unknown to the Arian nations, to those at least which passed into Europe; and it was introduced among them, in long after ages, by the Phœnicians.

The physical aspects of Greece and of Hindûstan were widely various; and great indeed was the contrast of their influence, as well as of that of their different climates, upon the generations of men that were brought, from age to age, into inevitable connection with them. Within the Arian horizon of the Indo-European mind, were immense mountains, mighty rivers, impassable forests, inextricable jungles and boundless deserts, with all the fervors of a tropical climate, its tempests, its wild beasts and its pestilences. Under such a constant series of lessons about the natural impotence of man, with such awe-inspiring and terrific shadows ever resting on his bosom, from the gigantic forms of nature by which he was surrounded, is it strange that, in the barren feeble state of heathenism, the Indo-European mind succumbed, in India, to the force of surrounding influences, and lay prostrate in conscious weakness at the feet of Fate. How different a realm for the growth of that divinely-gifted style of mind, was Greece! Its coasts furnished abundant points of departure for all the world beside: its rivers were short and narrow; its mountains, though many, were small: large enough to stand like closed gates in the way of hurricanes from the sea and of pestilences from abroad, as well as to furnish many a secret home for Liberty, sweet Mountain-Nymph; but not large enough to for ever remind men of their littleness and baffle all their aspirations of enterprise and hope. In India the lesson ever thundered in a heathen's ear by Nature so misinterpreted by him, was fear, despondency, helplessness; while, in Greece, the lesson read was hope, courage, effort. Whenever Christianity shall have the opportunity, to interpret rightly the great lessons of Nature in India: Christianity, with her eye of faith and voice of prayer and songs of praise even in the night: Nature will be found there as everywhere, to be man's helper on earth and his guide to Heaven. In some parts of the earth, the deep and solemn base of her wondrous diapason is struck; while in others only the lighter notes are heard; but all unite, each in its proper way, in grand chorus in the universal Hymn of "Glory to God in the highest." If God be left out of the human heart or nature is thought of as unoccupied by Him, discord is introduced at once into the vision of His works, and their influence, as felt upon the heart in such a way, is only perverted and evil. The advocates of intensely materialistic views of human history, like Buckle, forget in their great over-estimate of the normal action of nature upon man, that national development everywhere but in Europe, where it has been most free in its spirit and most grand in its proportions, has occurred only in circumstances where not only no preparation was made within, in the states and forces of the mind, for its real greatness or goodness, but, on the contrary, every possible energy was framed and set in motion, to prevent a divine result.

2d. The Italic Family.

Three distinct races originally peopled Italy, namely: the Iapygian, Etruscan and Italian. In later times Carthaginian arms, ideas and influences swept over Sicily, where Greek colonies had previously planted the institutions and customs of their native land, as also over all southern Italy; while in northern Italy on either side of the Po, in Cisalpine Gaul, men of Celtic blood were rioting on the abundance of what was then, and has been ever since, the garden of Italy. In Magna Græcia, at the lower end of Italy, the Greek was spoken, as, in Gallia Cisalpina at the upper end, a Gallic idiom was spoken; but, in the north especially, no such foreign idiom was cherished with hereditary interest and perseverance, as a badge of national distinction or affection. In the extreme part of south-eastern Italy, a considerable number of inscriptions has been found, whose language is essentially different from that of all the other dialects of the land. It possesses, like the Greek, the aspirated consonants. Its genitive forms aihi and ihi answer to the Sanskrit asya and Greek οιο, and indicate its origin, although not yet itself deciphered, to be quite certainly Indo-European. These inscriptions are regarded as Iapygian; and the race that spoke it are believed also to have prevailed at an early date in Apulia. As the emigrations of masses are, at the first, always landward; since seaward movements presuppose too great a knowledge of navigation, for the first barbarous periods of history; and as the Iapygians occupied the outermost verge of the peninsula, it is natural to suppose that they constituted the first race, that ever came from the East into Italy. Like the Celts, dwelling at last on the flanks of Western Europe, they were pushed farther and farther from their first resting-place, by each successive tide of emigration behind them, until they became lodged in the wilds and fastnesses of Messapia and Calabria, to be driven from these their last homes, rocky and ocean-bound, no more.

As to the Etruscans, it is a question of much doubt among scholars, what was the origin of this ancient and interesting tribe. Donaldson* has a theory on the sub-

* All praise to Donaldson, who is both learned and ingenious, for his efforts to unveil to English eyes the charms of the new and delightful science of classical philology. But since, in the absence of higher and truer standards in this department of study in our language, many are disposed to look, with false confidence and even admiration, to him for light; it seems well to caution alike the novice and the general student of language, to remember that whatever in Donaldson is general, and so lies within the field of this science at large, deserves acceptance from him as it would at the hands of any other good compiler or system-maker; but that whatever is distinctly Donaldsonian is of rather suspicious value.

ject, which he utters, like every thing else of his own invention, with great assurance. He regards the Etruscan language as in part a Pelasgian idiom, more or less corrupted by the Umbrian, and in part a relic of the oldest Low-German or Scandinavian dialects. They were composed, accordingly, in his view, of two main elements as a people, namely: Tyrrheno-Pelasgians, more or less intermixed with Umbrians and Rætians or Low-Germans: the former prevailing in the South, and the latter, in the north-western parts of Etruria. But the origin of the Tuscans, notwithstanding this bold analysis of their elementary constitution as a people, still remains an unresolved enigma. The alphabet of the Etruscan language is an archaic form of the Hellenic. While its grammatical structure, so far as yet ascertained, is manifestly Indo-European, there are so many and so great variations in the types of its words, as to have quite baffled all attempts hitherto at an accurate lexical analysis of their nature. The mystery will undoubtedly be unravelled in future years, as new discoveries shall be made of ancient inscriptions not yet disclosed to our view. It is certainly one of the many marvels of our day, that so much of the minute full history of the past has been recovered to modern eyes, from records buried for safe keeping under ground too deeply to be found and clawed up by any of the vengeful conquerors of the past, whose vulture-hearts would eagerly have pounced upon such prey. The East is full of such unopened piles of the treasured past; and so is Southern Italy. But as grammatical correspondence is the great test of relationship between languages, we are safe, whatever discoveries may be hereafter made concerning it, in assigning definitely to the Etruscan a place, although not one of high honor on account of its mixed and barbarous style of structure, in the Indo-European family. In respect to the heterogeneousness of its lexical elements, it is worth remarking that some languages mix much more evenly together than others; and that the style of modern lingual development, generally, is very much more mixed than in ancient days, as the nations of the world themselves mingle in peaceful intercourse more widely with each other. Whatever language it was that entered into combination with the original staple elements of the Etruscan, it must have been of a wild uncultivated sort, as the resulting product is at best but an unsightly hybrid. The stock of words incorporated from the Etruscan into the Latin tongue, was exceedingly small: not more numerous than the supply of Chinese words in English. They are such as balteus* a girdle, cassis a helmet, lituus an augur's staff, and Lar† a household god: all but the last names of special instruments.

* English belt.
† Scotch laird, and English lord or lady, in respect to which last compare, for form, dame and dam, (French, dame) with domina and dominus.

Some peculiarities serving to identify and isolate their language, as a separate branch of the Indo-European family, are these: 1. They had none of the medial mutes (b, g, d.) Hence they substituted the smooth mutes for them, in their equivalent forms of the Greek words in which they occurred, as in Tute for $Τυδεύς$, Utuze for $Ὀδυσσεύς$, Melakre for $Μελέαγρος$. 2. They frequently changed smooth mutes into rough, as in Atresthe and Thethis, Tuscan forms of $Ἄδραστος$ and $Θέτις$.

The Italian race occupied the central part of Italy. From this race that large peninsula obtained its name and character. They were at the outset its great leading race, and became ere long the conquerors of Italy and subsequently of the world. In them we see the great Western home-growth, in a separate form, of the same Græco-Italic people which swarmed in the Pelasgic period from the East into Europe: a large fragment of which remained behind in Greece, and became so greatly enlarged, refined and beautified in the Hellenic period, by the aid also of successive emigrations, from the more cultivated regions of the eastern coast of the Ægean. These successive emigrations none of them reached Italy, to overlay the broad and rugged proportions of her pioneer colonization, as in Greece, with richer and deeper elements of national advancement. The home-growth of the Greek off-shoot of the common original Græco-Italic stock, was maintained constantly under the powerful ministry of the most quickening and enlarging influences ever flowing in upon it, in both its nascent and formative state. The home-growth, on the contrary, of the twin Italic offshoot of the same parent stock, was perfected entirely by itself and with none of the overflow of a higher civilization, from age to age, upon it serving to enrich the soil upon which it was planted.

The two principal branches of the Italic race, when defined by a distinct growth of their own into fixed proportions, were the Latin and the Umbrian, which last includes also the Marsi and the Samnites or Oscans. The more deeply investigators penetrate into the different dialects of this race, the more closely do they find them to be connected with the Latin. While the remains of the Umbrian are very scanty, those of the Samnite or Oscan dialects are more abundant. Samnium, the home of the Oscans, is but a contraction of Sabinium, the land of the Sabines. The vowel-system of the Oscan dialect, as is evident from many inscriptions, was preserved much more intact than that of the Latin or Umbrian. Final consonants also were less mutilated. The locative case maintained its position, while the ablative kept its original d final; and the dative and accusative adhered much more closely to their primitive type, than in the other dialects. The Latin itself is, contrary to the once prevailing idea of its composite character, a simple, unmixed language like the Greek: as they are also each a distinct and strongly individualized demonstration under different influences, of the same original common tongue. In the Oscan and Umbrian dialects we see what the Latin must have originally been, before taking on any separate laws of development of its own.

Of the Volscian and Marsian dialects we have hardly sufficient traces, to be able to classify them with certainty. Of the Sabine, here and there a solitary ray shines glimmering in provincial Latin. The Latin stands related to all this Umbro-Samnite class of special dialects, as in Greek the Ionic to the Doric dialect; while the differences of the Oscan and Umbrian and their allied dialects may be compared with those of the Doric dialect, as found in the two regions of Sicily and Sparta. These different Italic dialects all point to their original union in one parent stem, in possessing as they do not only many roots in common, but also many exactly identical words; while their flexional forms also agree in the mode of their structure.

The peculiarities which individualize this whole family of dialects, as a distinct branch of the Indo-European stock of languages, are worthy of notice. They are such as these: Aspirates were not originally favorite with them, while with the Greeks and Etruscans they were. The finer breath-sounds, s, v, y, which the Greeks disliked, they cherished. Sibilants, indeed, constitute a marked feature of the old Italian languages.

THE INDO-EUROPEAN LANGUAGES. 77

Consonants they maintained at the end of a word with firmness. By the retrogressive tendency of their principles of accentuation in inflected and compound words, end-syllables were weakened and shortened in Latin, much more than in Greek. Vowels,* accordingly, at the end of words, except in flexion-endings where they form diphthongs or represent contracted forms, are short. The ingenious and compact mechanism of the Greek, in the preparation of the different tense-forms by prefixes, suffixes, vowel-substitutions and various consonantal changes, was unknown to them. The different tense-stems were formed, by compounding with the theme of the verb the auxiliary roots—es † and—fu. The dual ‡ number, both in the noun and verb, was rejected as superfluous. The ablative which was lost in Greek, was here retained; while the sense of the original Sanskrit locative was also engrafted on it frequently, and

* Hence the rules of prosody, that a and e final are short; while i final in the second declension (being contracted from Sanskrit sya in the genitive and in the plural nom. from Sansk. as) and also u final in the ablative (contracted from -ud, the original Latin ablative suffix) are long.

† Es, as in sum (for esumi); Greek $\epsilon\sigma$, as in $\epsilon\iota\mu\iota$ (for $\dot{\epsilon}\sigma\mu\iota$); Sanskrit as, as in asmi, I am: is the base of one of the two verb-forms signifying to be, which run through the whole range of the Indo-European languages; while the other is in Latin fu; in Greek, $\phi\upsilon$ (as in $\phi\upsilon\omega$), and in Sanskrit, bhu; English, *be;* Anglo-Saxon, beo; German, bin.

‡ Mommsen describes this in a quaint way. He says, literally translated, that "the strong logic of the Italians seems to have found no reason for splitting the idea of moreness into twoness and muchness."

so preserved with much more distinctness as a case than in Greek. The substantive-development also of the verb in the gerund, was peculiar to the Latin.

The Latin and Umbrian have been spoken of, as being closely related to each other. They are indeed ; and yet they are quite distinct from each other in many of their forms. The most important remains, now left of the Umbrian, are the seven Eugubine bronzed tablets discovered in ancient Iguvium, now called Gubbio, whence their name. The greater part of them is written in an old native alphabet from right to left, and was probably prepared about 400 B. C.; while the rest appears in the Roman alphabet, and is of a date, as is supposed, of about 200 years afterwards. The phonetic value of the same letters was greatly changed, during so short a period in the language. The ancient Latin and old Umbrian mutually explain many of each other's differences and difficulties. In the Umbrian the Latin q appears as p, as in pis * for quis who, and nep for neque nor. In the Samnite the genitive of words in us, is—eis, in the Umbrian—es, and in Latin—i † for -is In the Umbrian r and h are of much more fre-

* Cf, for a similar interchange of the labial and guttural, ἕπομαι and ἵππος Æol. ἴκκος, with sequor and equus (pronounced originally as if sekor and ekus); also Ionic κοῖος and κότερος with the Attic ποῖος and πότερος and Latin quinque (pronounced by the Latins kinke) with πέντε, five. In quispiam for quisquam, and nempe for namque, we have specimens of Umbrianized Latin.

† Dominus, gen. domini was originally domino-s, gen. domino-is; dat. domino-i, &c.

quent occurrence than in Latin. R is used, not only in the conjugation and declension of the verb as in Latin, but also in the declensions of nouns in different cases; while in Latin, except in nouns whose root ends in r, it is found only in the genitive plural. The Umbrians did not like l and b: never using l at the beginning of a word or b at the end. Terminations also in the Umbrian were greatly mutilated or destroyed. But in the retention of the locative and of the genitive suffix—s in the different declensions, the Umbrian presents itself before us, as having some resemblances to the older members of the Indo-European family, that are more antique than even those of the Latin.

The Umbrians occupied in ancient times the northern half of Italy, from the Tiber to the Po; and spread southerly in their course, along the Apennines upon their eastern slope. The Latin race extended in the same direction, along the western borders of Italy. The Romans called their own language Latin. Its designation as Roman, is not found in any author earlier than Pliny, and in him but once in a poem in his "Natural History." The Latins early covered the ground from the Tiber to the Volscian mountains; and from the names of places already existing there, they seem to have occupied Campania before the Samnite or Hellenic irruption into it. Latium proper occupied but a small district between the Tiber, the Apennines, Mount Alba and the sea, and was situated on a broad plain, as the name itself (latus) seems to indicate. This plain is surrounded on every side by mountains, except where it is bounded by the Tiber and the sea. It is level on an extended view; but, when surveyed in detail, it is found to be broken up into many unevennesses filled with innumerable little pools, which, from want of a sufficient watershed for drainage, breed in summer now as in ages past a fatal malaria, which overhangs its plains for months together, breeding disease and death. And yet on this narrow plain, with the sea on one side and the mountains on the other: such surroundings as environed also the Grecian mind: was to appear a race which should conquer the world by arms, as the Hellenes had by arts; and long after it had lost its civil power, should yet hold in its iron grasp the souls of men over all the earth: a race that in one form or another was destined to leave its impress on every people and every individual, every hamlet and every institution, in the civilized world. In this narrow space as their native home, the Roman eagles nestled and grew to greatness for almost a thousand years; and when those eagles ceased to appear in all the earth, there came forth in their stead from that same breeding-place of wonders, where it still lives and riots in its work of ruin, a scarlet-colored beast having seven heads and ten horns, bearing a woman drunk with the blood of saints and trampling upon the necks of prostrate kings and princes.

The climate of Latium is fitted to arouse the physical energies, and to induce an active busy restless style of life. It traverses a wide range of temperature throughout the year, and frequently in either direction through every point of the scale from the highest to the lowest degree, as in our North American atmosphere, in a few hours. The heats in summer are intense by day and at sunset are exchanged, as in our northern States, for a dewy and chilled state of the atmosphere that keeps rapidly cooling down for some hours. In the true season for out-door life, every thing around and above seems bright and exhilarating. Ethnology and philology thus maintain, in all countries, the closest possible connections with climatology. Indeed, as, on the bosom of a quiet summer stream, all the trees and herbage of the bank are seen mirrored in clear corresponding perspective, so, in the poetry and not in this only but also in the very history, character and language of each people, the skies and seas, the hills and dales, the flora and fauna, the mists and shades, the lights and heats and airs of surrounding nature are reflected. Man is deeply and tenderly receptive of her influence; and at the basis of all just interpretations of different national developments, viewed as historical problems, lies rightly understood a true, philosophic, divinely ordained materialism. It is, in other words, amid different types of nature that God casts, as in a mould, the different mental types of mankind.

Rome itself was situated on the Tiber, chiefly on its eastern bank. Down to the times of the Emperor Aurelian, it was built on seven hills; and from his time to the present it has extended over ten. It was, like the other great cities of ancient times, built for the sake of safety from invasion by water, at a little distance from the sea. To the Romans the world is indebted, beyond any other nation, for the principles of law and order and for the whole frame-work of organized social life. The Roman mind as instinctively tended towards mechanism in every thing, as a salt under appropriate chemical influences does to crystallization. The syntactical structure, accordingly, of the Latin, is as sharp, definite and uniform in its angles, as the laws of crystallogeny themselves would demand a given crystal always to be. The language itself is of a harder material, than the Greek. Its characteristics are gravity, solidity and energy; while those of the Greek are a wonderful vitality, elasticity, individuality and permanency. The Latin, by the greater contact of its people with other men, as they penetrated with their victories and their laws among them, while giving out everywhere its own light and heat to all parts of the conquered world, received in return an impress which was never left upon the more mobile Greek, from the other languages whose tides of influence it encountered.

The Greek had several beautiful dialects of its own, which blossomed in strong native luxuriance on its shores in the days of its power, like so many differently colored flowers on one parent stem; while in modern times it appears only in a single variety of the original stock, the modern Greek. Not so however with the Latin, which at the first stood alone in its own simple majesty without division or diversification, but has since, under the combined action of many influences, burst forth into an almost wild variety of forms, in the different languages of modern times.

The Latin language, as we have it, is far more unaltered and ancient in its features than the classic or Hellenic Greek; yet it must not be forgotten, that while the ultimate roots remained the same the forms themselves of the original words* were so altered in the Augustan age, that is, in the classic or golden age

* It will interest the classical reader to see a specimen or two of old Latin:

1. From the laws of Numa (700 B. C.): Sei qui hemonem loebesum dolo sciens mortei duit, pariceidas estod. This is in classical Latin: Si quis hominem liberum dolo sciens morti dederit parricida esto.

2. A Tribunitian law (493 B. C.): Sei qui aliuta faxit, ipsos Iovei sacer estod, et sei qui im, quei eo plebi scito sacer siet ocisit, pariceidas ne estod. That is: Si quis aliter fecerit ipse Iovi sacer esto; et si quis eum qui eo plebis scito sacer sit occiderit, parricida ne sit.

3. An inscription on L. Scipio's tomb (260 B. C.): Honc oinom ploirume consentiont Romanei duonorum optimom fuise virom. That

of Roman literature, as to require, for the right comprehension even of the scholars of that day, special helps and explanations. The oldest specimens of Latin literature that we have do not date farther back than 200 years before Christ; and in the 6th century after Christ, the Latin became extinct as the vernacular of the people of Italy. Even English as it was 300 years ago, or in the times of Shakspeare 250 years since, is very much of it unintelligible without a glossary; and this, with all the power of types and of the press to hold fast the ἔπεα πτερόεντα of modern speech. Even in the time of its highest culmination in the Augustan age, the Latin of the provinces was different from that of Rome itself; as that of the rural districts also was from that of the provincial municipalities. Indeed the Latin spoken by the masses was essentially a different idiom from that of the written classical Latin of the polished literary circles of Rome. The Latin was brought under the power of grammatical and critical culture, at a much later period than the Greek. In the progress of its growth it absorbed, in the south of Italy, some Greek idioms and in the north some Celtic : resolving them into the elements of its own greater enlargement. The triumph of Roman arms was followed always by the march of the Roman language, literature,

is: Hunc unum plurimi consentiunt Romani bonorum optimum fuisse virum.

So we find in the old Latin loidus for ludus, oiti for uti and quoius for cujus.

laws and institutions in their train. Like a stream of lava the flood of living influences pressed with irresistible force, sweeping every thing before it, into France and Spain and even into the fastnesses of Germany, and as far as to the distant shores of England and Scandinavia on the north, and the wilds of Sarmatia on the east: dissolving every thing in its way, or, at least leaving the signs of its fiery force on the crisped and altered forms of things, wherever it went. And yet the receptive, susceptible or passive side of Roman character, was almost as remarkable as its aggressive. The hard and stern elements of its genius and language were slow to receive impressions from without; but they were also equally slow, when having received, to relinquish them. The Latin accordingly not only degenerated at an early period in the provinces from its pure form, but also ere long settled down everywhere, even as the language of the learned in matters of State, Science and the Church, into what is called the Middle Latin. This phrase, like that of the Middle Ages covering substantially the same interval of time, is used to mark that transition-period in which the spoken Latin, wavering in form between its original pure state and the several dialectic aspects which it subsequently assumed in the different Romanic languages, possessed the elements of both the old and the new in combination, without the determinate preference which was afterwards given to the new. This degenerate form of the spoken Latin never became popularized, on the one hand; nor was it ever wrought into artistic shape, on the other, by scholars, but remained a heterogeneous compound of Latin, Græco-Roman and Germano-Roman elements. In schools, and especially cloisters, classical Latin was still cherished as a dear favorite of the past, whose voice seemed to them, like that of a sweet bird, flying down through the ages and singing as it flew. It found, like the sparrow, a nest for itself among the altars of God's house; and in the twelfth century, its song was heard again everywhere in the open air, in the sacred church-hymns of the times, as of a bird uncaged and at home once more in its native element, full of freedom and of joy.

It was in the tenth and eleventh centuries that the Latin was, as a spoken language, in the greatest possible state of ruin; and it was the energetic pressure of the German mind from the north, that most of all broke the weak ties which then held its elements together. Modern civilization is the combined result of the ideas, institutions and influences, contained in four great providential manifestations of national life and character: the Jewish, Greek, Roman and German; in which category although the German be last it is far from least. It is impossible to comprehend either the history of the past or the philosophy of the present, without a full acquaintance with German history which, strange to say, has been more neglected in this country hitherto than any other history. But the marks of German might and mind lie deep and strong over all the languages of southern, as well as of northern Europe.

When from the chaos of the Middle Ages the upheaval of modern society commenced, and the present nations of Europe began to exhibit in growing outline the general proportions, which they have since so distinctively assumed; the different Romanic languages, under the combined action of various local influences with the ever present influence of Rome, came to be severally enucleated. These afterwards grew up under the same influences in which they germinated, into separate well-defined forms, each beautiful in its kind, to cover with their different degrees of upward and outward expansion, as with a friendly shadow, the ruined greatness of their parent Latin stock, when it fell to lie forever prostrate under the hand of Time. Each of the five Romanic dialects, the Italian, Wallachian, French, Spanish and Portuguese, presents a different resemblance to its mother language, according to the quantity and quality of the alloy with which the Latin element in each is mingled. Each of them has specially preserved some separate cardinal characteristic of the old native stock, which it has kept with jealous care, as a precious proof of its original parentage. The Italian has still in possession its fulness of form and sweetness of tone: the Spanish has appropriated to itself its majesty and dignity, and the Portuguese its soft and tender strokes and touches: the French, on the contrary, best exhibits its elements of vivacity and its practical business-qualities, and therefore like it abounds in abbreviations and contractions, and is full of martial fire and energy; while the Wallachian has kept most of the old national disposition, to appropriate and assimilate extraneous influences and elements to itself. Each of these different languages has its different spoken dialects; although only the standard one in each ever shows its front, in the sacred precincts of literature.

Our modern languages are all, except the German, full of the most various mixtures. These mixtures in the European languages are of course all between those of the same Arian origin; and usually indeed languages of the same immediate family coalesce more readily, than those which are unrelated or but distantly related; as fruits may be made to grow most readily, when grafted on trees that are homogeneous in the style of their seeds. In the Modern Persian, indeed, we have a mixture of Iranian (the Old Persian) and Semitic (the Arabic); while, in the Turkish, there is a mixture of the Persian and Arabic with the original stock of the language itself, involving (and it is the only specimen of the kind in the whole circle of the languages) a combination of Indo-European, Semitic and Turanian elements in one.

A general view of the introduction of Germanic influences and elements into the Romanic languages is desirable, for a proper comprehension of their real constitution, and will, it is believed, be more satisfactory in such a form than if broken up into separate details, under the treatment of each different language by itself.

The German conquest of the Roman provinces occurred in the course of the fifth and sixth centuries, except that of Wallachia, where Gothic arms had long before made their power felt. In Italy, in the middle of the fifth century (A. D. 476–493), the brief supremacy of the Heruli passed, like a swift thunder-cloud, over the country, leaving only a temporary desolation in its track. Then came the Ostrogoths, who for 66 years (A. D. 494–560) ruled Italy with a rod of iron; and afterwards for 200 years (A. D. 568–774) the Lombards. The Lombardic dialect was, as is manifest from some of its relics, Old High German in the type of its consonantal structure. The Lombards began their wanderings in the course of the fourth century, from the northern shores of Germany and from Scandinavia, and, after many various adventures with the Bulgarians, Heruli, Gepidæ, Huns and Goths, settled quietly down in Pannonia, whence afterwards, under Alboin the 11th of their kings (A. D. 568), they marched into Italy and founded a kingdom, which endured, until overthrown by the Franks under Charlemagne, and left behind an enduring memorial of itself, in the name Lombardy, still given to the richest portion of northern Italy.* In the beginning therefore of the sixth century a Gothic kingdom was established in Italy, as also in Spain; and in Spain the succession of Gothic kings became (A. D. 531) elective. As Spain had been in earlier days traversed and scourged and conquered in different parts of her territory, by so many various races, as the Celts, Carthaginians and Romans: so, in connection with the great invasion of southern Europe from the north, race after race from the ever-swarming hive of Germany swept over the face of this then fair land, eager for the pleasures and prizes of conquest. In the beginning of the fifth century, we find the Suevi in full possession of Modern Gallicia, Asturia, Leon and a part of Lusitania, as well as the region formerly held on the east by Carthaginian arms; while in the south are the Vandals resting for a little while, only to gather strength for a still more vigorous movement onwards, conquering every thing before them as they spread beyond over the regions of northern Africa. In the north-east of Spain lay at the same time the Visigoths; hovering like a dark cloud, which, though appearing to the rest of the land at the time as but a little fleck of darkness in the distant horizon, was destined ere long to envelop the whole peninsula in its folds of gloom and terror.

* Grimm's Geschichte, pp. 473—485.

The German irruption into Gaul bore away every thing like an overflowing flood, then upon the soil, except the Latin language; so firmly established at that time over the people after so many centuries of Roman conquest and jurisdiction, and in itself so superior as the language of civilization, even in the eyes of the fierce northern conquerors as well as of the conquered; and which therefore maintained itself both in Church and State, as a beacon-light upon a high firm rock, unshaken amid all the swell of military commotions, in its place. And, as here in our own age the great peaceful German immigration, which is ever flowing in upon us, is constantly absorbed and assimilated to our common English type of language and of customs; so, in France slowly but surely the prevailing numbers and institutions of the country brought about, together with the advantages of a comparatively high civilization even in the hands of a conquered race, the final absorption of the new German element although an invasive one, into the grand all-comprehending unity of Roman life and law and language. The Roman type of social fixtures and usages was such, that its moulds were firm enough without, to receive any amount of fiery martial overflow into them, without breaking under the pressure, and sharp enough within, to make the cooling mass distinctively of its own pattern. By the year 486 the Franks had become masters of the greater part of Gaul. The first of the German tribes who were converted to the Christianity of the Catholic Church, was the Franks; and it was by this similarity of faith, that these German conquerors were most of all amalgamated with the older inhabitants of the land; as the development indeed of the new European nations, generally, was effected everywhere in the same way.* In the beginning of the fifth century, the south-western part of Gaul was in the possession of the Visigoths: the south-eastern part, of the Burgundians and the northern of the Franks: all Germanic tribes. Over the slow deliquescence of the German from its new home on Gallic soil and its final disappearance there, a veil of historic darkness rests, which has at least the advantage of hiding from modern eyes the offensive process of its dissolution. But "the position is not too bold," says Diez,† "that the German continued to be used in France, up to the division of the Carolingian kingdom (A. D. 840); and in the north, taking the song of victory of King Louis III. over the Normans (881) as a voucher, up to the end of the ninth century: which would make the time of its duration in Gaul from four to five hundred years."

Long after the German conquest the Byzantine armies tramped, from time to time, over lower Italy and Sicily and southern Spain; and yet no considerable mixture of people of different blood occurred in such a way.

* Gieseler's Ecc. Hist., vol. ii. pp. 131—3.
† Diez' Grammatik, p. 63.

The composition accordingly of the Romanic tongues is one, formed in the main of these staple elements: Classical or Pure Latin, Middle Latin, Græco-Romanic and Germano-Romanic words.

The Middle or corrupted Latin is, like the original or proper Latin itself, a very large element of all the Romanic languages. This was the common spoken dialect or patois, out of whose elements as their bases, those forms which arose in the times of Charlemagne and afterwards were generated. The great mass also of common unclassical Latin, existing in the language before the age of the Middle Latin, has a representation of itself, and that not inconsiderable, among these languages. Many of the forms also ranked under the Middle Latin, were but mere contractions of fuller classical or Greek forms of words: as cosinus (French and English cousin) of consobrinus; and colpus (Ital. colpo, French coup) of $\kappa ό λ α φ ο ς$; while not a few of the remainder were simply Latinized forms of words adopted from other languages, or forced into the speech of the Romanic races, by the busy or rough contact of the surrounding nations with them.

Great care is needed, in tracing Byzantine-Greek originals in the Middle Latin. Appearances of resemblance occur, at times, which are but appearances and entirely fortuitous; and as Latin and Greek were primarily of one immediate united origin, words even at so late a period may seem many of them to have been borrowed, which yet are as much vernacular to the one, as to the other. Like the principles of the common law, living of themselves unwatched and growing fresh and strong, without any of the trellises of statutory regulation or recognition to support them, beneath and around all the formalities of special legislation: so these words, never having shown themselves before on the high points of literary demonstration, may have yet kept, on the plane of thought and feeling lying below it, a fresh green life perpetually of their own. It is as true in etymological and ethnographic relations, as in other things, that "fools rush in where angels dare not tread."*

* Specimens of the different classes of elements to be found in the Romanic languages besides pure Latin:

I. Of ante-mediæval unclassical Latin.

Latin.	Italian.	Spanish.	French.	English.
badius, brown	bajo	bayo	bai	bay
Bassus, Prop. name, Cf. βαθύς, Comp. βασσων.	basso		bas	base
beber, for fiber	bévero	bibaro	bièvre	beaver
caballus, a nag	cavallo	caballo	cheval	cavalry / cavalier / chevalier / chivalry
capulum, a rope	cappio	cable	câble	cable
camisia, a shirt	camicia	camisa	chemise	chemise
cambiare, to exchange	cangiare	cambiar	changer	change
confortare (con-fortis)	confortare	conhortar	conforter	comfort
carricare, to load	carcare	cargar	charger	charge / cargo
gabalum, a cross			gable	gable
grossus, thick	grosso	grueso	gros	gross
pretiare, to put a price on	prezzare	preciar	priser	prize
Sapius, wise, for Sapiens	saggio	sabio	sage	sage

THE INDO-EUROPEAN LANGUAGES.

struppus, a band	stroppolo	estrovo	étrope	strap
unio (from unus)	unione		oignon	onion
vidulus, a knapsack	vuligia		valise	valise

II. Of Græco-Romanic elements:

Greek.	Latin.	Italian.	Spanish.	French.	English.
βλασφημεῖν		biasimare		blâmer	blame
βύρσα, a skin	bursa	bors	bolsa	bourse	bourse / disburse / purse
πύργος	burgus	borgo	burgo	bourg	burgh / burgess
λύγξ		lonza	onza	once	ounce
καμπή, a flexure	gamba	gamba	jamba / jamon	jambe	jamb / ham
κόλαφος	colaphus and colpus.	colpo	golpe	coup	
πέζα	petium	pezzo	pieza	pièce	piece
σπάθη	spatha, a broad tool or sword.	spada	espada	epée	spade
	spathula, shoulder blade.	spalla	espalda	épaule	epaulet
παραβολή	parabola	parola	palabra	parole / parler	parable / palaver / parole / parlance
σμύρις, emery		smeriglio	esmeril	émeri	emery
τρυφᾶν, to bore		trapan	trepanar	trepaner	trepan
τῦφος, smoke		tufo	tufo	étouffer / to suffocate	tufa
θρίξ, hair	trica and terza, plaited hair.	treccia	tresse		tresses / trick

III. Of Germano-Romanic elements:

German.	Middle Latin.	Italian.	Spanish.	French.	English.
bauen, to build. Old German, Buisc, building material.	boscus, a wood	bosco	bosque	bois	bosky / bush / ambush
brennen, to burn	brunus brown, lit. scorched.	bruno	bronce	brun	brown / bronze
Harinc, a corruption of Lat. halec.		aringa	arenque	hareng	herring
Hring and ring, a circle for fighting.		aringo / aringa	arenga	harangue	harangue

Of Germano-Romanic elements in these languages, there are two kinds of quite different chronological features. The first of these, as they were imported into these languages at the time of the first German immigration into the Provinces, are marked by the greater prevalence of the original a and i vowels in their forms, instead of the later introduced e, and the diphthong ai instead of ei, as well as the consonants p, t, and d for f, z and t. The second class of Germano-Romanic elements has on it the special mark, which the Germans call Lautverschiebung, or a mutation of the radical consonant or consonants; which is one of the great peculiarities of the Gothic languages, and which first became an established fact in them in the sixth century: so that this class of words must have been introduced into the Romanic languages after this time. In the French a third class also, German words, called Danish by the writers of the day, came in from the Normans in the north-western part of France. They readily amalgamated with the people of the land, and, so, gradually relinquished their own language for theirs, although depositing in it also many of their own words, especially those pertaining to maritime life.

German influence was felt, only on the lexical[*] and not at all on the grammatical features, of the Romanic

[*] Diez finds in the different Romanic languages about 930 pure German roots, some still alive in them, and some obsolete, independently of unnumbered derivatives and compounds; of which 450 occur in French; 140, not occurring elsewhere, in Italian; and somewhat

languages, which are of a firm, unimpaired Latin structure.

But each of the Romanic languages requires a separate consideration.

(1.) The Italian.

By far the great majority of all its words, to at least nine parts out of ten, are Latin. Of the Greek elements, which constitute a considerable portion of its remaining vocabulary, many must have doubtless come into it through the Latin. In the Sicilian and Sardinian dialects, where words of this nature most abound, it would seem probable that many of them must be the remains of that early contact with Greece, that grew out of their original colonial relations to that land.

The Italian since the second half of the twelfth century, when it first became enthroned in a permanent literature of its own, has changed but little; far less indeed than any of its sister languages. It is altogether in itself the purest specimen of the old common stock, and has spread out its boughs beyond the limits of its own native sphere, into the Tyrol and even into Illyria. It was at first called common Latin, afterward Sicilian and then Tuscan, and seems to have come into use by the cultivated classes in its present distinct form by the end of the tenth century. Its phonetic phenomena are remarkable, as are those even of the differ-

more than 50 each, in the Provençal Spanish and Portuguese languages; while in the Wallachian there are less than anywhere else.

ent dialects compared with each other. The department of phonology is in fact quite as full of wonders, in the modern languages as in the ancient. Italian literature is of broad and high dimensions. In it are hung up as in a temple, the votive offerings of many poets, philosophers and scholars: offerings, which, though made in the midst of smoking incense and of holy water, have but few of them any of that fragrance of holy feeling and purpose, with which so much of English and American literature is sweet-scented.

In respect to the different dialects of the Italian, the Lombard, the Genoese, the Florentine, whose form of speech constitutes the standard of taste, the Neapolitan, the Sicilian, the Sardinian and the Corsican, each carries a distinct badge of his nativity upon him, in the different tone or form or spirit of his speech. Language is too impressible to all the influences of every kind which separate men not only into various nations, but, also on every extended area, into different sections of the same nation, and which mark off the historic life of the same community into successive periods of growth, maturity and decline; to preserve for any great length of time or space, one unaltered, petrified, Egyptian style of form or features. It can no more be cribbed and confined in any one direction, however free and full, than humanity itself, whose utterance it is and which is ever swelling with vital forces, struggling for a newer and larger expression of themselves.

(2.) The Wallachian.

This descendant of the old Latin has been, almost wholly, made known to European scholars since the recent war at Sebastopol. The people call themselves Români and their language România. The region over which it spreads, consists of Wallachia, Moldavia and parts of Hungary, Transylvania and Thrace, or, in other words, both banks of the lower part of the Danube; and it is spoken by more than three millions of people. It is in its grammatical constitution more like the Italian than any of the sister languages. It is accordingly easy of acquisition in this direction; but, in respect to its lexical elements, it is not so readily mastered; as it contains large mixtures of Slavonic elements, forced into it by the pressure of so many languages of this class lying around it on every side. They have also adopted from them the Cyrillic alphabet. The Wallachians proper number now not far from a million souls. Like the Albanians and Bulgarians, they put the article after the noun. They use also, like the French, in the formation of different tenses, auxiliary verbs much more than did the Latin. The old Illyrian appears often also in broken fragments, in the Wallachian, and only in such a form; as it does likewise in the Albanian. The Danube divides the Wallachian into two principal dialects, northern and southern or Daco-Roman and Macedo-Roman. The northern is more pure, although having more Slavonic mixtures with it; and it is more cultivated than the southern, which has been overlaid with much foreign material, especially Albanian and Grecian. Many words also from various languages have, under the pressure of past conflicts as well as social and commercial contact with neighboring nations, become incorporated into the fabric of the language, so as to form a permanent part of its tissue; and many are the Slavic, Albanian, Greek, German, Hungarian and Turkish words that, like strange birds, sit and sing now in this language, in boughs out of which they have driven forever the native inhabitants of the wood.

The Wallachian took its rise, as one of the Romanic dialects, definitively in the Roman colonies sent into Dacia by Trajan, who made Dacia (107 B. C.) a Roman province. The original population of Dacia was of Thracian origin: the inhabitants of eastern Dacia being Getae and those of the West being Dacians proper. In the Wallachian the Latin greatly preponderates, while the old Illyrian still preserves a foothold in it, reminding us in these modern times that there it once dwelt; although its fires are now all quenched and its ancient walls destroyed. Wallachian, or Daco-Romanic literature began its distinct career in the year 1580; and, since that day, poetical and scientific works have appeared from time to time, although not in great abundance. The mass of its literature is of a religious kind.

(3.) The Spanish.

THE INDO-EUROPEAN LANGUAGES. 101

The original inhabitants of Spain were Iberians, probably a very early offshoot of the ancient Celtic population of Europe. Pictet* regards Iberia, and with good reason, as like Hibernia a compound of Ibh the land and Er, of the Erins or Arii; on which supposition, two marked instances occur in the West of the continued retention of the old family-name of this great class of languages. When afterwards subsequent generations of Celts came, in their separate historic character, as such, to be commingled with the descendants of those first settlers, they received from the Romans the name of Celtiberians. Phoenicians and Carthaginians very early settled on the coast, and, by ever fresh additions of men and resources, obtained ere long the supremacy of the land. After dispossessing them and conquering the fierce obstinacy of the natives, the Romans seized upon Spain as their own possession (133 B. C.), and held it as such for 600 years, until the Vandals and the Huns wrested it from the grasp of their effeminate descendants; who themselves also afterwards were compelled to give up this same tempting prize into the hands of the Moors. The Vandal or German invasion occurred in the beginning of the 5th century; and in the beginning of the 8th the Arabic; while, during the interval between them, the authority of Byzantium was acknowledged throughout the line of its seaward coast in the South.

* Kuhn's Beiträge zur Sprachforschung, pp. 94—5.

And what a mixture of elements, for growth and greatness, is here! So much more energetic however was the influence of the Latin element than that of the others, that, except in phonetic and logical relations, it moulded the whole language into conformity with its own spirit and type. The structure of the language and its accentuation are thoroughly Romanic, as is also the larger part of its lexical elements.

In the north of Spain there still lives, like a wild bird that has wandered away from the rest of its species, undisturbed among the recesses of the mountains, a strange language, the Basque, that has come down from an elder age and remained unmixed with the dialects that surround it. This Humboldt regards as the remains of the original tongue of Spain, which, chased away from the open fields and streams of the land by Phœnician and Roman arms, found at last a safe retreat for itself in fastnesses too deep and high to tempt their pursuit. Its present home embraces the provinces of Biscaya, Guipuzcoa, Alava and a part of Navarra. Among the sisterhood of the Spanish dialects,* the Castilian sits queen, and has its local habitation in the very centre of Spain embracing the provinces of Leon, Estramadura, Andalusia, Aragon, most of Na-

* Diez quotes Sarmiento's analysis of the constituent elements of Spanish to be as follows: Six-tenths Latin: one-tenth ecclesiastical and Greek: one-tenth northern or German: one-tenth Oriental and one-tenth made up of American, modern German, French and Italian. —*Diez' Grammatik*, 2d ed., p. 95.

varra, Rioja and Murcia. The Catalonian and Galician dialects which are next in value, are intermixed largely with elements serving to alloy their purity : the former with those of the dialect of Provence in France, and the latter with the neighboring Portuguese. In its forms of declension, the Spanish is more like the Latin than is the Italian; but less like it in the sound or sense of its derivatives. It was about the middle of the twelfth century, that Spanish literature began its distinct career, and with it that the Spanish language assumed a fixed form : although it was not until three centuries afterwards, that scholars began to elaborate the language as such. Its vocabulary is very largely interspersed with foreign elements, especially Arabic. By her very position, so near to northern Africa, where Phœnician Carthage dwelt of old in the pride of her power and delighted to make her a prey, and whence afterwards the Moor trampled with furious energy upon all her growing greatness : Spain was through all the formative part of her history held in subjection to the influence of Semitic* arms, languages

* The stock of the present population of North Africa is well described by Barth, vol. i., p. 195. "They all," he says, "appear to have been originally a race of the Semitic stock ; but, by intermarriage with tribes which came from Egypt or by way of it, to have received a certain admixture. Hence came several distinct tribes designated anciently as Libyans, Moors, Numidians, Libyphœnicians, Getulians and others, and traced by the native historians to two different families, the Beranes and the Abtar, who however diverge from one common source, Mazigh or Madaghs. This native wide-spread African race,

and institutions, beyond any other nation in Europe. The two languages, with which it thus came into close mechanical, if not chemical, combination for centuries, were the Phœnician or Hebrew, the noblest of the ancient tongues of that family, and the Arabic the noblest of the new. Its technical terminology is particularly rich in words of Arabic origin. Spanish literature is specially distinguished by two marked features: first the general ballad form of its poetry, and secondly the abounding prevalence of tales of chivalry and knight errantry. If ever the Lyric Muse had a home that she specially loved, next after Jerusalem when David filled it with the music of his harp, whose echoes have ever since filled the world beside, and Lesbos, where Sappho sang in her heathen home of earthly loves, like a songster that had wandered from her native skies and lost her tune though not her voice; it was in old Castile. Her strains were at first simple, tender and melting, but, after Arabic blood had mingled its fire with the Spanish, she became more bold and brilliant in her eye and mien. Under the influence of Moorish energy and daring it was, that the romantic literature of Spain sprang into being. In no other language of Europe, except the German which is full of the balm and bloom of the luxuriant East, is there such

either from the name of their supposed ancestor Ber, which we recognize in the name Afer, or, in consequence of the Roman name barbari, has been generally called Berber, and in some regions Shawi and Shelluh."

an Oriental richness of coloring, as in the Spanish. In the language of Schlegel, " Castilian poetry incorporated into itself foreign forms and borrowed charms, combining the most various Romantic dialects, until its glowing and fanciful creations at length expanded, like flowers of perfect brilliancy clad in every hue." In the fifth century the Vandals poured like a torrent through its rich valleys: in the sixth and seventh, Byzantium stretched its sway over its southern borders; and in the eighth the Arab held Spain, like an eagle, gasping for life in his talons. It was in the middle of the twelfth century that the great national Epic of the Cid appeared.

(4.) The Portuguese.

This language is in its structure of great beauty. It was modified from the simple Latin original, much more than either of the other Romanic languages, by the Provençal dialect; and is regarded by those acquainted with it as the flower of all those dialects: combining, as it does, in a most wonderful manner, both simplicity and sweetness with high artistic finish of construction. And here let us listen again to Schlegel's glowing words: "In its power of expressing tender feeling, it surpasses every other language. It is also singularly rich in appropriate words, the very tone of which, independently of their beautiful signification, seems to melt at once into the soul. Even the soft Italian appears rough in comparison with the Portuguese; and the Spanish stern and northern. It is by far the most simple of all the Provençal and Romantic dialects, yet inferior to none in highly artistic construction. The prose is simple, rich and laconic, yet without the slightest constraint; indeed, in every kind of style, ease and grace appear to be with that nation natural qualities." Unfortunately we are as ignorant of its literature, as of that of Holland : having scarcely one author within our reach, except the noble Camoens; in whose Lusiad, a great national epic poem, we find ourselves equally lost in joy and sorrow, as we converse in it with the poet and with Portugal: in joy at the splendor of his genius, and in sorrow that this beautiful production, like the last song of the dying Swan, though almost too sweet for earth, was but the prelude to the downfall of his country in the loss of India. Suddenly, like a star deserting all at once the bright sisterhood of planets in which it had before moved and shone, it wandered away from its place among the leading nations of the world; and is now remembered, only as having once had a lustre which it possesses no more.

Such phonetic discordances occur in the vowel and diphthongal combinations and derivations of the Spanish and Portuguese languages, as quite place them in respect to many points, at antipodes to each other. The Portuguese has far less Basque in it, than the Spanish; and has adhered much more constantly to its own original antique modes and degrees of development. It is accordingly an independent shoot of itself from the roots of that vigorous old mother-tongue of Rome, which succeeded in spreading itself over all Western Europe; and which, wherever it spread, was sure to exclude every thing that it could not assimilate to itself from the soil. It has in its composition a manifest mixture of French elements, brought in by Henry, Count of Burgundy and his numerous Court-retinue.

(5.) The dialect of Provence.

This was the language of the old Troubadours, and occupied a sort of middle ground between the other dialects, and was greatly modified and moulded by them all. Those poetical musicians of the Middle Ages spent their time in wandering about from court to court in France and on the continent; and, having no one place in which they might congregate and build up a lasting literature for themselves and for the world, they left behind them no written records of their own. Fortunately the airy spirit of this language, supposed but a little while ago to have been for ever exhaled from this world, has recently been found,* lingering spell-bound, although unvisited and unknown for many long centu-

* It is announced also by F. Dümmler, of Berlin, that he has published of late 300 Troubadour poems in the Provençal dialect, edited by Dr. C. A. F. Mahn; gathered, most of them for the first time, out of seven ancient manuscripts from the Royal Library at Paris, and four old English ones, which by a conjunction of fortunate circumstances have just come to light and into his hands.

ries in the very words and letters, which those old minstrels used and loved. As for itself it spread out like a vine of strong growth, throughout the southern part of France and beyond its native French limits, into all the neighboring parts of Italy and Spain. It was in the eleventh century, that the Troubadour poetry reached the acme of its excellence, scattering its fragrance for many years afterwards over all Europe. And even if the language had been obliterated from the records of the past, as was once supposed, its name and its influence would still have survived, having passed by a true transmigration in the style and name of that department of literature, called Romance, into all the languages of the civilized world.

The Provençal dialect spread, in France, over Gascony, Provence, Limousin, Auvergne and Viennois, and in the regions of Northern Italy over Savoy and a small part of Switzerland, as Lausanne and the Southern part of Valais. Specimens of the Provençal dialect are found of as ancient a date as the year 960; but they are only single sentences occurring in old Latin records. The song of Boethius, a fragment of more than two hundred stanzas, preserved in a manuscript of the eleventh century, although written probably half a century before, is to be found among Reynouard's collections with some smaller pieces of the same date.

(6.) The French language.

This is in many respects the finest reproduction

of the original Latin, that we find among the modern languages. It has a much smaller mixture of other elements in it than the Spanish, and much more than the Italian. The French character is not indeed as strongly representative as is the language, in its spirit, of its Roman original. The French mind has naturally the love of martial activity and pomp, as well as the instinct for organization and centralization, that characterized the Roman; but it has, with these tendencies also, under its more favorable atmosphere, and surrounded by its more enchanting* landscapes, an inclination to art and a sense of the beautiful, as well as an elastic vivacious style of social character, that are rather Grecian than Roman in their type. Gaul, originally settled by the Celts, afterwards conquered by the Romans, fell in the end into the hands of the Franks,† a tribe of Germans; and was continuously Romanized, from the time of Cæsar who first conquered it, all along the track of the successive dynasties *of* Rome or *for* Rome, civil and spiritual, that held their sway over it. The southern part of it, occupied

---

* In the language of Ruskin: " Of all countries for educating an artist to the perception of grace, France bears the bell; in even those districts of which country, that are regarded as most uninteresting, there is not a single valley, but is full of the most lively pictures."— *Modern Painters*, Vol. i., p. 126.

† In their very name Franks, we see that they were distinguished by their love of freedom and the openness of their character and conduct, as a strong conquering race conscious of their own power and virtue, from the feeble Celts and degenerate Romans whom they had overcome.

at first by the Basques, still retains its memorial of that fact in the very name Gascony* applied to it, which means literally the land of the Basques. In this region, and that of Low Brittany, the influence of Rome was least felt upon the people and their language. The original dialects of the French were many. In those of Southern France, bordering on Italy, the old Latin vowel-sounds were preserved full and pure. In Northern France they were changed like the consonants, and rejected to such a degree as to depart far from their first Latin type. Compared with the Spanish and Italian, the French has in it less Latin and more German.

The determinate amount of all its elements, it is difficult to decide. Of the Gallic words preserved to us as such in the old classical authors, a large number are still found clearly preserved in either the new or old French. The Old French, of which we have but few remains, is chiefly allied to the Gothic, but less in its vowel-system than its consonantal, which is much akin to the Old Saxon, although after the Carolingian † period it inclined more towards the High German. Having

* The interchange of g, in both Low and Middle Latin and the French, with b, v and w in German and English, is worthy of notice, as in Latin, Gulielmus; French, Guillaume; German, Wilhelm; English, William. So compare also French garder and English guard and ward, guardian and warden; also Latin vastare, French gâter (for original gaster), English waste, vast and devastate, as also French guerre and English war.

† Or, Carlovingian.

no monuments left now of those early Germanic dialects, the Lombardian, Burgundian and Suevian, and scarcely any of the French, it is hard to trace with distinctness the action or presence, to any high degree, of each or any of the Germano-Romanic elements that came into the French behind the Gothic, or even in parallel streams with it.*

There are in French some four hundred and fifty root-words, with many derivatives and compound words, some now living in the language and some obsolete, of direct German origin. The southern part of France not being overrun by the Norman invasion, lost all that class of words introduced into the north, and was therefore less Germanized. It has spread out its boughs beyond its own limits, over Belgium and a considerable part of Switzerland; while, in connection with the Norman Conquest, it has much modified the English, both by its great effect upon the Latin elements of our language itself, and also by the direct introduction into it of many of its own words. It is now also the universal language of social commerce

* The following are specimens of Gallic and Old French:
    G. alauda, a lark.   O. F. aloe.
    " sagum, a military clock.   " saie.
    " marga, manure.   " marie.
    " bulga, leather-bag.   " boge.
    " braccæ, breeches.   F. braie.
    " betula, birch.   " boule.
    " leuca, mile.   " lieue.
    " beccus, beak.   " bec.

throughout civilized Europe. The oldest specimen of antique French in existence occurs in the oath of Charles the Bald against Lothaire (A. D. 842), at Strasburg. The old French literature was at its height in the twelfth and thirteenth centuries.

Before turning away from the Romanic family of languages it deserves to be remarked, that by a comparison of them each with the other, the existence of the Latin, if wholly extinct, could be definitively ascertained from them, as an absolute foregone necessity. And, just as from the multiplied analogies of these modern dialects of the Latin, we revert infallibly to their union in a common parentage, so, the analogies of the different Indo-European families declare with the same certainty, that once there existed somewhere an unknown mother of them all, who is yet now revealed to us as having herself had high character and honor, only by the innate beauty and energy of her illustrious progeny.*

* A comparison of the numerals in the different Romanic languages:

Latin.	Italian.	Wallachian.	Spanish.	Portuguese.	French.
1. unus	uno	unu	uno	hum	un
2. duo	due	doi	dos	dois	deux
3. tres	tre	trei	tres	tres	trois
4. quatuor	quattro	patru	quatro	quatro	quatre
5. quinque	cinque	quinque	cinco	cinco	cinq
6. sex	sei	sese	seis	seis	six
7. septem	sette	septe	siete	sete	sept
8. octo	otto	optu	ocho	oito	huit
9. novem	nove	nove	nueve	nove	neuf
10. decem	dieci	dece	diez	dez	dix

THE INDO-EUROPEAN LANGUAGES. 113

III. The Lettic family.

Under this title are included the Lithuanian, the old Prussian and the Lettish.

1st. The Lithuanian.

This is a language of very great value to the philologist. It is the most antique in its forms, of all the living languages of the world, and most akin in its substance and spirit to the primeval Sanskrit. It is also at the same time so much like the Latin and the Greek, as to occupy to the ear of the etymologist, in a multitude of words not otherwise understood, the place of an interpreter: with its face fixed on the Latin and its hand pointing backwards to the Sanskrit. It has preserved its identity wonderfully with the Sanskrit, in respect generally to its radical, and, in the case of the noun, also its flexional forms. It has seven of the eight cases found in the Sanskrit: the ablative being wanting, which in Latin indeed is preserved, while two cases, the locative and instrumental, have been lost in a distinct form: the Greek has lost the three cases, which have disappeared variously from both the Lithuanian and Latin; while the German has lost still another, the vocative, and the English one more even, the dative: retaining only the nominative, genitive (or possessive) and accusative, or rather the possessive only: the nominative and objective not being cases in English in their form. The Lithuanian has also, like the Greek and Gothic, but unlike the Latin, the dual number.

The Lithuanians, living as they do on the southern shore of the Baltic sea, have been from the first, as much as even the Icelanders themselves, out of the path of the successive tides of emigration, that so much crushed and bore away the forms of other languages. Their language, accordingly, on account of the primeval regularity of its roots and structure, stands related to the various branches of the Indo-European family, especially to those of a modern date whose forms have been much mutilated, as a general exponent of their agreements and differences, or a sort of general solvent for the etymologist, of a multitude of otherwise unresolvable difficulties. It is like an universal interpreter, seeming to have the gift of tongues, since its tongue is so greatly like all the rest in preserving the pure primal model, from which they are all corrupted derivatives, as to seem in whatever language you hear the chime of its words, very much like an old-fashioned brogue of that language, ringing down loud and clear from ancient times. Its literature possesses neither height nor breadth, and is limited to a moderate number of popular songs, fables and proverbs.

In respect to the flexion of the verb, it has departed more widely from its original than in any thing else; having lost the principles of reduplication and augment, and of the change of the radical vowel in different tenses to indicate the several variations of time. The passive is formed by the aid of the substantive verb.

It has a middle voice formed by the use of s, si, which is a reflexive pronoun of the third person used in all the persons; as also in Latin the middle sense was formed originally, and derivatively from it the passive, by attaching this same reflexive s (i. e. se, the third person pronoun), euphonically changed to r, to the forms of the active* voice. The phonetic constitution of the language like that of its radical forms, has been wonderfully preserved by the fortunate isolation of the people from the great movements of the nations around them, unimpaired in its leading elements. The Lithuanian is now under the pressure of Russian institutions, influences and ideas, fast becoming mongrelized with that language.

The Lithuanians number in both Russia and Prussia, 1,500,000 people: not quite 200,000 living in Prussia. That their language should at last be found undergoing serious changes, who can wonder; for what can resist the onset of modern innovation, or rather the tendency of Modern Christianity to "make," and of Modern Humanity to receive, " all things new." " Behold," saith Christ, " I make all things new! " The world is destined to be in the end, for God hath spoken it, one great brotherhood; and, though, in some cli-

---

* Thus the passive forms, amor, amaris or amare, &c., restored to their original crude state, would be amo-se, lit. I love myself, amasse, amatse, &c. So the Germans use to a striking degree the reflexive forms, in our passive sense, as in sich schämen, (lit. to shame one's self,) &c.; and in French similar forms occur, as in il se vend cher. (lit. it sells itself dear,) it is sold high.

mates and in some races, the process of fusion goes on more slowly than in others, yet it is still everywhere, with the same certainty, at work towards the final issue. Perpetual changes in detail, but perpetual progress on the whole: these are the two great primordial laws of human progress.

2d. The Old Prussian.

This sister-language of the Lettic family perished, about two hundred years ago. The only memorial, now left of it, is a Catechism prepared by Albert of Brandenburgh. While not so ancient and pure in its forms, it was still much less corrupted than the Lettish. It had not so many cases as the Lithuanian and possessed no dual. It was spoken on the northern coast of Prussia, east of the Vistula.

3. The Lettish.

This is the popular language of Courland and of much of Livonia. It is properly but a derivative from the Lithuanian, like the Italian from the Latin. Its points of difference from it are, besides a general corruption of its forms, the following:—

(1.) It has the article as the Lithuanian had not.

(2.) It has opened a wide door to foreign words, particularly to those of German and Russian origin.

(3.) It has special euphonic laws of its own which it carefully follows.

(4.) Its grammar is much more modern in its type than that of the Lithuanian.

(5.) Its phonetic system has been much modified by Slavonic influences.

IV. The Slavic or Slavonic family.

The area covered by this class of languages in Europe is very large, extending from the Arctic Ocean on the north, to the Black and Adriatic Seas on the south; and from the Dwina on the east, to the Hartz Mountains on the west. It extends itself, also, in scattered districts through Asia, into the upper regions of North America. The name, Slavic, comes from the root, slu, Sanskrit, sru, (Greek $\varkappa\lambda\upsilon$, as in $\varkappa\lambda\upsilon\omega$, and $\varkappa\lambda\upsilon\tau\acute{o}\varsigma$; Latin, *inclytus;* Old High German, hlô), meaning to hear, and to hear one's self called, or to be named, to be celebrated. Its meaning is therefore* "renowned," "distinguished." The different stages of growth and strength in the Slavonic languages are well described by Schleicher, in his † "Geschichte der Slavischen Sprache," as being marked by five distinct periods:

(1.) The Slavic, in its primeval embryo state, among the elements of the unknown primeval Indo-European mother-tongue.

* And yet this is the very word from which, as in the French esclave and German sklave, comes our English word slave. So those great names, Cæsar and Pompey, are now the common names of dogs and slaves.

† This is a brief article, but quite valuable, of some 27 pages only published since his "Sprachen Europa's," in "The Oriental Journal of Literature and Art," and recently gathered with other brief philological essays, by Kuhn, into a sort of periodical collection, entitled, "Beiträge zur Sprachforschung," three parts of which have now been published.

(2.) The Slavic, as Slavo-German.

(3.) The Slavic, as Letto-Slavic.

(4.) The Slavic, as an individual independent language.

(5.) The Slavic, as itself the mother of different dialects.

The Slavonic languages are very intimately affiliated one with the other. With any one of their various dialects, except the Bulgarian, which has degenerated most of all, it is quite easy to make one's self intelligible in conversation with those speaking the others. There are religious manuscripts in the Slavonic language dating back as far as the eleventh century; and by a comparison of the present forms with those of that date, they are found to have been remarkably stable. The changes that have taken place have occurred chiefly under the influence of the vowels, especially the i and j sounds, on the consonants preceding them. By their influence many mutes have been changed into sibilants, or assibilated to those in juxta-position with them; and hence the superabundance of sibilants in those languages. The double consonants that occur so frequently in them, particularly in the Polish, while double to the eye, are like several similar combinations in English,* but single to the tongue.

The Slavic languages are rich in grammatical forms.

* As in English, know, knee, knife, gnash, gnat, pneumonia, &c.

THE INDO-EUROPEAN LANGUAGES. 119

They have the same number of case-endings with the Sanskrit, but do not use the article with the noun, or the pronoun with the verb. In common with the Lithuanian and German languages, they have a double form, the definite and indefinite, for each adjective.

The alphabetic characters of this family of languages are of two different kinds. The Slavonians of the Greek faith have what is called the Cyrillic alphabet, first introduced by St. Cyril : and it is used in the ecclesiastical Slavic now. Cyril was a Greek monk, who went from Constantinople (A. D., 862), to preach the gospel to the Slavonians. The characters of his alphabet are chiefly Greek, although considerably modified ; and new signs also are introduced, to represent sounds not found in the Greek. The Russians themselves also used the Cyrillic alphabet up to the time of Peter the Great, who boldly rejected nine of its characters, and then cut and carved what remained unsparingly into a more tasteful form. Not only the Russian, but also the kindred Servian alphabets, are formed with some alterations from this alphabet, and are of recent origin. The style of orthography used by the other Slavonians, as the Croats, Bohemians, Lusitanians, Illyrians and Poles, is of the Roman order like our own, although somewhat dialectic in each case. There is also a secondary form of the Ecclesiastico-Slavonic to be found occasionally, called the Hieronymic, from the idea that it was invented by Hieronymus.

It is however quite doubtful, when and by whom it was invented, and for what special purpose.

The Slavic family of languages consists, properly, of two leading branches:

1. The South-eastern Slavic.
2. The Western Slavic.

Some of the general points of difference existing between these two branches, although marked with many exceptions, are such as these:

(1.) An euphonic insertion of d before l, in those of the second division, but not in those of the first. (2.) The letters d and t before l and n, are rejected in those of the first, but not in those of the second. (3.) The labials v, b, p, m, when followed by j, take in the first an l between them, but not in the second.

I. The South-eastern Slavic branch:

   1st. The Russian.
   2d. The Bulgarian.
   3d. The Illyrian.

1st. The Russian language.

It was 300 years ago, that Russia succeeded in throwing off the Mongol yoke, which had for about two centuries, well nigh crushed out its very life; and, since the first full discovery then made of her own real inward strength, she has been marching forward in a lofty style of effort and of honor, in arts and arms, in learning and social improvement, and in every thing but religion. The same evil genius of hierarchical priestcraft stands in organized terror by her side, to poison continually the cup of all her sweets, that has drugged for so many centuries the papal nations of Christendom with its sorceries. Although Russian orthography has been greatly modified by the influence of ecclesiastico-Slavic elements; the pronunciation of Russian words has remained true to their early forms, so that it almost embraces in fact two languages in itself: one to the eye and another to the ear.

The Russian language, like the Russian empire, spreads over a very wide domain. It is with the Servian, the most harmonious of all the Slavonic tongues. Consonantal combinations which would otherwise be harsh, it often improves by the special insertion of vowels. While the modern Slavonic languages agree wonderfully with both the Latin and Greek, the resemblance of the Russian, especially, to the Latin is very striking. Donaldson quotes with approval a modern traveller, as saying that the founders of Rome spoke the Russian language. In the implication made, however, by such a quotation, that so unclassical a surmise is to be received as a literal historical truth, he shows the same credulity and the same tendency to philological marvellousness, that elsewhere often characterize his speculations. Such tendencies indeed are among the customary weaknesses of that class of skeptical minds, whether in natural, theological, historical, linguistic, or other science which he represents.

Already Russian literature, like Russian arms and Russian enterprise, has begun to show some of those gigantic proportions in which it is destined to lift up itself in full view, when, under a general equal evangelical system of social life, its people shall come to appreciate and undertake their true work among the nations. The Russian contains three separate dialects.

(1.) The Great Russian.

A special form of this dialect, the Muscovite, is the standard, in respect to both orthography and orthoepy, for all the dialects. The Great Russian is spoken from the Peipus Sea to the Sea of Azof.

(2.) The Little Russian.

This is spoken in the southern part of Russia, as in Galicia, and shows many traces of foreign influences upon it. It has been but very little used as a written dialect, and that chiefly of late, although it is easily recognized in ecclesiastico-Slavonic as far back as the 11th century.

(3.) The White Russian.

This is spoken in different parts of Lithuania, especially in Wilna, Grodno, Bielostok, &c., and in White Russia. It is a new dialect, and has grown up since the union of the Lithuanians with the Poles, and is full of Polonisms. The limits of its sway are much narrower than those of either of the other dialects, and it has made no throne for itself in books; nor has it constituted its products a part of the high commerce, that prevails in the world of thought.

2d. The Bulgarian.

This language spreads over the large and fruitful space, bounded on the north by the mouth of the Danube, on the east by the Euxine in part, on the south by a line running from Salonica to Ochrida, and on the west by the Pruth, or rather a line a little beyond its western bank. The Bulgarians have a solid deep earnest character, beyond the races that surround them, which must erelong bring them and their language, and all its archæology, into bolder relief than hitherto upon the page of history.

The ecclesiastical Slavonic or, as it is sometimes called, the Cyrillic dialect, which is but the old Bulgarian modified, although no longer a living language, is yet used by them at the present time, in common with both the Russians and the Servians, as the language of the Scriptures and of their religious books; so that, although in the ordinary business of life it is dead to the tongue, it is still alive to the heart. In all nations, old languages and old forms of language find their last hiding-place in the temples and services of religion, and there claim forever the right of sanctuary. Nothing but Time, which wears out all things, or the Spirit of Evangelical Reform, which can remove any obstacle, has ever sufficed to dislodge them from these cherished retreats.

It is in the old Bulgarian, that the most ancient religious writings of the Slavonians are found: the manuscript of the oldest date being a collection of the four gospels, prepared for Prince Ostromir in the year 1056. There are also old manuscripts of the language, probably older than this, in the Glago-litic alphabet without date, which, though of the same origin with the Cyrillic, is yet different in its graphic symbols. Schafarik regards them as the most ancient of all Bulgarian records; and Schleicher proposes to call the Bulgarian written in this alphabet, the Old Church-Slavic: as distinguished from the Bulgarian found in the Cyrillic alphabet, which he denominates Church-Slavic. Not that the writings in the Glago-litic alphabet were all made necessarily before Cyril's day, but that what were not so written were put in this old character from a sort of traditionary pride in its antique aspect.

The present Bulgarian is far inferior as a language, in the richness of its forms and the completeness of its structure, to the ecclesiastical Slavonic, and remains in its present state as it was three centuries ago. Its contour is plainly defined, as separate from all the other Slavic languages, by certain euphonic* principles and tendencies, which prevail in it.

* These are as quoted by Schleicher (Sprachen Europas, p. 207,) from Schafarik, the great historian of the Slavonic literature: (1.) The insertion of an s before t, when softened by an i or j placed after it, as in noszt for notj, night. (2.) The insertion of z (English zh), before a

3d. The Servian or Illyrian.

When written in the Cyrillic character, as by those of the Greek Church, it is called Servian; but when in the Latin alphabet, as by the Roman Catholics, it is called Illyrian: so much do men like names and fight for mere words.

Under this general title are included in one the Servian, Croatian and Slowenic dialects, which themselves also in turn might be resolved into still other dialects. Uniformity is not found to be a law of human development, in the department of speech, any more than in any other direction secular, or religious, practical or intellectual. The Servian dialect is very rich in vowels and so exceedingly musical to the ear. With the perfect sacrifice indeed of all scholastic instincts, and with none of that love of archetypal etymology so characteristic of the Greeks, who, while always at work artistically upon the forms of language to improve them, yet always left carefully on each new form some mark, that should forever in-urn the remembrance of the one that they had destroyed; the Servians, like the old Iconoclasts, break down old words and parts of words, and break them off with eager pleasure, if they can only thereby get a fuller, finer, sweeter sound. Thus consonants have been driven

softened d or instead of it, as in mezda for medja, limits. (3.) A peculiar adjective ending, in—ago. (4.) The use of the personal pronouns ti, si, instead of the attributions moj my; tvoj thy and svoi his, as in carstvo mi, my kingdom.

everywhere through the language, out of words where they had nestled for centuries. The Croatian and Slowenic dialects have no historical importance. The Slowenic is spoken by the people of Carinthia, Steiermark and Carniola. The oldest monument of the language dates back to the tenth century.*

II. The Western Slavic family.

This includes four special dialects, which, on account of the historical insignificance of most of those who have spoken them, we can dismiss rapidly.

* SLAVONIC CORRESPONDENCES.

Sanskrit.	Zend.	Greek.	Latin.	Lithuanian	Slavonic.	Gothic.	English.
vrikas, a wolf	vehrkas	λύκος	lupus	vilkas	vluku	vulfs	wolf
aham, I	azem	ἐγώ	ego	asz	az	ik	I
bhratar, a brother.	bráta	φράτηρ	frater	brolis	bratr and brat	bruother	brother
		φηγός	fagus		buku	bôka (German, buche, beech; buch, book.)	book beech
yuvan, youth,	yavanô		juvenis	jaunas	jun	German, jung	youth
ganda, the cheek or chin		γνάθος γένυς	gena	zandas	szczeka	kinnus	chin

In the following Slavonic words, who can fail to see the resemblance to familiar classical words, especially Latin: moryo, the sea: voda, water: kosti, a bone: volya, will: gosti, a guest: syny, a son: domy, a house: mator, a mother.

1. The Lechish.
2. The Tschechish or Bohemian.
3. The Sorbenwendish.
4. The Polabish.

The Lechish is so called, from the once powerful Lechs; and its domain was formerly much wider than now. The Polish and the Kashubish, a dialect of the Polish, are its present representatives. In this language sibilants abound; and as they are quite varied, the differences between them are often difficult of discovery except to a native's ear. Besides also being full of lisping and hissing utterances, it contains many nasal sounds; and is distinguished by a double vocalization of the letter l as either a palatal or a guttural, which is peculiar. Poland lost her place among the nations, by the selfish internecine strife of her princes and great men with each other; and though in the days of Knight Errantry her sons exhibited as energetic, manly, martial qualities, as those of any other people; yet, having been once laid prostrate by parricidal hands, she has never under the tyranny of her spiritual conquerors at Rome, or of her civil conquerors at St. Petersburgh, been allowed the privilege of a resurrection. She has never therefore figured as she might have done, upon the stage of history; and her language awakens no pleasant memories of travel and discovery, of research and spoil or of pleasure and profit, in the hearts of the lovers of learning. The fountains of knowledge and thought and truth and all beauty have been opened for them on other shores, and by other hands; and Poland is spoken of only with sadness.

A Russian and a Pole have so many grammatical and lexical forms in their two languages alike, although belonging to the two separate Slavic families, that they can each read the other's language about as readily as a Spaniard can the Italian. A Russian also, it is said, can comprehend easily the ancient Bulgarian. It has indeed been claimed by some writers, that all the various Slavonic dialects differ no more from each other, than did the various dialects of Greece one from the other.

The Tschechish is the speech of the Slavonic inhabitants of Bohemia, Moravia and north-western Hungary, and occurs sporadically throughout almost all Hungary. In respect to both of its two leading dialects, the Bohemian and Slowakish, but especially the former, it can boast of an historical organic identity, that dates back half way at least, towards the beginning of the Christian Era.

The Sorbenwendish, or Sorbish as it is called by the Germans, or Wendish as the Lusatians name it, prevails in limited parts of Upper and Lower Lusatia The Polabish, as the word indicates (po along and Labe the Elbe), was spoken more or less, anciently, by those living on both sides of the Elbe. It disappeared, as a vernacular language, about two centuries ago; al-

THE INDO-EUROPEAN LANGUAGES. 129

though some few families in that region still keep it alive among themselves.

The domain of the Slavonic languages has been always, with singular uniformity, on the middle ground between barbarism and civilization. Their literature also has been almost always borrowed from other nations: a habit, which, when pursued continuously by any people whether with willing enthusiasm or blind thoughtlessness, is sure to spread a blighting mildew over all the germinating tendencies and forces of native genius. Like all other people also, whether viewed individually or socially, who have lacked principles of self-reliance and earnest self-development, in a world so full on every hand of unequal and unjust rivalry, they have been jostled aside and dashed down by stronger races rushing against them, in their strife for the prizes of this world.

There are found in the interior of Germany at the present day, some Slavonic names of cities and rivers, even as far west as the Elbe: the only monuments now left of their ancient occupation of the regions lying westward of their present home in Europe. But as, on the one hand, they have succumbed to the influence of the more civilized and powerful races on their western borders, so, on the other, have the races less civilized at the east yielded to them; and Slavonic ideas and institutions, Slavonic law and order now rule over the whole northern part of the continent of Asia.

As the Greeks and Latins were originally blended in full combination with each other, as one primitive race ; so, the Slavonians and Germans, although never historically one, have yet been from the first in long contact with each other in large masses, and must have come into Europe, at a nearly contemporaneous period.

V. The Gothic, or Germanic family.

In the Gothic version of the Scriptures made by Ulphilas (A. D. 388) are all the remains that the world now possesses of that noble old tongue, the queen-mother of so many princely languages. The Goths were living at that time on the lower side of the Danube, around its mouth. In Herodotus they are called the Γέται,* and in Tacitus the Getae, and are

* In Menander's comedies, a Γέτος or Δᾶος is introduced as the standing representative of a slave, and as being brought from Thrace into Greece. The Γέτος was a Goth and the Δαός (Latin Davus for Dacvus, the fuller form of Dacus) a Dacian. Compare with Δᾶος for ΔάϝοϚ, also νέος for νέϝος Lat. novus and ὠόν for ὠϝόν Lat. ovum. Strabo expressly states, that Δάκοι and Δάοι are the same. When the Getae and Daci are represented as occupying separate regions, the division is always this: that the Getae live in the north-eastern part of the region, about the mouth of the Danube, and the Daci in the southwestern. As, from the title Getae, came Gothi, Getini, Gothoni, or Gothones, as they were variously called by Latin authors, so, from Daci came Dacini, afterwards Dani and the modern Danes represent the ancient Daci. In the middle ages indeed we find writers using Dacus for Danus and Dacia for Dania or Denmark. In Russia, also, a Dane is called a Datschanin, and in Lapland a Dazh.—*Grimm's Geschichte der Deutschen Sprache*, p. 132.

described as living in those times in the northern part of Thrace, between the Haemus and the Danube. In later times they divided into two portions: the Ostrogoths or eastern Goths, and the Visigoths or western Goths, the former settling in Italy and the latter in Spain. Their language however did not take root successfully in either country. A few Gothic memorials were left behind in Italy; and in Spain, besides a few hereditary baptismal names and the garnered pride of a few old noble families of Gothic blood, all records of their ancient dominion there are obliterated.

The Gothic stands related to the Germanic languages generally, very much as the Sanskrit to the Indo-European family. From want of any knowledge of the languages preceding them of the same class, they each have the historic aspect of a mother of that class; but strict philological analysis places them each, rather in the position of an elder sister standing so far apart in age and character from the younger sisters, as to fulfil in form the offices of a parent. An interval of four centuries separates the Gothic Scriptures, from any literary documents now extant of the other Germanic tribes.

The phonetical constitution of the Germanic languages appears in its most simple normal elements in the Gothic, out of which spread all the rest, as branches from one common stem.

In the Gothic languages are included:

1. The Low German.
2. The High German.

I. The Low German embraces:

(1.) The Norse, or Scandinavian languages.
(2.) The Anglo-Saxon.
(3.) The Frisic.
(4.) The Low Dutch.

1. The Norse languages include three Special dialects: the Icelandic, Swedish and Danish.

The Icelandic or Old Norse dialect is of a high antiquity. It was originally translated from Norway to Iceland, and has there wonderfully retained to the present time, its early characteristics. The Edda is the chief national epic of the old Norse, written, as is supposed, in the tenth century or about midway between our day and the beginning of the Christian era. Its heroes are all heathen.

The Swedish and Danish may be properly called the new Norse languages. These are greatly changed from their first estate, in every way. The Swedish is the purest Norse of the two. The Danish has been greatly affected by the contact of the German, and changed its old full a-sound in many words to e. The Norwegian dialect has been so entirely overtopped and overgrown by the neighboring Danish, that it has shrunk down into perfect insignificance, and deserves no separate place in history. The Danish prevails also in the Faroe, Shetland and Orkney Islands. As the Gothic family has had its home between the Celtic and Slavic families, its different languages show many signs of their influence upon them: the Norse languages exhibiting the most proof of Celtic influence and the German of Slavic.

The Norse family exhibits as such two remarkable characteristics:

(a) The suffixing of the definite article (hinn, hin, hit) to the substantive, as if a part of it, as in svein*inn* (m) the young man; eign*in* (f) the possession; and skeip*it* (f) the ship.

(b) A peculiar passive flexion. An original reflexive pronoun is appended immediately to the verb, giving it not as would be natural a reflexive sense, but a passive one. In this respect however these languages agree with the Latin, although in the latter the fact is more disguised. Thus brenni, "I burn" is in the passive brennist "I am burned; and brennum "we burn" becomes brennumst, "we are burned." The singular and plural forms are the same for the other persons respectively as for the first; and these are distinguished, only by the different personal pronouns prefixed to them.

(2.) The Anglo-Saxon.

The Anglo-Saxons first went to England, in the middle of the fifth century. In the place of its nativity, their language as such has disappeared. What relics remain of it on the continent are to be found, only as membra disjecta, in some few Low-German dialects. The English language however, which, for all the ends and wants of human speech, has never been surpassed by any language upon earth, is ribbed with its oaken strength. While it has large admixtures of words derived from the Celtic aborigines of England, and still more of Latin origin received from its Roman and Norman invaders, its predominant type is yet Anglo-Saxon. The original Britons were Celts, who were in the end attacked and repulsed by the Saxons or Teutons (A. D. 450-780), who themselves also afterwards succumbed to the Normans (A. D. 1066). These great historic facts are all clearly treasured up in the imperishable monuments of the language itself. The lexical elements of our language, however, are but its mere outside body; while its inward life and spirit are to be determined by its grammar, or the forms and rules by which its elements are combined together. Its grammatical constitution is Teutonic; and, taking our point of view here, we are able to see in reference to its lexicography, what is the natural or stable element in it, and what are the incidental or superadded elements. In every part of the language its inward chemical and vital agencies are all Teutonic. A very small portion of its vocabulary is Celtic; and of Latin it absorbed far less than any of the other provinces of Rome, although it imbibed so much: so that its lexical elements are chiefly Anglo-Saxon.*

* Harrison (on the English language, p. 55, 2d American Edit.,

It was in the fourteenth and fifteenth centuries, that it took on its full features as a noble independent language by itself, among the other languages of the world.

The speech, in which such an author as Shakspeare could find his native air and element, while honored by the great genius who enrobed himself in it, is yet proved thereby to possess adaptations to all the varied phases of human life and all the multiplied complexities of human thought and feeling, which raise it as a whole to a height above that of any other human tongue. Who would expect to see Shakspeare, when translated into Latin, French or Spanish or even German, appear with his own immortal beauty unimpaired? The same lustrous face would shine upon us, but only through a mist. Schlegel's translation of Shakspeare is indeed

Phila.) estimates the proportion of Anglo-Saxon terms in English, to be fifteen-twentieths of its entire bulk; which seems to the writer quite too high an estimate. It will amuse any true etymological scholar to hear an enthusiast for Anglo-Saxonism enumerate what he calls words strictly of that class, in which he will include by the score, because so short and pithy, multitudes of Latin-English words, like much (multus); very (verus); sort (sors); rest (re-sto); ay! (αιο); air (aer); day (dies); sex (secus); enter (intro); chief (caput); crutch (crux); pay (pacare); pray (precari); brace (brachium); pair (par); stick ($\sigma\tau i\zeta\omega$, in-$stigo$); axe ($\dot{\alpha}\xi\iota\nu\eta$); time (tempus); soap (sapo). strap (stroppus); cost (consto); rule (regula); other (alter, French autre); old (altus); race (racemus); space (spatium); new (novus); part (pars); sweet (suavis); stand, stay, state, estate, stable, stall stallion, constant, distant, instant, &c., all from sto, stare, to stand; and so safe, save, salve, salver from salvus, and have, behave, habit, inhabit, able, &c., from habeo.

justly celebrated; but the Shakspeare that he introduces to his countrymen is a German Shakspeare, and not the Shakspeare that we know and love as our own. As well might one attempt to deliver from some stringed instrument, tones that can resound only from the loud swelling organ; as to hope to express his utterances truly and in a style as if vernacular, in any other language than his own. In no language has a pyramid of literature so high, so broad, so deep, so wondrous, been erected, as in the English. In no other language are there such storied memories of the past. No other nation has wrestled, like the English, with Man and Truth and Time and every thing great and difficult; and no language accordingly is so full of all experiences and utterances, human and divine. Like that great world-book, the Bible, which has done so much to ennoble and purify it, it has an equipment for its special office, as the bearer of that book to all nations, grand and beautiful, in its adaptations to the wants of universal humanity. Few of the scholars and educators of our land, to their shame be it spoken, seem, although standing within the sphere of its beauties and under the glowing firmament of its literature, to appreciate in any worthy manner the glory of their mother tongue; which yet other nations, looking on it from without, admire so greatly; and which, in the eyes of future ages will appear in the far-off distance, radiant with heavenly beauty. While to the nations of Europe, whether approaching it on the Romanic or the Teutonic side, of which two languages chiefly, as of two distinct hemispheres forming one glorious orb, it is composed, it is more difficult than any modern if not also than any ancient language to be thoroughly mastered; to us, who first learned it in our mother's arms, it seems itself as natural a portion as any other of our own spontaneous vitality. Before it, as before the ideas which it bears like a flaming sword against all forms of despotism, the world everywhere bends in submission; and it is fast stamping its own enduring impress and enforcing its laws of personal and social life, on every part of the world civilized and savage. It has not indeed, like the German and other modern languages, the tendency or the capacity to enlarge its fabric, by new combinations and developments of its own materials. The German is, like the orange-tree, loaded at the same time with fruits and full-blown blossoms and nascent buds; while the English, like some thrifty fruit-tree in the temperate zone, is in one predominant state only at a time, and that has been one for more than two hundred years of full and golden fruitage. But, unlike languages possessing inward elements of self-enlargement, it has a wondrous faculty for appropriating to its own use and growth all the strength and beauty of all other tongues.

The three great languages of the world selected in the providence of God for the conveyance of His word and will to mankind, deserve from that fact a distinct enumeration and association with each other: the Phœnician or Hebrew, the language in which the Old Covenant was published; the Greek, that of the New; and the English, the language of modern civilization, religion and human progress beyond all others, and in whose words and by whose people the truths of the Bible are brought home to the business and bosoms of all nations. Like the angel seen standing in the sun, the English mind enlightened and sanctified stands bright and beautiful on the margin of modern times, holding up God's messages of light and love on high before the eyes of all men.

In ground-forms and the whole element of flexion and the details of a ramified syntax, the English,* when compared with the ancient languages, is poor indeed. Our words also are much mutilated, especially in the mode of their pronunciation. They appear everywhere

---

* It is certainly quite an interesting not to say surprising fact, that the English should in many of its forms, be more like the primeval Sanskrit, than the intermediate languages. Thus compare:

Sanskrit.	Greek.	Latin.	German	English.
bâd, to wash one's self	βαλανεῖον	balneum	bade	{ bath and { bathe
bhu, to be	φύειν	fui	bin	be
bhratâr, a brother	φράτηρ	frater	bruder	brother
bhar, to bear	φέρειν	ferre	bären	bear
bhrus, the brow	ὀφρύς	frons	braune*	brow
bhuj, to flee	φεύγειν	fugere		budge
duhitri, a daughter	θυγάτηρ		tochter	daughter
gâ, to go, and gam, to come	βαίνειν	venire	gehen	{ go { come
go, a cow gen. gavas	βοῦς gen. βοός	bos bovis	kuh	cow

* As in Augenbraune, the eyebrows: occurring only in composition.

throughout the language, to the eye of a scientific etymologist, bruised and broken in their aspect. Even our large stock of Anglo-Saxon words, which as a class are short and compact, are often condensed from an

Sanskrit.	Greek.	Latin.	German.	English.
jalas, cold		gelu	kalt	{ chill { gelid
hard, and hrid, the heart	{ καρδία and { κῆρ	} cor(d)	hertz	heart
gridh, to desire			{ begierde { gier { gierig	greed and greedy
kut, to cover,	κεύθειν		hüten	coat
kâravah, a crow	κόρυξ	corvus	kräche	{ crow { and { raven
laghus, light	{ ἐλαφρός { ἐλαχύς	} levis	leicht	light
lih, to lick	λείχειν	lingere	lecken	lick
lu, to separate	λούειν	{ solvere { (se + luere)	} lösen	loose
lubh, to desire	λίπτεσθαι	{ libet and { lubet	} lieben	love
madhu, honey	μέλι	mel	meth	mead
mah, to prepare	μηχανᾶσθαι	machinari	machen	make
naman, a name	ὄνομα	nomen	name	name
patha, a way	πάτος	passus	pfad	path
su, to scatter about	σείειν	serere	saen	sow
siv, to fasten together	κασσύειν *	suere		sew
smi, to laugh	μειδᾶν for σμειδᾶν			smile
stri, to strew	στορέννυναι	sternere	streuen	strew
svid, to sweat	ἱδροῦν (for σϝιδροῦν)	sudare	schweissen	sweat
svadus, sweet	ἡδύς (for σϝηδύς)	suavis	süsz	sweet
stabh and stubh, to press together. stambh, to support, and stambhas, a stem	{ στείβειν and { στέμβειν { to stamp on or down { στύπος { a stem, a { stump	{ stipare { { { { stipes { { stipulus	{ stapfen { { stampfen { { steif { stumpf	{ staff { step { stop { stamp { stump { stubb { stubble { stem
vash, to wish	εὔχεσθαι		wünschen	wish
yuyam, you	ὑμεῖς	vos	euch	you

* κασσύειν = κατά + σύειν.

original dissyllabic form into one monosyllabic in English. In consequence of the composite character of our language, its orthography and orthoepy are found at frequent variance from each other; while there are almost as many silent letters, not only in the middle and end of words but also when occurring initially, as in French; and the pronunciation of the same letters*

* The following letters are sometimes found silent:

(1) In the beginning of words: *b*, as in bdellium: *g*, as in gnat: *h*, as in humble: *k*, as in knee: *m*, as in mnemonics: *p*, as in psalm.

(2) In the middle of words: *c*, as in slack: *g*, as in daughter: *l*, as in balm.

(3) In the end of words: *b*, as in dumb and lamb: *h*, as in ah: *n*, as in condemn: *y*, as in say compared with ay: *w*, as in low.

Some consonants also have double sounds as *c*, which is sounded as *k* in cat and as *s* in city: *g*, hard in gun and soft, (as *j*) in gentle: *ch*, like *k* in Christian, like *tch* in chance and like *sh* in chemise: *x*, like *ks* in axe and like *z* in Xenophon; and *gh* as in though, laugh, hough.

Along also what a scale of variations does each of the vowels run, as:

a, in man, mate, many, father, water, caboose.

e, in mete, met, they, there, behold, inter, linen.

i, in pine, pin, lepine, bird.

o, in on, throne, attorney, move, lost.

u, in gun, astute, mute, full, busy.

How various too is the sound of the different diphthongs, as:

ai, in aisle, straight, air, again, complaisant.

au, in slaughter, laughter, hautboy.

ea, in lean, yea, meant, hearse, swear.

ee, in seen, been, committee.

ei, in sleight, feign, foreign, heifer, either, their.

ie, in die, believe, friend.

oo, in moon, soon, floor, flood.

ou, in bound, through, though, should, hough, cough, enough.

especially vowels, both singly and in diphthongal combinations, is exceedingly varied. The pronunciation of each word agreed doubtless, at some time in the history of the language, with its spelling: a fact which will serve well to show what great changes have occurred, within the very essential elements of its structure.

In this country especially, our people, language and institutions have been borne through such an unsettled pioneer experience, that a strange unscholarlike, if not indeed almost universal, indifference prevails among even our educated men, to exactness and elegance in the niceties of language. The noble old English tongue has assumed, in some large districts of our country, not only in its orthoepy* but also in its orthography, a distinct American type, and that not for the better but for the worse. It is not claimed indeed that in language, any more than in laws, usages and institutions, we should be servile copyists of those in the old home across the waters, who certainly have no better right, and as we are apt to think no better

* Witness the double pronunciation in England and America of such words, as desultory, leisure, detail, azure, isolate, demonstrate, and those words, in which a occurs in the same syllable before l, m, and st as in balm, calm, last, past, and also national, patriot, evangelical, courteous, fealty, either and neither, therefore, fearful, &c. As for changes in orthography all know, on what an extensive systematic scale Webster has undertaken to force them upon the language. Happily, the resistance to such innovations by him proved too great; and they are gradually losing, most of them, the little ground, which under his influential name they had begun to acquire.

capacity, to act well for themselves, than we for ourselves. Nor do we suppose that language can be compressed, either here or there, within fixed arbitrary modes of manifestation. Much less can it be maintained that language should cease its growth; as it seems to be an universal law of all growths in this world, that their stoppage is the beginning of their decay, which, stated more philosophically, is the beginning of their disappearance from the field of view, in order to prepare the way for something better in their place. America has the right and let her take it, for she surely will, to impress her own genius on the English tongue. To undertake to stop it, would be to fight the whirlwind. But let not provincialisms be accepted, for they are unnecessary, and in whatever language they appear, are abnormal within and unsightly without. Let not etymological principles, that is, grammatical, radical and phonetic analogies, which are not merely the ornaments of a language, but also its very essence and substance, be smitten and hammered down, by any rude barbarian zeal for squaring the forms of speech into phonographic correspondence with their pronunciation. As well attack the forms of sculptured life, fresh from the hand of Phidias or Praxiteles, and undertake to drive back the Spirit of beauty, now radiant in every feature, within the cold recesses of the marble where it had slept unwaked before, like Echo, sweet nymph of forest dells, slumbering unthought of in her leafy bower, until some friendly voice arouses her to answering words again. Whatever symbols of her greatness America carves upon the tablets of the English tongue, let them be no grotesque specimens of careless haste, or proofs of vulgar sensibility to forms of low life, in the world of speech. Let her signatures rather be here as elsewhere royal in their aspect: so that any who shall survey the vestiges of her influence, in whatever age or from whatever point of observation, shall be compelled to say with reverence and affection, Incedis Regina! There are those however who undertake to justify many and great abuses in this hemisphere, to the original, pure, historical Transatlantic English, which we have brought with us to our new home. The influence also of similar ideas and habits has run up, to a lamentable degree, into the whole style of our higher classical education, as it is generally conducted. Prosody, except in its rudest outlines, is openly disregarded and pronounced by teachers, who themselves are ignorant of its nice details, an useless appendage of classical study. Greek accentuation, similarly, is ridiculed by the same professional novices, who have not mastered it themselves; and who declare that it cannot be understood, or, that, if by long close study it should be comprehended by any one, the fruit would not pay for the labor bestowed upon its cultivation. But no men, more than educated Englishmen and Americans, owe it to themselves and their age and their mother-tongue, to preserve in its sacred beauty, unbroken and unspotted through all time, the temple of their literature and their language.

(3.) The Frisic.

This is kindred to the Anglo-Saxon and the Old Norse, and yet separate from them both. It was once spoken on the Elbe, and along the northern coast of Germany. It is found now as a living language, only in a few scattered districts in the Netherlands; and it is alive there only in the lips of men and not in their books, and so finds shelter only among the rude uneducated masses. The Dutch has entirely displaced its words, as current coin, by its own as having a far higher value.

(4.) The Low Dutch.

(a) The Netherlandish.

These include the Flemish and Dutch languages. The native home of the Flemish language is Belgium. As the French is the court-language of Belgium, and contains in itself great elements of vitality and wonderful tendencies to diffusion, wherever it once obtains a permanent lodgment, the Flemish is in such unfavorable contact with it rapidly waning away, and will probably ere long retain only the name of having been once cherished, as a household treasure, by its own people. Happily however, for dead languages like depopulated countries are full of mournful asso-

THE INDO-EUROPEAN LANGUAGES. 145

ciations, the Flemish language is a separate language from the Dutch, almost wholly in its orthography alone. As, therefore, they are in their real substantive essence alike and the words of the two languages are themselves the same, its spirit will still survive, when it has resigned its breath, in that fine rich Dutch language, of whose literature and of whose genius, as well as of the history of whose people although so strongly connected with our own, it is no praise to us, that we are so profoundly ignorant.

(b) The Saxon.

This is a modern title of convenience, for describing the staple or material of several kindred dialects, or rather different forms or stages of the same dialect, called the old Saxon, the Middle Low German and the flat or vulgar German (Plattdeutsch). The old Saxon was formerly spoken in the north of Germany. The Heliand, a poem written in the ninth century, is the only relic now left of it, possessing any value. It is a harmony of the gospels in mere* alliterative metre. The different dialects included under the old Saxon, receive in their bare enumeration all the honor that they deserve. They contain in them nothing that speaks of an heroic past or of a vitalized present.

2. The High German.

The etymology of the word, German, a name given

* A brief but good specimen of it may be found in Latham, on the English Language, pp. 26—7. Third edition.

to the people who bear it, by other nations and not by themselves, is yet a mooted question. Numerous have been the guesses made concerning it. Some have derived it from Kerman in Persia, now Caramania. But whatever affinities the German may have with the Persian, it is yet true that the Germans did not call themselves by this name, and so could not have carried it with them, from the place of their origin. Others have derived it from the Latin germanus (Eng. germain) kindred or cognate: a mere accidental resemblance in form, with no historical connection in sense; while others maintain that it originated in gher (French guerre, Spanish guerra) war, and mann, man; and others still find it in the vernacular Irman or Erman. It is, on the contrary, in all probability a Celtic word, as Leo has recently suggested, derived from gairmean a shout or war-cry, formed from gair to cry.* The name Deutsch, by which the Germans denominate themselves, and to which also the name Teutones is allied, is derived from the Gothic thiudisko (Gr. $\dot{\varepsilon}\vartheta\nu\iota\varkappa\tilde{\omega}\varsigma$), from thiuda ($\ddot{\varepsilon}\vartheta\nu o\varsigma$) a nation, and answers therefore to our word Gentile.

Like the Latin, the German languages supply the want of separate tense-suffixes, by auxiliary verbs. The only tenses formed on the simple verb-stem, are the present and imperfect. The Gothic retained the dual

* So in Homer a great warrior is often described as $\dot{\alpha}\gamma\alpha\vartheta\acute{o}\varsigma\ \beta o\acute{\eta}\nu$, good in shouting; which is an essential part of war with a savage.

and had also reduplicated forms; but these are so mutilated in the modern Germanic tongues, as not to be discoverable except by comparison.

Grimm states four points of discrimination, by which the German family of languages is individualized by itself:

(1.) The ablaut, or change of the radical vowel, in the conjugation-forms of the verb.

(2.) The lautverschiebung, or change of sounds and letters from one point to another on the same scale.

(3.) The weak conjugation of the verb.

(4.) The strong conjugation.

The High German has had three eras of periodic growth, in respect to the styles of its forms. 1. That of the Old High German, prevailing from the seventh to the eleventh century. 2. That of the Middle High German, from the eleventh century to Luther's day. The Niebelungen, the great German epic of ancient times, was prepared in the form in which we find it, somewhere about the year 1200. It contains however scraps of poetry, that probably date back as far as Charlemagne, two hundred years earlier (1000 A. D.). This is the Iliad of the Germanic tribes, written in the days of chivalry. Its heroes are those of the fifth and sixth centuries, and of a Christian type; and it is full of old traditions and marvels. 3. The New High German, or what we call the present classic German, born in its full complete state at the Reformation, and of it. Luther was its foster-father. Its words took their fixed and final form in his earnest, glowing, scholarly mind, and by his pen were "engraven in the rock forever." In his noble translation of the Scriptures, he not only scattered everywhere the seeds of divine truth but popularized also the usage of his mother tongue, in richer, deeper, stronger forms, than ever before; and by that translation, still recognized with national pride as the standard version of the Scriptures, as well as by the sweet hymnology that has flowered forth from its prolific stem around the walls of the sanctuary, the language has been preserved in the state in which he found and used it, with sacred care. Throughout all the stages of its historic development, the High German has been full of treasures, which the world has not been willing to forget. It is now, for both æsthetical and philosophical uses, more akin in its inward and subtle affinities to the Greek, than any other living language. It has a sort of divine aura around and within it. And if to one, not born in its presence or brought up under its power, who looks upon it from without with cool, critical survey, its charms seem so exquisite, even when compared with those of the other great languages of the world; how inspiring must be its influence on those, who from childhood have been taught to love it as their mother tongue: all whose thoughts and feelings, all whose wonder, joy and sorrow and all whose

THE INDO-EUROPEAN LANGUAGES. 149

loves and hopes and longings, for this world and the next, have been breathed from the first through its living chords! In original, constant productiveness and the capacity for an ever-enlarging home-growth of its own, and that of the most homogeneous character, no modern language equals it; and in this respect as in so many others, some of them more easily felt than described, it resembles the Greek. There is no modern tongue, which a mind thoroughly English in its type and tone, can so profitably receive into all its elements of thought and growth, as the German. It has great capacity for expressing nice discriminations and poetical conceptions; and to us of other nations, whose languages are the mere alluvial deposits of those of elder days: having none of the interior principles of spontaneous organic growth, that the German like the Greek possesses, taking on new forms and combinations as used by each new age and even by each new mind that assumes to itself the privilege of making them, as the right is universally conceded: it seems delightful indeed to come within the atmosphere and aroma of its fresh blossoming fulness of life. The mind feels, when surrounded everywhere by the living stir of its agencies and energies, joyously and strangely elastic in its moods: it has an instinct to climb and vault and shake off every sense of weakness, as when, in tender sympathy with nature, it stands and gazes on the first full outburst of new life and beauty in the spring. The heart is moved amid the splendors of its poetry, as it sometimes is under the power of some wild witching melody, which makes the soul feel, as if deep within itself there were another self, to which few things in this world had the power to make themselves heard or seen. In many-sidedness the German is not at all equal to the English. Its connections with the Latin are far less numerous: the Greek element does not prevail so extensively in it; nor have the modern languages impressed their form and influence upon it, as upon the English. The German has indeed, throughout, fewer admixtures of other languages in it, than any other European tongue, while the English has more than any other. While therefore in English almost all words have been first distilled through the alembic of the Greek, Latin, Gothic, German, French, Italian or Spanish mind; in German, with few exceptions, they all claim one common origin and bear in them the mark of a distinct national individuality. German literature is full of strength and beauty, to a degree even of almost Asiatic luxuriance. The more recent type, however, of the German mind is that of profound scholarship. The Germans are the self-chosen and world-accepted miners of the realms of science, and obtain the pure ore of knowledge, by willing, patient delving after it; which other nations convert into all the forms of intellectual commerce for the world's good. Instead of the sense of nationality, which other nations cherish so warmly and of which their poets sing in songs of their fatherland, as only those can sing who have lost a once dear treasure: a sense, which, by their minute division into kingdoms and duchies, has been destroyed among them: they possess a broad cosmopolitan taste and consciousness, and have accordingly undertaken to be the stewards of the world's intellectual riches, and purveyors to its mental wants.

VI. The Celtic.

This class of languages has not been appreciated until very recently, as having the connections, which it really does possess, with the great Indo-European family. To Dr. Prichard, that fine English investigator into the natural history of man and into ethnology, is due the honor of having first discovered their true connection with it. It was ingeniously guessed at the outset by Sir William Jones, to be one of the Indo-European family. But, as guesses are as likely to be false as true and have as such no science or substance in them, the merit of the discovery is as great, as if no such surmise had been previously made; since, in Prichard's day, it had lost all its qualities of value, whether authoritative or suggestive. Bunsen claims, as has been stated, that the place for the Celtic, in the history of languages, lies midway between the Old Egyptian, which he regards as the most primeval language yet discovered, and the Sanskrit: "The Celtic," as he claims, "never having had the Sanskrit development; so that, while it exhibits a systematic affinity with it in some respects, it shows also in others a manifest estrangement from it." The Old Egyptian, it is conceded, exhibits many inward resemblances to it in several respects; and on any and every view, the Old Egyptian of the Semitic family, and the Sanskrit and Celtic not of that family, point in many of their common characteristics to a possible unity, at least, in one ultimate origin; and it is not at present absolutely certain, in what way we should state the true relative order of their sequence.

It is manifest that the Celts led the van of occidental emigration through the wilderness of primeval Europe, and spread over Gaul, Switzerland, Germany, Spain and Britain. The greater part of Europe indeed was inhabited in its earliest historic period, by different tribes of Celts. They were found however by the races that followed in their train, most numerously in Germany, France, Spain and Great Britain; while traces were found of them also even in Greece, Illyria and Italy. They had no letters and in fact despised them, as unworthy of a warlike people; and therefore had no way of preserving their laws or history or scanty literature, except to deposit them in the archives of their own hearts. Hence they undertook to hand them down, from one generation to another by song. Their poets they called bards: a profession that included all who felt moved by any strange wild impulse within them, to an earnest utterance of themselves to others; and its ideal was best realized in a sort of native spontaneous combination of the poet, the musical composer and the practical singer, in one and the same person. Many such poets there were among them, in the course of those long centuries so voiceless now to us; and their poems were sweet, like the carols of summer birds, to the hearts of those wandering tribes. The ancient Druids, the instructors of Celtic youth, sometimes devoted many years to teaching them those wild native songs; and the primitive Celts were justly distinguished, as having been addicted beyond most rude early races to poetry; and bards were held in high honor, both among the primitive Gauls and Britons.

The chief monument of ancient Celtic verse, still left standing on the earth, is that of Ossian; which is now generally allowed by those best acquainted with Gaelic literature, to be genuine. He was indeed, as he is commonly called, "the prince of Scottish bards." Certainly, if Macpherson could himself write such a poem, so noble in itself and so wonderfully set, in respect to its ideas and all their surroundings of men and manners, in the age to which it pretended to belong, he would have no reason to be ashamed of acknowledging its authorship, and no motive to bestow the honor gratuitously upon another of whom nothing was known but his name. To one of the Wolfe-school of doubters, who can make himself believe that Homer is a name for a class of giant-geniuses, instead of one alone, and so that the Iliad is a fortuitous concourse of many poems from several authors, no evidence could probably ever suffice to assure him of its genuineness. But to one who feels an argument, the proof seems sufficient for the reasonable conviction, that Ossian really made the poem, which Macpherson only translated.

The Celtic possesses now but a sporadic existence. Its present remains are the Kymric or Welsh, and the Gaelic, the native tongue of the Scotch Highlanders, and the Erse or native Irish; in which, especially the last, we have modern specimens of the most ancient type of languages of this stock. The Celtic departs most in the style of its poems, of all the languages hitherto enumerated, from the primeval aspects of words as found in the Sanskrit. The institutions that the Celts founded and the very vocabulary that they used, were early overborne by Roman conquests, ideas and influences. They nowhere maintained a firm foothold, against the influx of the races that succeeded them, except at the most advanced outposts of the continent: whence there was no region beyond into which they could be driven except the sea. That German element also in modern society, which has so largely modified all the aspects of the civilized world, came in ere long upon them with all its force, and overlaid them with its own peculiar character. And yet the Celtic has left at the same time its manifest impress upon the German; which, having existed geographically midway between the Celtic and Slavonic nations, has also partaken of their characteristics mutually but much more of the Celtic than of the Slavonic. In the Teutonic languages generally, there is found a greater mixture of Celtic words, than in any other class of languages. The Teutonic races followed more exactly in the track of the Celts receding before them, than any others. The German and Celtic languages have likewise, aside from their common inheritance of the same great original staple of Indo-European words, many words that they have directly borrowed each of them from the other. It is not therefore always easy: so changed are words often in passing from one language to another, whether passing early or late in their history: to say, whether the correspondences which are found are in some cases original or derived.

The Celtic is spoken still, in the central and southern parts of Ireland, in the north-western parts of Scotland, in the Hebrides and the islands between England and Ireland and also in Wales, and on the continent in Brittany. The Celts are all now under the British yoke, except those living in Brittany over whom France rules. And, as they form in their geographical and historical position alike, the advanced guard of all the nations of Europe, it is both natural and logical to conclude that if of Arian origin, as is probable, and not of an antecedent date, they constitute the first cleavage from the great primary elemental mass of Indo-European mind. Not only does the Celtic differ more from the Sanskrit, than any of the other languages of the Arian family, but it is also the least complete and mature of them all, in its own individual features. The Celts never invented any alphabet for themselves, and never borrowed one for their own separate use, as did the Greeks from the Phœnicians, from any other people.

The Celtic * family includes,

1st. The Kymric.†

* This is Diefenbach's classification of them. He is one of the most recent investigators in this field, and is one of the highest of all authorities in philology: like Bopp, Pott, and the Brothers Grimm among the elder lights in this field, and Schleicher, Kuhn, Curtius and Aufrecht among its younger leaders.

† CELTIC CORRESPONDENCES.

Sanskrit.	Greek.	Latin.	Gothic.	Celtic.	English.
bhu, to be	φύω	fui	(Ang.Sax.) beo	Welsh bu, Irish bi	be
danta(s), a tooth	ὄδους stem ὀδοντ	dens stem dent	tunthu	dant	tooth
hanu(s), the jaw. cf. ganda	γένυς	gena	kinnus	genau	chin
sara, salt and salan, water	ἅλς	sal		Irish salan, Welsh halen	salt
pada(s), a foot	πούς stem ποδ	pes stem ped	fotu	ped	foot
aśva(s), a horse	ἵππος Æol. ἴκκος	equus		Irish each, Welsh eap	
niśa, night	νύξ	nox		nochd	night

THE INDO-EUROPEAN LANGUAGES. 157

2d. The Gadhelic.

1st. Under the Kymric are included

(1) The Welsh.

(2) The Cornish, which was confined to Cornwall, and ceased to be a living language about sixty years ago.

(3) The Low-Breton or Armorican, which prevails in French Brittany. This whole class of Kymric languages is separated very distinctly from the kindred Gadhelic; and they are sometimes denominated also the Britannic dialects.

2d. Under the Gadhelic are included also various dialects. Gadhelic is formed, as Pictet thinks, from gaedel and gaodheal, meaning hero, from gaodaim to rob, or plunder: a hero and a robber being among lawless men synonymous. This derivation is preferable to that of Charles Meyer, who regards Gadhel, Gael and Gallus, as all derived from the old Celtic root gwydh to follow, and so pointing to the nomadic habits of the primitive Celts, or their great perpetual tendency to clanships.

(1) The Gaelic proper, or High Scotch.

(2) The Irish or Erse.

In the words Eirinn,* Erin and *Ire*land Pictet

† The flexion of the word Eirinn is in Irish as follows:
  Nom. Eire also Ere.
  Gen. Eireann, Eirenn and Erenn.
  Dat. Eirinn, Erinn and Eiren.
  Acc. Eire.
The classical forms of the name as Ἰερνίς, Ἰερνή, Ἰουερνία, Hibernia

claims, notwithstanding Pott's hasty laughter at previous etymologists for having broached such an idea, that we see the old family name Iran or Arii, still flying on the flagstaff of one great branch of the Celts, who first left their common home. The Irish language possesses, beyond any other of the Celtic languages, the most ancient forms of words. What the Germans call the umlaut,* prevails here abundantly.

(3) The Manx, or that spoken in the isle of Man.

In the Celtic declension of the verb, the three persons are expressed sometimes by the personal pronouns, combined as suffixes with the verb-stem, as in the Sanskrit and also in mutilated forms in the other Indo-European languages; and sometimes, as in English, by the separate use of the pronouns before the verb. A declension of the noun cannot be said to exist at all, in some of the languages of this family, as the Welsh and Low Breton. The relations of words to others in a sentence, are expressed by changes in their initial

&c. are composite. Thus Hibernia, Pictet regards as compounded of Ibh the land, and Erna of the Erins; and so in the Greek form 'Ιουερνία, the syllable ου is a softening of the Irish bh, or Latin b in Hibernia; and the form 'Ιευρή is for 'IFερνή. The stem ibh may be connected, he thinks, with the Sanskrit ibhya wealthy, opulent, cf. Gr. ἴφιος strong, mighty: so that the stem of the word Iren or Irish would mean the good, the brave. Pictet's article is interesting, and may be found in Kuhn's Beiträge zur Sprachforschung, pp. 81—99.

* This means a softening of a radical vowel of a word, into an e sound, to denote a difference of person in a noun, or of tense in a verb; as in our words brother and brethren, foot and feet, tooth and teeth, was and were.

THE INDO-EUROPEAN LANGUAGES.

parts, and those changes are phonetically adapted to the terminal characteristics of the words preceding them: the direction taken by the law of assimilation in this family of languages, being exactly opposite to that, taken in the other branches of the Indo-European family.

In the Celtic languages, constant modifications are made by words placed in combination, one of the other, like those denominated Sandhi in Sanskrit. Consonantal mutations are much more varied in Welsh than in the Irish; and words beginning with vowels are subject also in Welsh to changes, similar to those made by Guna in Sanskrit. A comparison of the Numerals in Welsh and Irish with those in Sanskrit is worthy of attention.

	Welsh.	Irish.	Sanskrit.
1.	un	aen	aika
2.	dau and dwy	da / do	dwi / dwau
3.	tri and tair	tri	tri
4.	pedwar and pedair	keathair	chatur
5.	pump	kuig	panchan
6.	chwech	se	shash
7.	saith	secht	saptan
8.	wyth	ocht	ashtau
9.	naw	noi	navan
10.	dêg.	deich	dasan

The Welsh and Æolic Greek make nearly the same kind of consonantal substitutions: as p (π) for Sanskrit ch as in $\pi \acute{\varepsilon} \nu \tau \varepsilon$, Æol. $\pi \acute{\varepsilon} \mu \pi \varepsilon$, Welsh pump, Sansk.

panchan; and the gutturals c, g, k for sh and s as $\delta\acute{\varepsilon}\varkappa\alpha$; Welsh dêg; Sansk. daśan; and $\varepsilon\ddot{\iota}\varkappa o\sigma\iota$: Welsh ugain : Sansk. vinśati.

Similarly the Latin and the Erse are quite alike in their consonantal phenomena. They neither of them adopt the p of the Welsh and Æolic Greek, but have c or q instead of it, as in Latin quatuor, Erse keathair, four : Sansk. chatur : Welsh pedwar : Gr. $\tau\acute{\varepsilon}\tau\tau\alpha\varrho\varepsilon\varsigma$, Æol. $\pi\acute{\iota}\sigma\upsilon\varrho\varepsilon\varsigma$; and so quinque (pronounced originally kinke) : Erse kuig, compared with the Greek and Welsh as above. The Teutonic dialects agree generally more with the Welsh and Æolic Greek, than with the Latin and Erse. A few specimens of Erse and Welsh correspondents with the Sanskrit equivalent will make their differences still more apparent.

Sanskrit.	Erse.	Welsh.
jani, a woman	gean,	
virah, a hero	fear	
matri, a mother	mathair	
nabhah, æther	neav	nêv
dhara, earth		daiar
ukshan, an ox	agh	yeh
druh, a tree	dair	derw
danta(s), a tooth		dant
dvar, a door		dôr
mri, to die	marbh	marw
vid, to know	fis (knowledge)	wydha (to learn)

We have now passed in review the different families of the historical languages of the world, in as rapid a manner, as justice to their several degrees of excellence and honor would allow. The original Indo-European language, so called from its many Asiatic and European descendants, whose names, for want of one more apposite, are united in it; by whatever name it was called by those who spoke it, before they called themselves Arians, and wherever they lived under the power of those energetic influences, which the history of the languages descended from it shows it to have possessed, must have been one of great splendor within and without. And, as the reflex influence of a kingly language is one of the strongest of all stimulating influences that a nation can ever feel, in the mode of its development, wondrous indeed must have been its adaptations, for the purposes of an ever-growing mental life and commerce among men. In it were the germs of most of the many great languages, that have since come and gone upon the face of the earth. Whatever words have been really added to the original stock, except in the way of new combinations of words already belonging to it, must have been wholly or chiefly onomatopoetic; in which, as in the words hiss, crash, splash, murmur, men have simply uttered from their own tongues, by way of imitation, the same sounds which they had already heard in nature.

It is worth the while, in conclusion, to consider even though in a brief manner, the lessons which are taught us by historical philology. They are these:

1. The Unity of the race.

Nations and tribes that have no features physical, intellectual or spiritual in common, are yet found, by a comparison of their languages, to be bound closely together in the bonds of a common primeval brotherhood. Every new discovery in philology reveals new and wider connections between them, and harmonizes the voice of history with that of the Scriptures: just as in geology each new advance of the science serves to prove still more fully, that the genesis of nature was exactly the same as the Genesis of Revelation.

2. The greatly determining influence in man's history of the material, passive and receptive side of his nature. Human language wonderfully exhibits the play of physical influences upon us, in respect to our speech and our ideas, our experience and our employment, our pleasure and pain, our social state and our social progress. It almost says, that man is the sport of circumstances. This it would say absolutely, were it not for the counteractive power of that gentle but ever-active providence of God, which, while not disturbing at all the working of the most delicate, minute, unguarded elements of free agency in our nature, yet always broods over each individual, to influence him to the best possible improvement of his nature; and to combine the actual results of his untrammelled choice and action, in harmony with that of every other one, in the production of the greatest possible amount of good to all. There is thus a true materialism which phi-

losophy must recognize, as one of the fundamental bases of all her theories of man, whether viewed individually or collectively. Not more truly is man himself a compound being, composed of body and soul, or the body itself a duality in the details of its structure, than human experience and human development are two-sided, active and passive, material and spiritual. Without doubt, as men come to be more and more under the constant action of mental and moral forces, by the all-penetrating and widely-diffused power of Christianity, the sphere of climatic influences will be greatly abridged and their potency much impaired. Similarity of religion and of education will induce, in very different latitudes, similarity of views, feelings and habits. The mind was made to rule the body and to have dominion, not only over its activities and energies, but also over its ever-changing states and moods. An intellect and a heart set on fire of Heaven and glowing with a spirit of high service to God and man, are adequate to any triumphs over the infirmities of the flesh, or the power of matter and of time. And yet, in that golden age of the future, in which Heaven and Earth are to be wedded to each other in one prolonged and happy union, each zone will still have its different air and sky as now, its different fields and floods, its different advantages and defects, and all its wide variety of sights by day and of voices by night. And, when we remember how much more God undertakes to educate the mass of men, by the beauty of nature than by any other appliance even revelation itself, except the overflowing bounty of his providence, it is natural to believe, that in no coming age of the world will objective influences cease to mould, very greatly, the growths and manifestations of human character and of human society. In the past, however, most nations, even those of the highest development, have used, and indeed possessed but to a very limited degree in their culture, the full power of the light that Christianity contains in itself for the illumination of mankind, or of its heat to warm their sluggish natures into that generous divine growth of which they are capable. In the wild neglected state of Heathen life, in which as the very word itself implies, human society is one vast moral heath, physical influences are all-powerful, if not always upon the heart yet upon the temperament, as also upon the experience, employment and character, of those who have no elements of thought, feeling or purpose competent to resist the force of external agencies upon them, much less any transforming power within, that can make all things minister to their joy and work together for their good.

3. The low degree of man's inventive power.

The very word inventive indicates in its etymology, that he stumbles by chance upon his discoveries. The history of the arts of life, as well as that of the natural sciences, each wonderfully illustrates this fact, but neither of them more strikingly than that of language.

All the new forms to be found in any language are but new combinations of elements in previous existence, and but slightly and in the most accidental manner generally, modified to a new use or to a new form of expression for an old use. No new language is ever made, or was ever made, out of original underived materials by man; for the reason, that he is not only incapable of such a work, but also that, from the very sense of his incapacity for it, he is, as any man may know by appealing to his own consciousness for a verdict, immovably averse both to the effort and to the very thought of it. How amazing, accordingly, seems the stupefied atheistic wonder of some sceptical German philologists, at the fact, so incomprehensible to them and to any one else who does not see in language the handiwork of God, that the earlier languages of the world were so much more complete in their forms, than those of modern times!

We do not pretend indeed to solve all the mysteries of language. We walk in every science, and when in the pursuit of any truth, in but a narrow zone of day, whether using the torch of reason or the upper lights of revelation. Is it asked: whence, if language be of divine origin, comes the order of successive relation in different languages to each other, the monosyllabic, agglutinated and inflected? To this question several answers may be given. We might, for example, rest quietly in the admission and even the plea of human ignorance. Questions about the internal connections of things are more easily asked in every field of inquiry, than answered. Man, although having lived for six thousand years upon the earth, yet knows, to this day, nothing of its deep interior, save for the shallow distance of one mile; and, amid all the wonderful results of chemical analysis, no one can possibly tell in what life or light or electricity consist. We accept any thrust at human ignorance in general, and return it also with as good will as it is given upon the objector. But, so far as the divine origin of language is concerned, it is as easy to conceive of God's having created different types and orders of languages, as of his having made by distinct ordaining fiats, as he evidently has, so many different species of animals of the same genus. That Great Being, whose creative impulses have in them a royal measure of vitality: who gives to every zone its own distinct flora, in such unmeasured abundance, to every animal all his varied elements of activity and enjoyment, and to every man the whole vast complicated apparatus of his faculties, resources, opportunities and blessings: multiplying, on every hand, variety in species as well as in genera, unfolding one order of life within another, and joying at all times in the infinite overflow of His power and skill and love in all things: surely He may find a pleasure, in erecting different stages for the manifestation of man as a social being, that is too subtle for our penetration, and too high for us to undertake to climb up into the secret chambers of his plans.

Suppose moreover that the agglutinated and inflected languages were conceded to be of a derived nature, and, in their special forms, of absolute human construction, yet the divine origin of language itself could be asserted and vindicated. The development-theory of the origin of language claims as such, not merely a successive manifestation of related and improved forms, but also that this is the whole theory of their first origination, as well as of their consequent progress. Unfortunately for the advocates of the development-theory, in respect to the different forms of vegetable and animal life, there is no such commingling of types, as there should be on such a view, in nature; but each type, on the contrary, stands by itself, a bold distinctive token of a separate creation: so that hybrids are monsters, which, like the Gorgon and Chimæra dire, can easily be dreamed about but nowhere found. So, in the realm of language, the different classes of families stand apart by themselves, in large well-defined groups: no one of them losing itself in another, or being untrue in its growth to its own normal type of manifestation. But is all language to be regarded, as having been in its first state a mere mass of word-germs: a huge pile of fortuitous, unconnected, crude syllabications? If any are pleased with such a philosophical analysis of the different styles of human speech, can they persuade themselves to alight, with confidence in their speculations, upon such a theory, as a matter of historical verity. If the Chinese system of mere separate monosyllables thus represents the first period of its manifestation, how happens it, that in four thousand years there has been no advance in that part of the world on such a supposition, as in all other parts, beyond its first beginnings? Nothing else has remained stationary in that strange land, unless it be the kindred art of painting. The Chinese have arrived surely at as high a point in enterprise, literature and the arts of life generally in the aggregate, if not in some single particulars, as any heathen nation before them. Whence then such a long-continued petrified state of the language remaining, like a rock, still unchanged in its original simplicity, amid a sea of changes around it?

On the theory, that every language was not only a mass at first of monosyllabic germs, so that the organism of all speech must have commenced, like the reproductive processes of vegetation, in a sort of monadic cell-life; but also that man himself has been, in each case, the creator of those germs: where, we ask, and when, lived that wonderful generation of men, who had the superhuman genius to evolve such a world of prolific germs out of nothing? The mystery of the creation of language, if of human origin, is by such an hypothesis only thrown farther back in time. It is also rather increased than diminished, by such

THE INDO-EUROPEAN LANGUAGES. 169

a fancied duplication of the modes and elements of its formation : first by germs of man's construction, and secondly by their multiform evolution in so many languages, in such a wonderful abundance of complicated word-growths. To create the germ of a tree is even a greater miracle, than to create a tree itself : since, not only the future existence of the tree is thereby determined, but also all the agencies, principles and processes fitted to secure it, are compacted together in so small a space and harmonized in their adaptations, to the wide array of circumstances and influences, by which it is surrounded. A botanist, who, after analyzing the elements of a plant into its ash or unorganized base on the one hand, and its organific elements on the other, should tell us, that these each came forth, in spontaneous succession, from the bosom of nature to their proper place and work, without any designing or ordaining hand to guide them, would receive for his recompense our pity, if not our contempt. But is not a theorist very much like him in his positions who contends, that the bases of words as such were made by men themselves, and that afterwards the organific principles, which form the constitution of the inflected languages, were also created in the same way, and combined with them in such a beautiful union : the more beautiful in clearness and completeness, the farther back that we go towards the dawn of creation?

Men have nowhere shown, within any historic

period, such amazing skill. The contributions made by any one generation in modern times to the stock of language, are exceedingly narrow, except in the single direction of scientific terminology; for which the constant progress of the sciences, all of them so new in their origin or in their present style of effective demonstration, is ever making new demands. And such additions are not new words in themselves, but only importations directly from the Greek and Latin, into English or some other modern tongue. And yet we of our day, and not they who lived before us in times of less experience and progress, are the old men of the world; and what we, in the manhood of historic humanity, are unable to do, they certainly, who were so much younger in their attainments, had not power to accomplish. The history of language also is always, as it floats down the stream of time, a history of abrasion and curtailment, in respect to its structural elements.

To suppose that Adam was made by his great loving Maker but an adult infant, to develope language, his first social and mental necessity, by slow gradations from unmeaning inarticulate cries in the first place, mere syllabicated whines and hiccoughs, is a theory, that neither honors man in its statement, as it respects his real wants, or God, as it respects his disposition to provide for them. That same benignant Father of mankind, who always works a miracle when it is demanded, for the same reason that He refrains from working one, when it is not: who confounded the speech of those who were building the tower of Babel: who wrote with his own finger on the tables of stone: who inspired prophets and apostles to speak unto all men the things that they received from Him; and who gave the gift of tongues to the disciples, on the day of Pentecost, for the purpose of better spreading the truth, as it is in Christ: he surely would not leave Adam at the outset to himself, as a poor, ignorant, helpless being, to grope from one unavoidable mistake into another, in respect to the very simplicities of life, and, when accompanied by his mate made for high companionship and discourse with him, to eke out by slow degrees, in a few unformed and broken syllables, a poor and pitiable intercourse, but little better than the mute association of two animals together.

While Adam was yet alone, God is represented as bringing before him "every beast of the field and every fowl of the air, to see what he would call them, and whatever Adam called every living creature, that was the name thereof." Surely here is a being, who is no infant in knowledge or in speech, but who is treated rather by God himself, as one who knows well the scope and power of words. And, as God looked upon His works, at the end of each of the great days of creation to see that they were all very good; so, in the record here furnished he seems to call upon Adam to use the speech which He had taught him; as if looking on, to enjoy the pleasing result of His own contriving skill. As a matter of plain undeniable fact also, each successive generation, in all times and places, has learned its language from the one immediately preceding it; and, as we run backwards with this rule of analysis to the first man and find him standing alone in the garden of Eden hearing God's commands, not to touch the tree of knowledge of good and evil, and giving names at His summons to every beast of the field, are we not forced, both by logic and fact, to ascribe the authorship of language as such to God? He moreover, who made man for intercourse with Himself, and therefore walked with him in open vision in the garden, would surely give him language, to use for the purpose; and He, who afterwards made a coat for him, when having no implements yet prepared himself, with which to conceal his nakedness, would give him words, with similar love and care, with which to clothe his thoughts and feelings.

It is no reply to this general course of argument to say, that children now-a-days learn language, by first of all uttering monosyllables, and, from such feeble initial attempts, grow up into the full use of all the mysteries of speech. For children learn even such simple monosyllables, by imitating sounds that they hear, and that too under the constant effort of their parents and others, to lead them forward step by step in their progress. In mutes accordingly, as all know, the ear is at fault and not the tongue or larynx: they are dumb, only because they are deaf; or, which is the same thing, they cannot speak, because they have never heard others speak. Language is accordingly, one of the imitative arts of life.

There are but three possible theories, concerning the origin of language: the development-theory, which we have attacked and, as we believe, overthrown; the theory of its divine origin which we hold, with both intellectual and moral satisfaction; and still another, which seems utterly preposterous in itself, but which yet no less a scholar than Max Müller soberly advocates: its origination, as an unique complete product by itself of a single human mind, especially in reference to each of the two great families of inflected languages. Hear his singular words: " In the grammatical features of the Arian and Semitic dialects we can discover the stamp of one powerful mind, once impressed on the floating materials of human speech, and never to be obliterated again in the course of centuries. Like mighty empires founded by the genius of one man, in which his will is perpetuated as law through generations to come; the Semitic and Arian languages exhibit in all ages and countries a strict historical continuity, which makes the idioms of Moses and Mohammed, of Homer and Shakspeare, appear but slightly altered impressions of one original type. Most words and grammatical forms, in these two families, seem to have been thrown out but once, by the creative power of an individual mind; and the differences of the various Semitic and Arian languages, whether ancient or modern, were produced not so much by losses and new creations, as by changes and corruptions which defaced in various ways, the original design of these most primitive works of human art."

Does it not seem strange, that such a scholar can seriously maintain a view so singular as this: that, from one man's mind alone the great primal language, now lost in itself but represented in various proportions by the several members of the Indo-European family, came, at a full and sudden birth, into existence; and that too, with such inward and outward characteristics, that subsequent ages have been able to add nothing to them or subtract nothing of value from them; and that, from another superhuman mind of equally gigantic proportions the original mother-language of all the Semitic dialects came, with equally grand and fixed, although so diverse elements and energies, into being. Hear him still again in the same strain. He says, in an article furnished for Bunsen's Philosophy of Universal History,* "on all the Arian languages, from Sanskrit to English, there is one common stamp, a stamp of definite individuality, inexplicable, if viewed as a product of nature, and intelligible only, as the work of one creative genius." All this he utters, while having

* Vol. I. p. 475.

present to his thoughts, at the very time, such a conception of these languages as he thus expresses: "no new root has been added, no new grammatical form been produced in any of the Arian provinces or dependencies, of which the elements were not present at the first foundation of this mighty empire of speech." He views accordingly the Semitic and Arian languages, as "the manifestations and works of two individuals, which it is impossible to derive from one another."

And what a divine intellect must such an one have possessed! and what an age, fortunate beyond all others, must that have been that had two such giants in it, debarred by mutual ignorance and the wide interval that separated them from any communication with each other, yet each employed in the magnificent work of conceiving for himself the form and substance of a language, which was to be ever afterwards the supplying fountain, each in a separate sphere of relations, of a long procession of kingly languages, that should draw all their life and strength from its fulness. Is not the supposition as monstrous, as that of the ancients, in supposing Atlas to bear upon his shoulders this solid globe on which we dwell?

There is indeed a wonderfully scientific and artistic unity of plan, in the structure of the Indo-European type of language, as also in that of the Semitic: and the argument is conclusive from the unity of analogies here, as in nature, to unity of authorship, and that authorship divine. The work of originating language is too high, for man's weak faculties.

The hypothesis that language is of any other than divine origin, necessitates at once the farther supposition, that immense periods of time have existed, for the development of the great leading languages of the world, especially those of a high and finished organization, as the families of the inflected languages. This Bunsen sees and boldly accepts, as logically he must upon his theory. He says "a concurrence of facts and of traditions demand for the Noachian period about ten millennia before our era, and, for the beginning of our race, another ten thousand years or very little more."

We find little or no difficulty in supposing, with him and others, the deluge to have been local, although vast and overwhelming, where it prevailed, in Northwestern Asia. Just principles of interpretation, at any rate, seem to allow the possibility of such a theory; but not so with the history of our race, as given in the Bible, where a formal record is made of the successive generations of the race, step by step and name by name, with the birth and death and age of each representative of his own period in the series.

A signal proof of the smallness of man's inventive powers in the department of language occurs in the fact, that even our low vulgar words, which never creep into a dictionary or upon any page, that has light and beauty enough in it to deserve a day's continuance in any place of honor; words, which, at first thought, one would suppose must be the slimy product of English depravity: are yet thousands of years old. They are found, with but little change of form in Greek and Latin, preserved, together with other specimens of ancient corruption, amid the altars of Heathen worship or the bowers of Heathen Song. Like the so ancient sports of boyhood, as the outdoor game of ball and the indoor game of chess, which were played in Babylon, Athens and Rome, just as they are now among us, they make us feel that after all there is nothing new beneath the sun.

4. The necessity, for the proper comprehension of any one language, of a thorough survey and analysis of its connections with other and older languages. Comparative philology is a science, of even more interest, than comparative anatomy. In its three chief departments: comparative grammar, comparative lexicography and comparative phonology, it reveals wonderful resemblances between the older and newer languages, one and all of them, even in the most minute details. Etymology, taught and studied on thoroughly scientific and philological principles, is, not only one of the most engaging, but also, one of the most profitable of all studies. The time is near at hand, and may it come soon, when, in our universities and high

schools, the languages can no more be taught, in a narrow, mechanical and profitless manner; and when mere verbal accuracy in translation, and the careful skimming off of a few facts and principles of syntax, form the surface of the lesson, shall not be deemed adequate results to be gained, in so high a department of study. A professorship of Sanskrit, embracing the whole field of comparative philology, is, as a part of the true ideal of classical instruction, an absolute necessity in every college; and it must ere long be recognized as such, in every institution that aspires to the character, of doing honestly and earnestly its true work in the world. There is surely no one department of instruction, in the collegiate course, that, in respect to all the elements and uses of a liberal education, can compare, in importance, with that of the languages. And to be found ignorant, amid all the lights of modern philology, of the multiplied connections of Greek and Latin one with the other, as well as of their connection with the Sanskrit before them and with the modern languages behind them: to make no use or but little use of these great facts, enlightening and inspiring as they are in the work of instruction, should entitle him, who thus dishonors his high calling, to exchange at once his false position, as a professed guide to others, for the true one of a learner for himself, in respect to its first principles. With the educated men of the country, are lodged its fortune and its fate. And republicanism of the highest form claims, as one of its chief supports, a broad and columnar style of scholarship among them.

TABULAR VIEWS.

I. OF THE DIFFERENT LANGUAGES OF THE WORLD, IN GENERAL.

II. OF THE LANGUAGES OF ASIA AND EUROPE, IN GENERAL.

III. OF THE INDO-EUROPEAN FAMILY, IN PARTICULAR.

IV. OF THE SPORADIC LANGUAGES OF ASIA AND EUROPE.

TABULAR VIEWS.

I.—GENERAL TABULAR VIEW OF THE DIFFERENT LANGUAGES OF THE WORLD.

First. Those of the Unhistorical Continents: Africa and the Americas.

    I. The African.

        1st. The Berber Languages: Native in Fezzan, Tripoli, Tunis, Algiers, Morocco, &c.: Semitic in their origin.

        2d. The Caffre Languages.
- (1) The Congo: spoken in Lower Guinea.
- (2) The Sichuana: the language of the Bechuanas.
- (3) The Hottentot.

        3d. The Languages of Soudan.
- (1) The Nubian.
- (2) The Galla.
- (3) The Senegambian.

    II. The Aboriginal American.

These never have been, and probably never will be, classified into any thorough scientific system.

They are polysyllabic and polysynthetic to a high degree; and so, exactly antipodal to the monosyllabic languages.

Second. Those of the Historical Continents: Asia and Europe.

    I. The Monosyllabic.
    II. The Agglutinative.
    III. The Inflected.
    IV. The Sporadic.

II.—TABULAR VIEW OF THE LANGUAGES OF ASIA AND EUROPE.

First. The Monosyllabic, or Family-Languages.
    I. The Chinese.
    II. The Indo-Chinese.
        The Brahman, Siamese, &c.

Second. The Agglutinative or, Nomadic Languages.
    I. Those distinctly Agglutinative.

        1st. The Tataric Family.

The Northern Division of the Turanian Family.
(1) The Tungusic languages; spoken from China, northward to Siberia and the River Tunguska.
(2) The Mongolic: The Eastern; Western; and Baikal dialects.
(3) The Turkic: Dialects, the Osmanli; Karatschai; Nogai; Kumückish, &c.
(4) The Samoiedic.
(5) The Finnic, or Tschudic: Dialects, Ugric; Permic; Bulgaric; Lappic; Finnic.

The Southern Division of the Turanian Family.
(6) The Tamulic.
(7) The Bhotiya: Gangetic and Lohitic.
(8) The Täic.
(9) The Malaic.

    II. Those not so distinctly but yet essentially of the same rude style of mechanism.

        2d. The Caucasian Family.
            (1) Iberian: Georgian; Colchian; Suanian.
            (2) Abchasic.
            (3) Lesgic.
            (4) Mizshegic.

Third. The Inflected or State-Languages.
    I. Semitic.
    II. The Indo-European.

The Semitic Languages.

    I. The Egyptian or Khamitic.

        1st. The Old, or Hieroglyphical, or Ante-historical Egyptian.
        2d. The Later Egyptian.
            (1) Hieratic.
            (2) Demotic.
        3d. The latest Egyptian, or Coptic.

    II. The Old Assyrian or Babylonian: differing as such, only in their orthography.

    III. The Berber dialects of Africa.

    IV. The Canaanitic.
        1st. Phœnician.
        2d. Hebrew.
            (1) Ancient Hebrew.
            (2) Rabbinical Hebrew
        3d. Punic.

    V. The Aramæan.
        1st. Chaldee.
        2d. Syriac.
        3d. Samaritan.

    VI. The Arabic.

        1st. Æthiopic, or Abyssinian.
            (Arabic, mixed with African elements.)
        2d. Maltese.
            (Arabic, mixed with Italian.)

III.—TABULAR VIEW OF THE ARIAN OR INDO-EUROPEAN LANGUAGES.

First. The Arian Family-pair.

  I. The Indian.

    1st. Sanskrit.

      (1) Ancient.
         a The Vêda-dialect.
         b Classical Sanskrit.

      (2) Later.
         c Pali.
         d Pràkrit.

      (3) Modern.
         e Hindûstanee.
         f Bengalee.

    2d. Gipsy.

  II. The Iranian.

    1st. The Persian Languages.
      (1) Old Persian.
      (2) Zend.
      (3) Pehlevi.
      (4) Pazend or Parsi.
      (5) New Persian.

    2d. The Kurdish.
    3d. The Ossetian.
      (Geographically a Caucasian language.)
    4th. The Armenian.

      (1) Old Armenian.
      (2) New Armenian.

Second. The Græco-Italic or Latino-Greek Family-pair.

  I. Greek.

    1st. The forming, or Dialectic period.
      (1) Æolic.
      (2) Doric.
      (3) Ionic.
      (4) Attic.

TABULAR VIEWS. 187

2d. The full-grown, or Hellenic period.

3d. The Alexandrine period.

4th. The Roman period.

5th. The Byzantine period.

6th. The Modern Greek or Romaic period.

II. The Italic Family.

    1st. The Iapygian.

    2d. The Etruscan.

    3d. The Italian.

        (1) The Umbro-Samnite Dialects: Umbrian; Samnite or Oscan; Volscian; Marsian.

        (2) The Latin.

            § I. Its own different phases.

                1st. Literary Latin.

                    (1) Anteclassical.

                    (2) Classical

                    (3) Postclassical.

                2d. Middle Latin.

                3d. Common Latin: (afterwards Italian.)

            § II. The Modern Languages derived from the Latin.

                1st. Italian: (Dialects, Lombard; Genoese; Florentine; Neapolitan, Sicilian; Corsican; Sardinian, &c.)

                2d. Wallachian.

                    (1.) Daco-Romanic.

                    (2) Macedo-Romanic.

                3d. Spanish: (Dialects: Castilian; Catalonian; Galician.)

                4th. Portuguese.

                5th. Provençal.

                6th. French.

                7th. Rhæto-Romanic.

                    (An uncultivated patois of Italian elements mixed with German, found in the Canton of the Grisons in Switzerland.)

Third. The Lettic Family.
    I. The Lithuanian.
    II. Old Prussian.
    III. Lettish.

Fourth. The Slavic Family.
    I. South-eastern Slavic.
        1st. Russian.
            (1) The Great Russian.
            (2) The Little Russian.
            (3) The White Russian.
        2d. Bulgarian.
        3d. Illyrian.
            (1) Servian.
            (2) Croatian.
            (3) Slowenic.
    II. Western Slavic.
        1st. Lechish or Polish.
        2d. Tshechish.
            (1) Bohemian or Moravian.
            (2) Slowakish.
        3d. Sorbenwendish.
            (1) Upper Lusatian.
            (2) Lower Lusatian.
        4th. Polabish.

Fifth. The Gothic, Teutonic or Germanic Family.
    I. The Low German.
        1st. The Norse, or Scandinavian.
            (1) Icelandic, or Old Norse.
            (2) Swedish.
            (3) Danish-Norwegian.
        2d. The Anglo-Saxon (English.)
        3d. The Frisic.
            (1) Netherlandish.
            (2) Saxon.

II. The High German.
    1st. Old High German.
    2d. Middle High German.
    3d. New High German.

Sixth. The Celtic Family.
  I. The Kymric.
    1st. Welsh.
    2d. Cornish.
    3d. Low Breton, or Armorican.

  II. Gadhelic.
    1st. Gaelic Proper, or High Scotch.
    2d. Irish or Erse.
    3d. Manx.

IV. TABULAR VIEW OF THE SPORADIC LANGUAGES OF ASIA AND EUROPE.

First. Of Asia.

    I. The Caucasian Languages.

        (See Division II. of Agglutinated Languages.)

    II. The Thibetan:

        A hybrid between the Chinese which it resembles in its roots and the Tatar family, which it resembles more in its structure.

    III. The Japanese:

        Somewhat mingled with Chinese; but in its grammatical constitution more Tataric than Chinese.

Second. Of Europe.

    I. The Basque: In the Pyrenees—the remains of the Old Iberian.

    II. The Albanian or Arnautic:

        A seedling of the original Græco-Latin stock: Dialects, the Geghian and Toskian.

II.

THE HISTORY OF MODERN PHILOLOGY.

II.

THE HISTORY OF MODERN PHILOLOGY.

PHILOLOGY* is that science which treats of the origin, history and structure of the words composing the classical languages and those connected with them, whether cognate or derived. It comprehends what is usually included in the separate departments of etymology and grammar, as well as both the history and the philosophy of language. The present state of philological research, vast as are its results, is rather that of splendid preparation for a complete scientific construction of its elements, than any such absolute construction itself. Its

* The following Articles on the history of philology, although incomplete, are yet interesting and worthy of perusal: Wiseman's Lectures on Science and Religion, Nos. 2 and 3: Edinburgh Review, Vol. 94, (1851,) pp. 297—339: Bunsen's Philosophy of History, Vol. 1, pp. 44—64: Humboldt's Cosmos, Vol. 2, p. 142; Donaldson's New Cratylus, pp. 21—54: Winning's Comparative Philology, pp. 16—32: Weber's Indische Skizzen, pp. 1—38. In the preparation of this article the author has been careful to go as far as possible to first sources, and to form his judgment from personal examination, and on an independent basis; and for the analyses and criticisms made of the works of the various writers quoted, he alone is responsible.

discoveries are too new and too disconnected, to be put as yet into a perfect edifice of worthy proportions; while the opportunity also for making fresh acquisitions is still too great, to be favorable for that high repose of thought in which science loves to dwell, and to gaze with deep, calm survey upon the wide circumference of things.

Philology, like her elder sister Philosophy, has had for centuries a name among scholars; but like her, also, while honored with this formal remembrance, she has herself remained unknown, until standing within the horizon of our own day. From what beginnings, in what ways, and by what men, she has been conducted to her present seat of exaltation, it will be pleasant and profitable to learn. The various senses of the word philology ($\varphi\iota\lambda o\lambda o\gamma\iota\alpha$) at different times, exhibit in a general, though faint outline, the chief phases of its history. In old classical usage, it meant the love of literature; afterwards the scholastic mastery and exposition of language; more recently a sort of general amateur study of language, as a matter of mere pleasant curiosity; and last of all, the scientific exploration and comprehension of its interior mechanism, in relation both to its original elements, and also to their varied transformations, through a wide range of comparative analysis.

Grammar, that great central determinative basis of all true philology, Grecian scholars at Alexandria, in

Egypt, were the first to construct into any distinct scientific form. With both synthetic and analytic thoroughness, they collected and compacted together the materials furnished them by their mother tongue, which they so much idolized; and defined with clearness the actual inward structure of their own language, as an independent mechanism by itself. This new science the Latins afterwards borrowed; but they early lost it, as having any controlling influence over their educational discipline, and even over their own speech; for in each one of the modern Romanic languages, which are but the Latin moulded with a few commingling elements into forms better adapted to express the wants and tastes of later generations, like old garments refashioned for new uses, we find an almost perfect obliteration of the many-angled and complicated syntax of the original Latin.

It was in the cloisters of the middle ages, as in a conservatory, that the Latin was carefully sheltered from the rude storms without, and cultivated in all its native beauty. Here scholarly eyes watched with jealous care, by day and night, over its preservation. Here ancient words were kept as precious coins. Here Grammar, on whose wide and firm supports all the drapery of language rests, as a rich vine with its clusters of fruits and flowers upon the strong frame beneath it, was valued rightly for its many high uses, and from hand to hand and heart to heart, with heroic earnestness, this sacred relic of the elder times was carefully borne down from one age to another for the behoof of those who should live in the better days that were to come. And come they did, and that with observation. At the Reformation, the deep, slow heat, which for ages had been spreading as in a subterranean mine through all the scholarship of the world, burst forth with its long accumulation of energy.

The leaders of this great awakening in modern society, as of the next greatest event since that day, the exodus of the Puritan Church to these shores, were the leading classical scholars of the times. The new era, accordingly, of modern linguistic scholarship in its open and progressive manifestations, like that of modern social piety, is to be found in one and the same eventful period.

Luther and Melancthon, not to speak of others, were themselves fine classical scholars; but, under the pressure of the times upon their consciences, they rather used the scholarship that they had previously acquired, for immediate desired results in other directions, than devoted their strength to its greater enlargement.

But Reuchlin in Germany, Erasmus in Holland, aud Budæus in France, each in his own land, held high the banner of classical study before the eyes of many followers.

They were succeeded by some others who surpassed them, as each generation should its predecessor, if not in the quality of their scholarship, yet in its vastness; as Muretus, Scaliger, Casaubon, Salmasius, Bentley, Porson and others, whose names will never be forgotten for their great attainments as measured by the opportunities of their age, and much more for the deep enthusiasm out of which they grew. High aims always deserve and secure respect. They are, indeed, the only title to it; and no standard for measuring a man could be more false, in multitudes of instances, than the common one of success or failure. But the scholarship of those days either contented itself with its own conscious pleasure, or was almost wholly occupied in disentombing old authors, whom time had buried in oblivion, or in filing away excrescences and corruptions from the text, as first obtained, by a more careful collation of manuscripts. Throughout the whole of the eighteenth century, and especially the latter half of it, the linguists of Europe, like the votaries of science who had been long searching for the philosopher's stone and the elixir of life, were eager to discover the one mother-tongue of all the languages of the world; and whilst scholars decided variously, according to the different amount of their research, or the different quality of their mental constitutions, the majority believed that it was the Hebrew, as that contained the oldest literature of any language which they knew, as well as the earliest records of our race. Others however thought, with equally good reason, that it was rather the Armenian, as that was the language of the people living around Mount Ararat, where, from the times of Noah's ark, their ancestors had lived in unbroken succession. To one who would see the trail of these ideas extending down even to our own times, it will be worth the while to examine, in connection one with another, Parkhurst's Greek Lexicon, Nork's Latin, and Webster's English Dictionaries. The Hebrew is represented in them all as moving like a king in a grand triumphal march, with the other languages walking humbly in its train. In another direction, also, much effort and learning were expended by scholars in that century, as by geologists fifty years ago who were everywhere seeking to find traces of the deluge, in the attempt to discover sure proofs of the confusion of tongues and of peoples, by the dispersion at Babel.

As infidels also have sought to make each one of the natural sciences in their turn, when they first began to make any clear utterances of their own, bring in their testimony against the Scriptures, so too in philology they hoped to find a victorious enemy to Christianity. But Chronology, Ethnography and Etymology have all been tortured in vain, to make them contradict the Mosaic account of the early history of man.

During the last century great interest was felt throughout Europe in comparing as many different languages as possible, though only on a narrow scale of words, one with another. Leibnitz, who died an old man in 1716, that great philosopher, or rather universal genius, entitled by his contemporaries on account of his large learning a living dictionary, was very zealous in the study of Ethnography, and carefully collected all lists of words that he could obtain in different languages, for the purpose of comparing them together. He founded the present Academy of Sciences at Berlin, the home of modern philology, for the purpose of promoting the study of language, on broad philosophic principles, by tracing out with care their analogies, and through them also the genealogy of mankind. His place in the history of philology is that of its early prophet, foreseeing in dim outline the wonders of this new continent in the world of letters, but which, in his distance from it, he could picture to his eye only as a beautiful far-off dream-land. But with what sacred fervor did he, standing within the shadows of his own unilluminated age, wave his hand to the generations following him, in the direction of his ecstatic though faint vision of the future. Catherine II. also, Empress of Russia, ordered a special list of many of the most common Russian words to be prepared, and to be carefully collated with their equivalents in as many languages as possible; and, after undertaking herself to draw up formal tables of comparison in different languages, she transferred the long labor to Pallas, an eminent naturalist, who, as the result, published in 1787 and 1789 a work entitled "A Comparison of the Vocabularies of all the Languages of the World."

But in 1784 an event occurred, which made at the time but little show, and yet drew after it the most surprising consequences: the formation of the Asiatic Society at Calcutta by Sir William Jones, who had gone to Calcutta a year before, as a great admirer and connoisseur of Oriental poetry, in order to perfect his knowledge of Indian literature. Before his day, the term "oriental languages" had included only the Semitic dialects. Under the auspices of the Asiatic Society, the Chinese language and literature were thoroughly studied by the best French scholars, and the languages and literature of India by those of England. Those earnest students of the Sanskrit, however, we must leave for a time at their work, and look at the developments meanwhile of European scholarship at home.

In 1806, Adelung's Mithridates appeared, or at least the first volume of it: the second being issued in consequence of his death by Vater, in 1809, under whose auspices and those of the younger Adelung a third and a fourth volume appeared in 1816 and 1817. The languages of the world are here classified and described; and all helps for their acquisition then known are stated. Copies also of the Lord's prayer are presented in a great variety of languages for examination; but no scientific basis for a comparative study of them is indicated or conceived. These collections form, therefore, but a mere unarranged mass of curiosities, no higher in character than in mineralogy would be a collection of stones from different lands, divided into classes according to their mere resemblances of color or of shape. Neither Adelung nor Vater were any thing more than good linguists; and Vater, indeed, was not in any high sense entitled even to such a name.

Gradually, and in the form of many successive details, the true light was now beginning everywhere to dawn upon those that were seeking for it. The instinct and the effort to seek more light are always the needful preparation for obtaining it. In the study of the Persian, wonderful resemblances were found to both the Greek and German: the Latin and German also were compared together lexically, and found to possess many surprising points of connection; and the feeling began to be common among scholars, that, in the pursuit of mutual analogies in different languages, was to be found a path to much sure spoil. Amid such investigations and under the combined action of many minds, throughout Europe and Asia, the new and true philology slowly but steadily rose into being, at the beginning of the present century. German scholars claim that it should be called Indo-German, instead of Indo-European, and thus bear on its very front perpetual praise to those great Germans, who have brought its wonders into view. But it is to English enterprise and scholarship in the first place, that the world owes the discovery of the elementary facts, which German industry and skill have since so fully developed and woven into such a web of manifold and marvellous beauty to a linguist's eye. On any view, however, the title used for these new etymological developments should be one descriptive of the breadth of their relations and results, rather than of the genius of those who have made them known. "Great is Truth," whether seen resting tranquilly on her shield upon the page of history, or moving in majesty along the pathway of human advancement; and everywhere let her be honored, for she is divine, while it matters little whether any man or any set of men either stand or walk, in a vain show by her side.

And what now of those busy explorers of the Sanskrit, for many silent years in India! Much, in every way. Sanskrit literature is voluminous, in the form of poems, plays, fables, systems of philosophy, and works on astronomy and medicine. No one of the other Indo-European languages has ever possessed metres so varied and so complicated as the Sanskrit. The hymns of the Vêdas especially, written at the period when the Arian tribes first began to traverse the fields of Northern India, have an interest altogether their own: as we not only stand in them on the farthest outermost position in the whole realm of profane literature, facing the very dawn of the post-diluvian world; but we also see there primeval humanity unfold in simple, careless earnestness, its hopes and fears for this life, its pleasures and pains and all its anxious doubts and surmises about the future. These, as the result of the conquest of India and the transplantation of English minds to its soil, some of the best scholars of the latter part of the last century studied critically, under thorough native scholars. It was in 1765 that the East India Company obtained, by the treaty at Allahabad, their first sovereignty of Bengal; in the management of which they determined to rule the people in conformity with their own laws. Warren Hastings accordingly, then Governor General, caused a Digest to be made of their most important books of laws by eleven Brahmin Scholars, which was first translated into Persian and afterwards into English, and published in London in 1776 under the title, Code of Gentoo Law, in the preface of which Halhed, the editor, first spoke of the Sanskrit to European ears as being the original language of these ancient books; but without any knowledge of his own at the time of its character. Foremost among the first students of Sanskrit were Sir William Jones, a man of great learning and high cultivation, Mr. H. T. Colebrooke, author of a Sanskrit grammar, and Sir Charles Wilkins, also the author of a Sanskrit grammar, and the first to print Sanskrit in Europe. In searching the recesses of Sanskrit literature, like travellers rummaging the pyramids of Egypt or the ruins of Nineveh, to see what they could find, how were they amazed and delighted to discover at every step the most strange and beautiful correspondences, not only with the Latin and the Greek, but also with their own mother-tongue, and indeed with almost every language of which they had sufficient knowledge to make it a term of comparison. As early as in 1778, six years before the formation of the Asiatic Society at Calcutta, Halhed expressed his "astonishment" in his Bengal grammar, "at the similitude of Sanskrit words with Persian, Arabic, Latin and Greek, throughout the whole groundwork of the language." But Sir William Jones was the first to announce to the European world the connection of the Arian languages one with another, saying, that "no philologer could examine the Sanskrit, Greek and Latin, without believing them to have sprung from some common source, which perhaps no longer exists. There is a similar reason, though not quite so forcible, for supposing that both the Gothic and Celtic had the same origin with the Sanskrit. The old Persian may be added to the same family." This surely is a very bold, clear statement made at the outset, partly as a matter of ascertained fact, and partly as a matter of well-conceived theory, of what has since been so fully discovered and verified by so many scholars, with such brilliant success. The first direct translation made from the Sanskrit itself into English, was that of the Bhagavadgîta, a philosophic episode in the great Sanskrit epic Mahâbhârata, furnished by a young merchant, named J. Wilkins, in 1785; and was followed by another two years later, of a book of fables called Hitopadeśa. In 1789 Jones published a translation of the Śakuntalâ, a great drama full of tender and sweet thoughts; whose gems, when spread before occidental eyes, created a new and wide-spread interest in a literature so ancient and foreign, which possessed such riches. Sir William Jones died in 1794 letting his mantle fall, as he passed away, upon Colebrooke, a man remarkable both for his intellectual force and his unwearied industry. Colebrooke early published a translation of the chief one of the Sanskrit Koshas, called the Amara Kosha, "the most celebrated," says Wilson, "in all India, and having the widest circulation." This was but a vocabulary, made by an author named Amara Sinha, and not a dictionary; being arranged in separate sections and chapters, according to the topics in the text that it accompanied. Colebrooke is called by A. Schlegel, "a man who had shown himself a tasteful connoisseur of poetry, in the ancient and modern Asiatic and European languages," and no one to this day has exhibited a better appreciation than he, of the genius of the Sanskrit tongue. Several of his best articles have been grouped together, from "The Asiatic Researches" and "The Transactions of the Asiatic Society," into a volume, entitled "Essays on the Religion and Philosophy of the Hindûs," a new edition of which has recently appeared. Horace H. Wilson, still living, then assistant secretary to the Asiatic Society in Calcutta, published in 1819 a

Sanskrit and English dictionary in London, translated and improved from one originally prepared by learned natives, for the College of Fort William in India, almost immediately after its foundation, as one of its first necessities, having been begun in 1800, and finished in 1809. This translation, which has since reached a third edition, was hailed with joy by Schlegel, " as one," to use his language in his Indische Bibliothek, " by which we are at once brought forward to an immeasurably advanced position."

And how was the spark of the new light, thus brought from India by English hands, kindled in Germany? For there only has it been fanned into a broad all-illuminating flame. It was Frederic Schlegel, whose zeal for linguistic progress, during a brief visit to England in 1803, made him the depositary of the sacred treasure in behalf of his countrymen. From Mr. Alexander Hamilton, then recently returned from Calcutta, he obtained a slight knowledge of the Sanskrit, which he afterwards increased somewhat by farther study at Paris. Although the knowledge thus gained was slender, yet it was put to a noble use by him on his return to Germany, both in his own intentions, and in its final results, by his production of " An Essay on the Language and Philosophy of the Indians," which he published in 1808, and which first aroused his countrymen to this new and great study. And, although all the facts that he gave them were what a philological novice could carry home as a single sheaf in his hand, and the subsequent discoveries of his successors have made whatever was new in his statements, appear meagre and antiquated enough; yet the impulse that he gave to his generation has been spreading with ever widening force, from that day to our own. The highest and brightest path of modern scholarship now, is that on which he then started alone with a strong adventurous foot. As for his essay itself, it was a tissue almost equally of fancy and fact; and, judged by the light of our times, its scientific aspects are almost contemptible. But yet that great fundamental principle, which he was the first to state with distinctness, that *correspondence in the grammatical structure of different languages proves their identity, beyond any other kind of resemblance*, remains still intact, and will ever remain the basis of all real scientific philology. He also pointed out clearly the general fact that there is such a science as the comparative anatomy of language, in reference especially to the Sanskrit, Persian, Geeek, Roman and Teutonic languages. His services can never be forgotten by the lovers of comparative etymology, as he it was who first summoned his own people, a nation of scholars, into this new field of research where so much intellectual effort has since been so well rewarded; and whose earnest, joyous spirit in entering upon it seems to have been transfused into all his successors. His half poetical and half philosophical "Essay" was exactly adapted to do the work, which was needed at that period of German scholarship: to summon its energies, then just beginning to unfold themselves with power in other directions, in an earnest, enthusiastic manner into this new, wide-opening, enchanting field of intellectual toil and discovery. And that we may know all the better the man, to whom the world owes so much, let us pause for a moment and listen in silence to his words, as he stands before our thoughts, venerable, not only for his own greatness, but also for the wonderful issue of his life. "It had been," he says, " my intention to publish an Indian Chrestomathy, in the original character and in Latin, which should contain, besides the elementary principles of the language, a selection of extracts from the most important Indian works, with a Latin translation, notes, and a glossary. Every thing was prepared for this publication, and, besides the grammar and the two vocabularies, I had also copied in the original character and prepared for insertion a more than sufficient number of such pieces. I endeavored, by carefully copying the finest manuscripts both in the Devanagari and Bengalese character, to attain such perfection as would enable me to furnish in writing, very good models for the use of the type-cutter. But I found, notwithstanding, that the preparation of the types would require far more efficient assistance, than it was in my power to procure. The sacrifice of personal predilections, for the sake of any particular scientific object, brings its reward with it; but it is vexatious, to be compelled to pause midway, in attaining the desired goal, from the want of extraneous assistance. I must therefore be content, in my present experiments, to restrict myself to the furnishing of an additional proof of the fertility of Indian literature, and of the rich hidden treasures which will reward our diligent study of it: to kindle in Germany a love for, or at least a prepossession in favor of, that study; and to lay a firm foundation on which our structure may, at some future period, be raised with greater security and certainty."

Such were the aims, such the spirit, and such the labors of this first leader in philology. And to this hour no men put forth so much effort with so glad a heart, as the votaries of comparative philology. Pictures in still life do not appeal to many eyes, as do those of martial fire and fury; and so the steady long continued heroism and patient benevolence of a student's heart, earnestly and lovingly at work for many years by day and night, to give the world the benefit of its best thoughts and discoveries in new and untried fields of research, are among the specimens of human nobility, which may be often little prized or noticed here, but which are held in high account in heaven. It is in the silent depths of such hearts, brooding over things before unknown, that the ideas which afterwards rule the world are born. It is he who works, as well as he who prays, in secret, that the Great Father above rewards openly. The roots of all upward growths are out of sight under ground.

His brother A. W. Schlegel made, after him, deeper and more thorough researches than he. From 1819 to 1830, he published at Bonn his "Indische Bibliothek," (Indian Library,) which was a sort of private bulletin, issued occasionally by an enthusiastic scholar as he could get sufficient materials for a number, of the last results obtained from time to time in Sanskrit research. And well do its contents show,* with what versatile talent and high gratification, he undertook to spread the light of his new discoveries through his native land. In 1825, he set up a press for printing the Râmâyana, a great Sanskrit work. He

* Vols. I. II. III. contain among other articles the following: 1st. The present state of Indian philology. 2d. Indian poems. (1.) Introductory remarks on Indian epic rhythm and German hexameter. (2.) The orthography and pronunciation of Indian names. (3.) Two poems on the genealogy of the goddess Ganga. (4.) Notes and observations. 3d. The issue of Sanskrit works. 4th. The history of the Elephant. 5th. The Indian Sphinx. 6th. Etymological study. 7th. An extended notice of Wilson's Sanskrit Dictionary. 8th. A full notice of the transactions of the Asiatic Society in respect to Geography, Botany, Ethnography, Antiquities, &c. 9th. Two articles by Humboldt on the Sanskrit gerunds. 10th. A general review (in 1824) of the whole field of Indian philology. 11th. The correspondence of H. H. Wilson, from Calcutta, containing brief notices of some Hindu dramas. 12th. Indian tales. 13th. The Indian Sphinx. 14th. Two long articles by Humboldt, on the Bhagavad Gitâ. 15th. Review by Lassen of Bopp's Sanskrit Grammar.

went at this time to France and afterwards to England, in order to perfect himself in his oriental studies; and, on his return to Berlin in 1827, devoted his energies with renewed effect to their advancement among his countrymen. He and his brother Frederic were the founders of the modern Romantic school of German literature. He was himself a very voluminous and at the same time valuable writer on art, history, and language. These brothers were both of a warm, poetic, mental constitution; and in such hearts, when cultivated, philology is always a welcome guest. A man of dry nature, all whose instincts and aptitudes are only mathematical or logical, may manipulate well the forms of words; he may analyze with thoroughness their syntactical combinations; he may be able to state, with the accuracy of an exact statistician, the antiquities of a language, and map out with precision its various geographical details. All that can be done mechanically he can do; as one without a soul for music, or an ear to know its discords from its concords, may yet play skilfully upon an instrument, so that its harmonies shall warble in every heart but his own. He may thus be a cold and skilful anatomist of language; but he is no artist. He lacks that divine enthusiasm which the ancients, in the very word itself, described as "God in us;" and that inner sense of the beautiful, without which science, nature, art, and even thoughts and treasures from above wear but a dull and leaden aspect, compared with their enchanting loveliness to him, whose heart knows how to revel, like a bee in the bosom of a rose, in their inward charms. But to one of a true ethereal temper, whose eye is open and purified to see God everywhere and "good in every thing," and whose soul thirsts for beauty as a child does for love, language like every thing else that God has made for man's use in his outward and upward efforts on the way to the land that is above, is full within and without of His manifest wisdom and love. As the sea mirrors the sky, so to such an one every thing earthly reflects the heavenly. The inner beauties of things shine through all their outside forms to such hearts, as to spirit-eyes.

Francis Bopp made his first appearance as a philologist, in 1816, in a work of high merit, entitled "The Conjugation-system of Sanskrit, Greek, Latin, Persian, and German Languages." It was this production that first effectually opened the new era of comparative philology. But as his great work, the Comparative Grammar, which constitutes properly the foundation of the new science of philology, in its present form and dimensions, was not published until many years afterwards; the demands of both chronology and history will be best met, if we turn away from him for a time while brooding over his precious toil, and consider the character and labors of other leading scholars who began now to appear upon the stage.

Rasmus Rask of Denmark, was a man of splendid

capacities by nature, and of large attainments for his years as a scholar. His star rose brightly now above the horizon, but unfortunately soon sank again from sight. He had a strong taste for philological research and criticism; and this he had stimulated and strengthened by the careful comparative study of the Icelandic, Anglo-Saxon and Frisian languages. His principal work is entitled "The Origin of the old Norse or Icelandic Languages," which was prepared in 1814. He discovered also and showed the close relationship between the Germanic and classical languages. He set out (in 1816) from Petersburgh with great zeal, on a tour of general philological exploration, and, arriving at last in Persia and India, investigated thoroughly the Zend, and prepared the first grammar of that ancient language of Persia; while he also brought home with him some of the best manuscripts of the Zend Avesta. He made besides some interesting but incomplete efforts, to delineate the comparative features of German, Greek, Latin and Lithuanian grammar. Rask did not know Sanskrit, and so built his arch of comparative philology without its true keystone. Bopp, however, acknowledges his genius in classifying, as he did before him, (in 1819,) the Indian, Median, Lithuanian, Slavonic, Gothic and Celtic languages, as all belonging to the Arian family. Rask also clearly defined the place of the Zend as a sister language of the Sanskrit, instead of being, as some had begun to think, a corrupt patois of it; while he showed at the same time the derivation of the modern Persian from it, as of the Italian from the Latin. Like the great Buttmann, Rask was endowed by his Maker with linguistic sensibilities and capacities equal to those of the best scholars of any age; and, as Buttmann* on the one hand lived, for the world's misfortune, before the time most open and appropriate to so exalted a genius in the study of language, so Rask on the other remained but long enough on the stage of life, to show mankind what a bright light was extinguished upon the earth, by his departure from it. But Rask is worthy of distinct remembrance also for his zeal, in exploring the Turanian as well as the Arian languages; and he was the first to do so with any enthusiasm or effect. These he regarded as all resting on a wide-spread original Scythian base. Professor Castren afterwards, who was a sort of earlier edition of Lieut. Kane, in respect, on the one hand, to his personal qualities: as the boldness of his enterprise, the firmness of his will, and the delicacy of his health; and on the other to the outward mode and sphere of his labors: travelling alone as he did in the frozen north in his own sledge, over the snows of Siberia and along the borders of the Arctic Ocean: published in various volumes, between 1844 and 1850, the results

* Could Buttmann but have had the lever of the Sanskrit in his hands, what marvels would he not have raised up, out of the hard long trodden pathway of Greek grammar and Greek philology, over which so many had heedlessly tramped in their ignorance, before him.

of his wide and long research in this branch of languages; and they confirmed for the most part the learned convictions and statements of Rask. The Teutonic researches of Rask, though ended at a very imperfect stage in their accomplishment, have been since so well completed by Grimm, as to leave little for years to come to be expected farther in this direction.

In 1819, Jacob Grimm commenced publishing his magnificent work, a Teutonic Grammar, embracing the Scandinavian as well as the German languages, and drawing his authorities from the whole wide, long range of German authorship, from Ulfilas' translation of the Scriptures, (A. D. 388,) the only relic in existence of the old Gothic, down to his own day; and finished his great labor in 1837. The scholarship of the work is wonderful, for its breadth, accuracy and ingenuity. It is not too much to say, that the world has never exhibited a finer specimen of the true scholar, according to the highest and fullest ideal, than he is. His "scale," or law of correspondences of sound in the different Indo-European languages, is one of the highest triumphs of inductive analysis that have been ever furnished in any science. Bopp's first incidental suggestions in this direction he perfected into full ripe science; and, in constructing his "scale," made it with such nicety, as to its own characteristics and all its gradations, that, while the sphere of its use has been much extended since, no improvement has been made upon it at any time, in respect to its own essential nature. He has thus in effect given not only definiteness and certainty but also breadth and power, to the science of comparative etymology. The laws of analogy he has shown to pervade as truly human language as nature herself. The style of these discoveries, as of the mind that made them, is altogether Newtonian. While the finite mind cannot create analogies, it reveals itself in one of its highest forms of disciplined strength, in being able to trace them with clearness, in the demonstrations which the Infinite Mind has made of Itself in their appointment.

But behold the Scale and the interpretation of it!

GRIMM'S SCALE.*

	Labials.			Gutturals.			Dentals.		
Greek,	B.	P.	PH.	G.	K.	CH.	D.	T.	TH.
Gothic,	P.	PH.	B.	K.	CH.	G.	T.	TH.	D.
Old High German,	PH.	B.	P	CH.	G.	K.	TH.	D.	T.

For the Latin the scale runs as follows:

Latin,	B.	P.	F.	G.	C.	H.	D.	T.	(F).
Gothic,	P.	F.	B.	K.	H.	G.	T.	TH.	D.
Old High German,	PH.	F.	P.	CH.	H.	K.	Z.	D.	T.

The interpretation of the scale is this: that the several letters corresponding perpendicularly displace each other, or are substituted for each other, in the equivalent forms of the different languages respectively especially when initial. Thus the Gothic and the Lower German dialects substitute, in relation to the

* Grimm's Geschichte der deutschen Sprache, p. 276.

Greek and Latin, and measurably also to the Sanskrit and the Zend, aspirates for original tenues, (as, h for k, th for t, and f for p) : tenues for medials, (as, t for d, p for b, and k for g); and medials for aspirates (as, g for ch, d for th, and b for f.) It must not be supposed that these interchanges are observed in every case, with absolute uniformity. To what law, except that of love in things moral, and of attraction in things physical, are there not exceptions allowed and even constituted? But such are the general principles that prevail in respect to the mutual interchanges of letters, in these several languages.

EXAMPLES.

Sanskrit.	Greek.	Latin.	Gothic.	Old High German.	English.
aham, for agham	ἐγώ	ego,	ik	ih	I
	ἀγρός	ager	akrs	achar	acre
svan, a dog		canis	hunths	hunt	hound
dasan, ten	δέκα	decem	taihun	zehan	{ ten / tithe
danta(s), tooth	ὀδούς	dens	tunthus	zand	tooth
trayas, three	τρεῖς	tres	threis	dri	three
	δάκρυ / δάκρυμα	{ lacryma / archaic / dacrima	tagr	zahar	tear
	λείπειν	linquere	leiban	lipu	leave
vê, to weave	ἰτέα for Ϝιτέα	} vitis		wida	{ withe / with / wither
ad, to eat	ἔδειν	edere	itan	ezan	eat
	ἀμέλγειν	mulgere	miluks	miluh	milk
pâda(s), foot	πούς	pes	fotus	fuoz	foot
pula (s), much	πόλυς	plus	filu	filo	full
upari, above	ὑπέρ	super	ufar	ubar	{ upper / over
sad, to sit	ἔζεσθαι	sedere	sitan	sizan	sit

Such analogies, found in hundreds of instances, cannot be accidental. Thus Grimm virtually founded a new and widely influential department of linguistic science, which he denominated Lautlehre or the doctrine of sounds, or phonetic correspondences and substitutions. Besides his Teutonic grammar, he has published a work entitled "Mythology and Researches into German Antiquities." He has also written a very interesting history of the German language, as seen from the stand-point of philology, which he published in two volumes, at Leipsic, in 1853. This work is held in high honor in Germany, and yet the regret felt is universal, that his vast labors as a student and author have prevented him from perfecting the work, in fulness of form and finish of detail, more nearly according to the model of his own thoughts. On whatever subjects his mind is employed, it makes close research over a wide range of inquiry. He spares neither time nor pains, in making coast-surveys of German literature, and taking soundings in all its seas, and mapping out carefully all the discoveries which he makes, for the world's good. He is now, with his brother William, preparing a comprehensive dictionary of his vernacular tongue, beyond both for height and breadth the plan of any dictionary prepared or conceived for preparation, in any language: a work of Herculean toil, which none but an intellectual giant could for a moment feel himself adequate to achieve. Slowly but surely the vast work rises under their hands. May they live to put on its topmost stone! And yet so broad are the foundations laid, and so huge is the structure that is to rest upon them, that one could hardly expect that they would live, were they men in middle life, to see its consummation. Jacob Grimm, though still full of the fire of his youth, is a septuagenarian. How sublime is German scholarship, in both its patience under present labor and its trust in the future for the cherished result! and neither the changes of life nor its shortness frighten it back from any efforts, however long or hard, which seem worthy to be made. What an interval of many years often stretches between the first and last volume of a standard German work! and how many, who have eagerly seized upon the first, have through many long years kept continually looking for its successor, and died without the sight!

The one man, however, who by his wide research and vast learning and wonderful insight and ingenuity, is entitled beyond all others, to the name of being the founder of modern philology as a science, is Francis Bopp: not so old a man as Grimm, yet perhaps hardly so full of his native strength. The one work, in which Bopp has specially developed the wonderful proportions and relations of this new science, is his "Comparative Grammar of the Sanskrit, Zend, Greek, Latin, Lithuanian, old Slavonic, Gothic and German," which he began to publish in 1833 and finished in 1849. Little did Bopp dream in his earlier works, what a mine of inexhaustible riches he had struck, and what a sensation he was ere long to produce among the scholarly minds of his age. It was in these works that he came at the very outset upon the vein of phonetic correspondences in different languages, from which afterwards both himself and others deduced such vast results. Like other great discoveries, it was stumbled upon! This is the very meaning of the word invent: they *came upon it*, as a traveller upon a prize by the roadside. A few similar cases of transformations, substitutions and interchanges in consonants and vowels, sufficed to suggest inquiry and comparison upon a wide scale to those earnest students: as the result of which they found a vast mass of natural hieroglyphs treasured on the walls of each language that they investigated; the hidden alphabet of which they also discovered, preserved in the very characters themselves. Bopp is now preparing, with many improvements, a new edition of his grammar, and has published three parts of it already, since August 1857. Others have made great achievements in separate fields of research, but Bopp was the first, and has ever been foremost, in developing the comparative features of the old and new languages of the civilized world, Asiatic and European; and that on no partial or fanciful basis, but by an astonishingly wide and satisfactory scale of comparisons. He analyzes the whole grammatical structure of the Indo-European languages; separating words everywhere into their roots, their formative and derivative suffixes, their case-terminations and person-endings: opening into view in each language its whole interior frame-work, and showing them all to be, both generally and specially, alike in their organism; and the student feels on the one hand, that he stands on terra firma, while surveying the scene of strange and multiform correspondences of all languages around him, and on the other that he is gazing everywhere on unmistakable realities, both old and new. To their difference of form he applied, with magic effect, the phonetic principles which he practically developed, but never scientifically methodized. He was also the first to strike out that new and valuable idea in philology, that the organific principle of language is to be found in its pronominal elements; so that these contain the whole material of flexion, whether in the verb or in the noun both substantive and adjective. Bopp is one of the few men whose lives form eras in the progress of humanity. The study of his comparative grammar is like a constant festival to an inquisitive, scientific, scholarly mind. He travels, like one voyaging on the Rhine or the Nile or passing through a series of lovely landscapes in "la belle France," through scenery that at every point is full of beauty or of wonder.

Bopp has become in effect the founder of a wholly new order of classical literature. Language has been constructed, under his guidance and influence, into a science having a definite area and horizon. Its territories have been explored with care; and where its riches lie, and what they are, is well known. Like Bacon in philosophy, he has brought in philology the reign of theory without facts to a perpetual end. Up to his day, the streams of etymology were the favorite resort of all sorts of fishers after whims and fancies, and the most fantastic absurdities were treated as scientific verities. But, by his long and earnest pursuit of facts, the most surprising affinities have been found to exist between the Sanskrit and all the other members of the Indo-European family. And the Sanskrit itself is found to be not their parent, but rather their elder-born sister, although so much older and of such a different bearing as to have well-nigh the mien and place and care of a parent among her younger sisters; for the Sanskrit also gives decided proof of a derived existence, at a far earlier date, from the same common stock. And the Sanskrit, now treasured in books, is found to be the Sanskrit of a later date than that to which the affiliated Indo-European languages bear such strangely full and minute resemblance: so that sometimes the Latin itself is more faithful to the archaic radical type of the word, as careful phonological analysis shows, than the Sanskrit itself in its present form.

It has been quite impossible to get a copy of Bopp until within a short time: almost fabulous prices having been given for a stray copy that could be picked up in any part of the world. An advertisement of such a copy for sale would attract at once as eager a host of buyers, as would the sight of a chamois left dead in the mountains, of hungry eagles. A single broken volume of a copy was snatched after, wherever found, at any price. For those unacquainted with German, an English translation by Eastwick (2d edition, London, 1854) can be obtained at a cost of $16, and though very dear it is well worth the purchase. In 1834 Bopp published his Sanskrit grammar, and in 1845 a second edition of it, and it is still the best Sanskrit grammar to be had. In 1836 appeared his "Vocalismus, oder sprachvergleichende Kritiken," &c., or philological criticisms on Grimm's German grammar, and in 1847 his " Glossarium Sanskritum " or " Sanskrit Dictionary; in which all the Roots and most common Sanskrit Words are unfolded and compared with Greek, Latin, German, Lithuanian, Slavonic and Celtic Words." His last new work is the "Vergleichendes Accentuationssystem," published in 1854. It is a comparative view of the system of accentuation in Sanskrit and Greek, and, like all his works, full of evidences of acuteness and ability. It was immediately followed by an ingenious work, published by Professors Henri Weil and Louis Benloew, in French, at variance in many of its leading positions with Bopp's, entitled "Theorie generale de l'accentuation Latine." Bopp has been, however, most successfully controverted in some of his views by Prof. Whitney, of Yale College, in a paper read before the American Oriental Society, and published in their Journal, Vol. v. pp. 195 ff., as well as also in Germany in Kuhn's Zeitschrift.

Bopp's services therefore as a linguist have had, as we have shown, two great directions: the thorough advancement of Sanskrit scholarship as such, and the establishment of the science of Comparative Grammar; which not only rose at the outset almost spontaneously as if a fairy castle, out of the elements of Sanskrit study, as soon as they were thoroughly mastered, but has ever since rested on them for its foundations, as there it must forever rest. A. W. Schlegel and his admirers, like Lassen, have confined themselves to the investigation of Indian literature and antiquities and the issue of critical texts of Sanskrit works; while Bopp and Grimm have gone with the torch of analytic philosophy into the depths of the Sanskrit language itself, as well as into those of all the related languages, in order to find their hidden riches.

Wherever Bopp's discoveries are known, language will be studied and taught on entirely different principles and with very different results from what have been ever before witnessed. Each language must now be studied, not only as it is in itself, but also in its various relations; and he who studies but one language must stand on the outside of the gate of even that, and only dream, but never see, what is within its walls; what of beauty! what of vastness! what of life! Something, indeed, far different from the mere mastery of a few authors in a given language, is to be comprehended in the idea of studying not only language in general but any language in particular.

Augustus F. Pott, now Professor at Halle, should ever, both for his contemporaneousness and his merit as a writer in philology, be associated with Bopp and Grimm. They form, indeed, by themselves, a splendid constellation in the firmament of this science. His great work was published in two volumes, in 1833 and 1836, at Lemgo, entitled "Etymologische Forschungen," &c., or "Etymological Investigations in the Field of the Indo-Germanic Languages, with special Reference to the Changes of Sound in the Sanskrit, Greek, Latin, Lithuanian, and Gothic Languages:" the first volume of a new edition of which, much enlarged and improved, has recently appeared. Pott has the honor of first entering the department of Lexical Etymology, on any broad scale, with the torch of Indo-European analogy; and yet neither he nor any European writer has ever attempted to this day, to determine its principles, or group its facts into the form of a high and noble science. When, accordingly, Etymology is spoken of in this essay as a science, it is so denominated from deference to its own inward claims to such a designation; and not as a recognition of any attempt, ever made by German philologists to construct its elements into a distinct system. In 1846 Pott published a work of much merit on the language of the Gypsies, clearly establishing its membership in the great Indo-European family of languages. He has recently (1856) published an additional work of considerable interest on the Etymology of surnames, entitled "Personennamen und Familiennamen." Pott is a man of great erudition in philology, and a critic of the first class; while being also an original investigator, like Bopp and Grimm, although not on so large a scale.

William Humboldt in 1835 wrote a learned and philosophical treatise on "The different Modes of forming Human Speech," in which he presented, with clearness and effect, a true comparative estimate of different languages; representing the Chinese or monosyllabic, and the Indo-European and Semitic or inflected languages, as the two contrary poles of linguistic development, and holding up to honor the most thorough critical method of philological analysis as the only mode of studying language, deserving of the name. All such early utterances of a high sort in this department of study we hail with delight, as they show at least the quality of the men who made them; their genius, their philosophy, their scholarship, and the ideals which they set up before their own minds. And in the kingdom of mind, not as in that of commerce and in common life, where men are estimated according to their successes, but as in the kingdom of God, they are to be judged to their honor or their shame, according to their aims and their efforts."

But while in Germany the science of philology was thus rising to a conspicuous height before all eyes, in France also a few earnest devotees to its interests began now to appear. Two especially deserve distinct mention, Burnouf and Eichhoff. Eugene Burnouf published, in 1835, some of the results of his acute researches in the Zend, as compared with the Sanskrit, and established by careful induction the scale of correspondences between them: showing that the Zend is more like the Sanskrit than any other language, and that very often, by merely changing the Zend letters into their fixed Sanskrit equivalents, you may obtain the same precise word as in Sanskrit. He extended accordingly Grimm's law of substitutions and equivalents, so as to embrace the Zend with the Sanskrit. He also gave himself with much earnestness to the work of editing various publications of the Zend, restoring in each case the manuscripts with critical care; and prepared a Zend grammar, and was indeed strictly the founder of all true Zend philology. F. G. Eichhoff published at Paris, in 1836, a work entitled, "Parallèle des Langues de l'Europe et de l'Inde," or "A Comparative view of the Languages of Europe and of India." This was afterwards translated into German by Kaltschmidt, who greatly admires his views, and who published also in

1845, a second edition of it. Eichhoff's work is designed to present a comparative view of the Indo-European languages, both grammatically and verbally, and to be at the same time as comprehensive and condensed as possible. But, while being well deserving of possession, it is very unequal in its merits in the department of verbal etymology: at times rising to the highest point of excellence, and at others sinking below the average level of philological accuracy and skill. He is so charmed with the love of new discoveries, and even of suppositions that look like discoveries, that his etymologies are of too mixed a character to be of uniform value. To one, however, who will use Eichhoff with true discrimination, he will furnish real help in the study of philology. Since Burnouf and Eichhoff stand together in solitary grandeur, as leaders in this new science in France, it will please the reader perhaps to let Eichhoff come forward and speak of his plans in his own person. Says he, "'Who does not love etymologies? The imagination of what scholar would not involuntarily wander from one enterprise to another, out of one century into another, in order to find the remains of a perished language; remains which are the fragments of the people's history.'* These words," (says Eichhoff,) " of one of our first scholars and most ingenious critics, strikingly indicate the plan of this work, which proceeds from the double point of view

* Le Clerc, the dean of Philosophy at Paris.

afforded by philology and history. These two philosophies march forward in the world with equal steps and mutual support. The life of a nation reveals itself in its language: the true picture of their changing fortunes; and, where the history of a people is silent, where the thread of tradition is broken, there the ancient genealogy of language gives us light, which outlives the wreck of empires, and eternizes the origin of a people and their memory. Language, the living organ of so many extinguished races, suffices to solve many enigmas, which without it could not be resolved; so soon as one, after obtaining a thorough knowledge of the special speech of each single nation, procures some common measure of comparison, which makes them all comprehensible at a glance. Deeply buried in the East, after having ceased to be a living speech for more than three thousand years, and being equally long forgotten in Europe, a language has been found, which, in its inward spirit, in the completeness of its forms, in its riches, and especially in its agreement throughout with our European tongues, is full of wonder. A true comprehension of the languages of the world, is one of the necessities of our century; and it is no profitless task to aid in affording it. Following accordingly the dictionary and the grammar, in the leading languages of our system, (the Indo-European,) I have brought them together into one view, and developed them, sometimes singly and sometimes comparatively, and arranged together their component parts, in a comprehensive and complete synopsis." He dedicates his work to "Chézy, the founder of Sanskrit study in France, and Merian, the promoter of comparative philology," as being in a sense the authors and guides of his own thoughts in this direction. It is pleasant surely to look through even such a loop-hole into the developments of French scholarship at that time, and find there the same ardor in pursuit, and the same joy in discovery, which have ever characterized the German students of philology, and indeed the students of philology generally throughout the world. There is in fact so much of poetic material in this science, and so much of its inspiration in those who pursue it, that they might well be called the prose-poets of the world.

But to return to Germany again: Albert Giese published in 1834 a work upon the Æolic dialect, of great interest. It is in this dialect that the Greek retains most of its primitive character and manifests its common heritage with the Latin, in all the elements of their equal Græco-Latin or Pelasgic parentage. Giese lived only to publish himself the first volume of his work, the second being published by his friends, from preparations for it that he left behind him.

In 1837 Albert A. Benary gave to the world, as the result of his critical studies, a work entitled "Die römische Lautlehre sprachvergleichend dargestellt," or the phonetic principles of the Latin language philologically viewed. Beside the intrinsic merits of this production as a fine specimen of thorough scholarly research, it has also the honor of being the first distinct work of modern times on phonetics, not only relatively to the Latin, but also absolutely in itself. In modern times I have said, for in ancient days phonology was well understood by Sanskrit scholars. He dwells on two main points particularly of the phonetic system of the Latin: diphthongation and aspiration. The whole phonetic system of the Latin he regards as consisting of five principal features: 1st. Its disinclination to diphthongs. 2d. The small range of aspiration. 3d. The limited use of consonantal combinations in initial and medial syllables. 4th. The reciprocal influence of vowels and consonants upon each other, by their very nature and constitution. 5th. The weakening of end-syllables under the influence of consonants, as also under that of vowels. The first two of the above elements he discusses in this work, so far as yet published. In treating of Latin diphthongs he shows that being in their very construction binary, they are composed always of a fixed radical element, and of a movable one attached to it; and then divides them all into two classes: those formed by contraction and those formed by Guna.* Here he unfolds in full philosophic form the principles, sug-

---

* Guna means, in Sanskrit grammar, the lengthening and strengthening of an i- or u- sound by a prefixed short a- sound, by which they become respectively ai and au.

gested and confirmed by a wide and full survey of the facts of the language, illustrating each step by full examples. Under the head of aspiration also, he is very minute and clear and interesting. Any fuller analysis of his work would not be consistent with the general design and scope of this essay. There is a good deal of valuable etymological material, strown incidentally throughout Benary's work. No Latin scholar can study it without real profit, in the way of enlarging his conscious grasp of the analytic constitution of the language.

Albert Hoefer published in 1839 a volume entitled, "Beiträge zur Etymologie und vergleichende Grammatik der Hauptsprachen des Indo-Germanischen Stammes," or considerations on the etymology and comparative grammar, of the principal Indo-German languages. It is an able original work in the special field which it traverses. The whole vast scope of philology embraces a wide range of many related topics, and touches language, phonetics, ethnography, chronology and climatology, at so many points and in so many ways, as to afford room for an almost unlimited variety of special investigations and results. Hoefer's work differs from Benary's in this, that while Benary treats of the special phonetic system of the Latin, he spreads his inquiries with philosophic exactness over the whole field of phonetics. The two main topics that he discusses are, 1. The philosophy of vowels, with an investigation of the principles of Guna and Vriddhi,* and the declension-forms of the Sanskrit. 2. The history of liquids in their relation to vowels and to consonants. To most readers doubtless there will seem to be, in the announcement of two such topics of investigation, nothing suggestive of either light or joy. It is not he who, never having climbed a mountain, stands beneath and looks up at its bold, bare peaks, that knows what food the glad spectator can there find who has ascended to the heights above heights, where the clouds thunder and roll and break at his feet, and who gazes down, like one of the watchers of the upper air, upon the world of his own former home below.

Besides the writers of whom we have hitherto spoken, a few other names are deserving of special mention, though with varying degrees of merit in this immediate connection.

H. L. Ahrens wrote in 1838 on "the conjugation in $\mu\iota$, in the Homeric dialect." In 1839 he published his first volume on the dialects of the Greek, which is his principal work, following it with the second in 1843. The two volumes embrace the Æolic and Doric dialects, which are discussed with remarkable ingenuity and research, and not without reference to the principles of Indo-European philology.

Düntzer also appeared at this time. His principal

† Vriddhi consists in prefixing a long a to i or u.

works are "The Philosophy of Latin Etymology" and "The Declension of the Indo-Germanic Languages." Düntzer is clear and ingenious, but, like most of the other writers already enumerated, except the first three that stand so high above the rest, Bopp and Pott and Grimm, has been so surpassed by subsequent writers as to wear now quite an antiquated aspect. Twenty years in fact serve generally to make scholarship in any direction appear as old in Germany and as well nigh useless, except historically, as they do most of our periodical literature at home.

Kaltschmidt, the satellite of Eichhoff, published in 1839 a Greek Etymological dictionary of some merit: more, however, in respect to the amount of personal labor expended than in respect to the benefit to be reaped from it by the public; for in the department of Etymology, on which it was specially intended to throw a high light, it is very deficient, being quite as full of fanciful characteristics as of those of real scholarship. Kaltschmidt has less of the standard characteristics of a real authority in philology, than any other name mentioned in this earliest group of the immediate followers of the first leaders in philology.

Their writings had been sown broadcast over the land, and the precious seed had germinated in many minds.

A new generation of scholars has now come upon the stage; men who had the advantage of starting in their studies where their predecessors had ended; men who are, at this very time, in the full vigor of their early manhood.

Among these no name is more conspicuous than that of Lorenz Diefenbach, the former pupil of both Bopp and Pott. He is a philologist of the first class. His chief works are his "Celtica" and his "Vergleichendes Wörterbuch der Gothischen Sprache," or comparative dictionary of the Gothic language, published in two volumes, at Frankfort, in 1851, which is a standard contribution, not only to the Gothic language, but also to comparative philology. It is a vast cabinet of rare linguistic curiosities: the most extensive museum of comparative etymologies to be found in the world, not excepting in its present state that magnificent German dictionary of the Grimms; which, however, when completed, will stand by itself, as a vast pyramid of learning and labor, overshadowing all other human productions in the amplitude of its scholarship. Diefenbach is a noble follower of noble guides. Bopp does the most justice of them all to the Sanskrit front of this great argument: Pott to the Latin and Greek side of it; while Grimm and Diefenbach bring up the rear in splendid array with the Gothic and the Celtic.

August Schleicher stands also in the first rank of the more recent philologists. His principal works are "Philological Investigations," published in 1848: "The Languages of Europe in a Systematic View," a work of much scholarship and interest, published in 1850; and also "Litauische Grammatik," or "A Lithuanian Grammar and Chrestomathy," published in 1856, which, like Diefenbach's Gothic dictionary, and Zeuss' Celtic grammar, is a splendid contribution of thorough original investigations to the science of philology. He is now at work, and has been for a long time, (as he announces in a note to a brief article, on the history of the Slavic languages, in Kuhn's "Beiträge zur Sprachforschung,") on a history of the languages of the Gothic or Germanic family.

George Curtius' name also deserves honorable mention here. He published in 1842 a dissertation on the "Formation of Greek Nouns," which was followed in 1846 by an admirable work on "The Formation of the Tenses and Modes in Greek and Latin," containing many fine specimens of philological analysis and argumentation. Beside contributing several articles of much interest to philological journals, he is the author of a "Griechische Schulgrammatik," published in 1852, (third edition, 1857.) His most interesting work, however, is his last, (1858,) entitled "Grundzüge der Griechischen Etymologie," the first part of which only is yet published. Here, after a fine introduction on some interesting points connected with the range and limits of etymology as such, the danger of false analyses and of a careless use of the Sanskrit in solving etymological difficulties, euphonic mutations, etc., a scholarly view of more than six hundred Greek roots is presented, with their Sanskrit, Latin, Gothic or other correspondences, with brief notices of the views of other leading philologists confirmatory or adverse. When this work, which has just arrived in this country, is finished and translated into English, as it surely will be, American scholars will have the means at hand of a thorough exploration and mastery of " the elements of Greek etymology."

Friedrich Diez is the author of a " Grammar of the Romanic Languages," which is the standard, supplanting all others in this study. The second edition of it, enlarged and improved, is now passing through the press. He is an original and thorough investigator in a great field of research. No writer has explored as he has the lingual riches of the Italian, Spanish and French languages. His etymological dictionary also of the Romanic languages, published in 1853, is a noble structure, standing by itself in solitary majesty on the field that it occupies. A quotation from the preface to this dictionary, will best show his style of mind and of scholarship. "The object of etymology is," he says, "to trace back a given word to its origin. The method adopted for the accomplishment of this object is not always the same. There is, as it is easy to see, a critical and an uncritical method. The uncritical draws its explanations, as a matter of good luck, out of a mere external resemblance of form, or forces them, where there is little resemblance and even entire variance, through a mass of elements specially contrived for the purpose. Such a faulty mode of procedure, by which, notwithstanding, where wit and genius have not been wanting, a happy hit has been sometimes made, has brought the whole science of etymology into discredit with some; while it has commended itself to others by the ease of its applications: since any one without preparation for it can enter upon such a work. The former err in their aversion, and the latter in their inclination to it. In contrariety to the uncritical method, the critical acts in subordination to the well-discovered principles and rules of phonology, so as not to swerve a foot's breadth from them, unless plain, actual exceptions shall justify it. It strives to follow the genius of the language itself, and to draw out from its bosom its own secrets. It takes a careful gauge of each letter, and seeks to discover the value that attaches to it in each position. And yet how little often can it accomplish! How doubtful are its results! The highest point reached by the etymologist, is the consciousness of having acted scientifically. For the attainment of absolute certainty he has no security. Some insignificant new thing may hurl down from him under his feet, to his mortification, a result previously gained with great labor. This will happen to him in every extended investigation: it is indeed among the daily experiences of the etymologist, from which even the most keen-eyed are not free. Therefore, modesty! even when every fact seems to support our theories." Here is presented in full view a self-drawn picture of the patient, scholarly, earnest spirit of the scientific etymologist. How different from that of the ancient empirical dealers in words as cheap, frivolous wares! It is when studying such works as his and Bopp's, Grimm's, Pott's and Diefenbach's, that one stands on the summits of modern philology, where the whole field of its wonders lies spread out before him.

Germany is at the present moment full of earnest investigators, in every part of the whole wide field of philology. In every university there is, as there ought to be, a provision for instruction in comparative philology. This new science is not only giving law to grammar, lexicography, classical study and linguistic research, but also to history and ethnography. Under its light the history of Rome has been rewritten with new clearness and beauty by Theodore Mommsen, as has that of Greece by Ernst Curtius; and under its influence must our own histories of the classical past be written still again for the proper illumination of English and American scholarship.

Ernst Curtius is, like George Curtius, a philologist of high attainments. He resided for four years in Greece, for the purpose of better pursuing his researches into the history of Greece. He was a pupil of O. Müller, and has been the private Tutor of Prince Frederic William. He is one of the finest living writers of Germany. He endeavors, both scientifically and studiously, to open the myths of the legendary periods of ancient history, and to extract the hidden kernel of their real truth; while Mommsen rejects them altogether, and falls back on the mere historic guidance to be obtained from the disentombed remains of language, in the archaic periods of the past. For ourselves, we must say, that we sympathize rather with Curtius than with Mommsen, in his conceptions of the intrinsic value of the early legends of Greece and Rome.

The great investigators, who have most opened the wonders of philology to the eyes of their admiring countrymen, are still living, to marvel at the effect of their labors upon their age: beholding changes quite as great in the community of scholars to which they belong, as the pioneers of the west have seen, in the brief but brilliant history of our new settlements. Three works especially of those already mentioned, made a distinct epoch by their great influence each by itself on the public mind of Germany: Frederic Schlegel's Essay on the Speech and Philosophy of the Indians; Grimm's Teutonic Grammar, and Bopp's Comparative Grammar. Most of the great philologists of Germany appear more or less frequently as the authors of occasional papers, in the " Zeitschrift für vergleichende Sprachforschung," &c., or " Journal of comparative Philology in the Department of the German, Greek, and Latin Languages," now in its seventh year; edited at first by Theodore Aufrecht and Adalbert Kuhn, but now by Kuhn alone, and published every two months at Berlin. In this journal, the last and best results of the most recent investigations appear, in a condensed form. Here the delighted reader meets with frequency with such men, in high discourse, as Bopp, Grimm, Pott, Aufrecht, Kuhn, Kirchhoff, Benary, Curtius, Schleicher, Ebel, Ahrens, Benfey, Förstemann a Danish scholar, and many others of the same spirit, if not yet of the same reputation. This journal will be welcomed, as a friend whose face is full of light, by every earnest student of its contents.

Aufrecht and Kirchhoff have recently prepared in combination a work of high critical qualities, entitled " Die umbrischen Sprachdenkmäler," or "The Remains of the Umbrian Language," published in 1851, by which much light is thrown on the early Latin. It consists of an explanation of the Eugubine tables, and of the various remains of the Umbrian still to be found, which are treated in the most careful elaborate way.

Benfey is learned and often exceedingly ingenious, and, like all such minds in other fields, exceedingly venturesome also at times, and so, quite unsafe as a guide to a novice. He has published a Greek Etymological Dictionary, and also a Sanskrit grammar not equal to Bopp's though succeeding it, which still remains the standard in this study.

Heyse has written a work on "The Philosophy of Language," well deserving perusal: it is thoroughly philological in its type. For a compendious scientific survey of the facts and principles of philology, in its broad general relations historically, phonologically, grammatically and lexically, it is, for so brief a work, one of great worth to the student; and not only quite superior to Rapp, but unequalled yet by any other in the same field. From him and Schleicher, if he can obtain no more helps to philological information, the young student in this charming field of investigation can procure a very good outfit of facts and principles, for wider and higher attainments, whenever means or opportunity can be secured. Heyse is the author also of a German dictionary, which, for ordinary use, not only for purposes of exegesis, but also of etymology, is of high value. Grimm says indeed of it, in the introduction to his own great national dictionary, what he does also of all others in the same field, that he has brought little if any thing new to the previous stock of knowledge possessed by the learned. But, while this is true, it is also true that he has thoroughly gathered together and methodized the various results of the most advanced scholarship of his day; and, while the honor is not so great to him, for brilliancy of intellect, as that of being a new discoverer, the advantage is very great to others, who obtain at his hands what they would have otherwise to search long and hard to obtain from many sources.

The philological acumen and attainments of Adalbert Kuhn, although of the highest sort, have been exhibited thus far chiefly in brief but sterling articles, a large number of which have appeared in the "Zeitschrift" which he edits. He seems to be quite objective in his aims and full of a spirit of usefulness. He does not wait for great occasions, or feel that when he acts he must move in state, and either do some great deed or do none at all. He appears on the contrary always intent on filling up that which is behind, and ever scattering the new light to others that has greeted his own vision. Albrecht Weber, Professor of Sanskrit in the University of Berlin, is one of the first Sanskrit scholars in Germany. He is the conductor of a periodical called " Indische Studien," now numbering four volumes, containing various interesting articles on Indian literature of value particularly to Sanskrit scholars as such. He is also the author of a collection of brief articles, entitled " Indische Skizzen," consisting of a sketch of " the recent investigations on ancient India," an article " on Buddhism," another on " the connections of India with the lands in the west ; " and a fourth on " the Semitic origin of the Sanskrit alphabet." Weber ranks for character with Curtius, Kuhn and Schleicher.

Rapp, professor at Tübingen, has published recently in three parts a work which he entitles "Grundriss der Grammatik," or "An Outline of the Grammar of the Indo-European Family of Languages." He is ingenious and learned. One of the main defects of this book is his adoption of phonographic equivalents for both simple and compound vowel-sounds in different languages: turning every language to the eye into the same form that it has to the ear, so that not one of the many languages compared appears in its own home-dress and with its own native mien; but they are all, with their different stature, complexion, airs and motions, exhibited in one uniform, homely phonetic garb. It seems strange to think by what arbitrary laws of taste or criticism, a scholar could have persuaded himself to undertake such a system of wholesale violence to those old familiar languages, on whose faces, as on that of the moon at night, so many loving eyes have looked with admiration, in all ages. In no way could he have made himself more unintelligible to a beginner, or more distasteful to one who had passed through his novitiate in philology. Two classes of minds relish phonography: those who, being satisfied with only incidental superficial views and general outlines instead of minute details, delight in saving all the labor of thought that they can; and those that have such an intense love of the beauty of abstract order, that, for the sake of its gratification, they are willing to see the ancient, well known, beloved forms of words broken to pieces, in order that they may be reduced to their simple, ultimate, radical type. Many, indeed, would greatly rejoice to possess a grand scientific dictionary, composed of the elementary themes of words, with a synoptical view of the variations more or less from them in different languages, arranged in true philological order; and doubtless, when philology has attained its full development, such a dictionary will be prepared. But even then phonography will not furnish the torch, that shall illuminate to the scholar's eyes the pages that will contain the record. In the same spirit of unholy freedom with which Rapp has thus handled the sacred forms of words that have come down to us, unscathed by time or human conflict, from the far-off past, he has also undertaken to build up a sort of Cyclopean structure of his own fancies, far back in that unknown, ante-historic period, when the Sanskrit itself had not yet appeared upon the earth. From a comparison of kindred forms of the same radical in different languages, he finds among them what he deems a preponderance of authority for a given elementary constitution of the word, and from such data makes the majority absolute witnesses, over a stifled minority, about the formative necessary stem of the word, in that original mother-tongue. Indeed, his whole aim terminates in a vain effort to constitute his own guesses, by the aid of as many phonographic correspondents as possible, into the framework of the first language of the world. In the realms of science how absurd are such structures, built up of mere empty suppositions! nor are they relieved of their unsatisfactoriness by the prefatory remark with which he introduces them, that they are the results of many years of devoted study. Presumptions, of even many years' quarrying, are not the stones of which to build any part of the temple of science. Rapp and Diez represent in many things two opposite poles of scholarly character: the one bestowing too much honor on mere fancies for their novelty or beauty, and the other rejecting them at once, with sharp logical precision amounting almost to critical vengeance. Rapp is pithy and often witty, and, like most wits, greatly pleased with a new conceit. As one incidental specimen of this trait of his character, among many, consider his classification* of diphthongs.

* "There are," he says, " two classes of them. I call it a genuine diphthong when the movement is from the central a towards the circumference, and indeed in the first place in the direction from a to i. Here lie the diphthongs æ, eī, commonly written ei, ai and the nasal æ; on the way from a towards u, ao ëu (commonly written ou), au and the nasal ao; and on the middle line from a to ü, aŏ, ëü, aü and the nasal ao. A special kind of genuine diphthongs consists of those which make a lateral movement from the negative to the positive side as åe, oe, ai, oi, åü, oü, ui and the nasal œ. The second principal kind make a backward movement, from the circumference towards the centre; and are called illegitimate or deceitful diphthongs, and are somewhat inflexible and the first sound is somewhat prolonged, so that they incline towards a triphthong, &c., &c. To some undoubtedly all this will appear very clear and beautiful; but to the apprehension of the author that light is

Ernst August Fritsch wrote in 1833, on the oblique cases and prepositions in Greek, and afterwards several treatises on different grammatical points, as the formation of tenses, modes and oblique cases, but his work of chief merit is his last: "A Comparative Treatment of Latin and Greek Particles," the first part published in 1856, and the second in 1858. In this he discusses the etymology of the adverbs, conjunctions and suffixes of these languages. It is the best treatise to be found upon this subject, and much excels Düntzer in this same field. This part of Bopp's grammar also is one of its most interesting parts, as, indeed, it is of the new philology generally; since its testimony is so minute and unequivocal to the truth of its great leading positions. In all the principal works of philology, that appear now from time to time, the department of phonetics claims a distinct and full representation. The authors, who have treated it most fully in a separate form, are Benary and Hoefer. In the new edition of Bopp's grammar, special attention is devoted to it at the outset, as is also in Rapp's. It will indeed force itself into notice everywhere, in all true philology; for its connections are vital with it in every part of its framework.

To present a still longer catalogue of names in this

most desirable on all subjects, that serves best to reveal them as they are, instead of bedizening the eye with its own marvellous brilliancy.

connection would be tedious, as it would be without profit; for in those already detailed, the elements of philological study have been sufficiently indicated, as well as both the modes in which and the men by whom it has been brought to its present advanced stage.

The history of Indo-European philology in England is very briefly written. A few names describe the narrow orbit of its development. Beside the first scholars already mentioned as so earnest in making the Sanskrit known to their countrymen, as Sir William Jones, Wilkins, Colebrooke and Wilson, the list of more recent authors in modern philology is equally limited in number. They are all told, but these few: Prichard, Rosen, Donaldson, Garnett, Winning, Max Müller and Bunsen, the last two of whom are Germans, though writing in England and in the English language, as was also Rosen.

James C. Prichard, M. D., a practising English physician, was a man of good natural endowments, and earnestly devoted to thorough philosophical and philological research. His one great idea was to establish, if possible, the unity of the race. He published accordingly an essay (in 1808) on the varieties of mankind, in which he first made himself favorably known as a philosophical writer. This he enlarged from time to time in successive editions, until in the last (1836–1847) it had swollen into the five large volumes entitled "Researches into the Physical History of Mankind." The one work, on which his fame specially rests among scholars, is that denominated "The Eastern Origin of the Celtic Nations proved by a Comparison of their Dialects with the Sanskrit, Greek, Latin and Teutonic Languages;" which was published in 1831 as a supplement to "The Researches" abovementioned. He is minute and thorough in this work, in the comparison of Celtic, Sanskrit, Latin and Greek themes and flexion-endings, both formally and euphonically, and his labors in this direction have a high scholarly value. Like Rask and Burnouf, Prichard was removed prematurely from his labors on earth; but his memory, like theirs, will not perish.

Dr. F. Rosen, a pupil of Bopp, was for many years Professor of Sanskrit in the University of London. The round of his labors and services seems to have been filled up with practical instructions in philology to his pupils, brief articles in the Penny Cyclopædia of London, and the translation of the first eighth part of the Rigveda, which was published in 1838, and formed a new epoch in Sanskrit studies throughout the world. Previous translations of Indian literature had represented only the later and somewhat degenerate periods of Sanskrit development; but now the mine of Vedic thought, as well as that of its distinct dialectic forms, was struck; and all Europe has been ever since ablaze with interest in this new direction.

Donaldson has carefully studied grammar, language,

and history, in the light of Indo-European philology; and has felt, like every one else who has so studied them, an almost irresistible impulse to communicate the pleasure experienced by himself, as widely as possible, unto others. Such a fire cannot easily be kept shut up within one's bones. He has accordingly written a book entitled "Varronianus," on the history and structure of the Latin language, and another of similar nature upon the Greek, entitled the "New Cratylus," and both a Latin and Greek grammar for schools, of which the latter is decidedly the better, being built up more fully in its ground-forms on the basis of thorough philological principles. Donaldson is both learned and ingenious, but at the same time often fanciful. He has indeed fulfilled no mean office, in acting as an usher, to introduce the new philology to the acquaintance of so many English and American minds. He has added little, however, to the world's general knowledge of either its facts or principles: while he is, on the contrary, chargeable with the fault of needlessly leaving many parts of this great science in a state of very learned obscurity. It is doubtful whether any one who does not rise in his scholarship above the horizon of his works, so as to be able to look down critically upon them from a higher point of view, can fail to feel, as the priest of ancient Egypt made the crowd that stood wondering without feel, in their day, that there must be a veil over the truths on which they most long to gaze with clear, full vision. To those who adore mystery for its inherent beauty, this may be acceptable; but not to those who believe that truth is the proper aliment of the human mind, and that, then, it is most adapted to make it grow to all nobleness of stature and of strength, when it is most unmixed with other elements. And Donaldson seems to see the reflection of his own image from his works, through the same haze in which he has invested many of the treasures of philology to the eyes of his readers. He is guilty of the sin, deemed so unpardonable in an author, of public self-praise. A single extract or two will exhibit it in all its fulness, especially to one who realizes, from the small number of English scholars in this field, how absolutely his language must be understood as referring to himself. In speaking of the progress of philology in England, he says: "We can point to conceptions more original, and to results more important than any which have signalized the efforts of the learned elsewhere. It is not to be denied that we had great advantages at starting, and that it would have been very disgraceful if we had not learned to profit by them."* So also (on page 39 of the same work) he says, "Our apprenticeship to German philology has ended in producing a number of original workmen, at least equal to a majority of those in whose school they had been trained." In connection with the above ex-

* New Cratylus, 2d Edit. p. 45.

tracts, the reader should peruse at the same time his exquisite tirade (pp. 35, 6, 7.) upon the Germans, which he concludes with this remark, "that German scholars limit their chances of improvement by the narrow boundary of their own nationality; and that consequently they are not more favorably situated than our English scholars were, some forty years since." Was ever a wholesale slaughter of a whole nation of scholars committed in such cool blood and with such self-gratulatory satisfaction? Instead of making fresh inductions and generalizations for himself, like Bopp and Grimm and Diefenbach, he has merely acted the part of a theorist, in weaving out of the materials furnished him by others the web of his own philosophy; while working on it at times also figures of the most unreal and fantastic shape.

Winning, although somewhat praised by Donaldson, from want of other compeers in this great study, was but a writer of the third class for merit, as Donaldson himself is but of the second. He directly contradicts, in the latter part of his work, (published in 1838,) the positions which he formally took and defended in the first part; and while we praise him for his straightforwardness, in openly declaring the change that had really occurred in his views, this is all which we can possibly admire. He should have rewritten it at once, so as to make it throughout harmonious with itself. No true scholar will thus pilfer the time and comfort of his reader, to whom such treachery is the same, as to a traveller would be that of a guide, who should lead him for a long time in a direction exactly opposite to that in which he ought to go, and at last, after many a weary hour, suddenly inform him that all his toil and patience hitherto had been expended but in vain. And now hear him honestly stultify himself. He says, (p. 160,) after having, through the long track of nearly one hundred pages, maintained the contrary, " Although I now attach not the slightest historical importance to the division of the European languages into Median* and Persian, yet it is still evident that there

* It will amuse the philological reader to see his "table of languages." Behold it.

IRANIAN.

Sanskrit, Zend, Persian.

I. IRANO-INDIAN.

Sanskrit, Hindustanee, Bengalee.

II. IRANO-EUROPEAN.

Zend, Persian, Slavonian, Lithuanian, German, Celtic.

1. SLAVONIAN.

Russian, Servian, Croatian, Wendish.

2. LITHUANIAN.

Lithuanian, Lettish, Old Prussian, Latin (!).

3. GERMAN.

(1.) LOWER GERMAN.

Gothic, Scandinavian, Dutch, English, &c.

(2.) UPPER GERMAN.

Old, Middle and New High German, Greek (!).

4. CELTIC.

Erse, Gælic, Welsh, Bas Breton, Basque.

Of these he considered the Slavonian, Lithuanian, and Lower German as of Median origin, and the Upper German as of Persian; while, as to the Celtic, he regarded the Erse, Gælic and Manx as Medo-Celtic; but the Welsh, Cornish and Bas Breton, as Perso-Celtic.

were three original Iranian dialects, viz.: Sanskrit, Zend, and some third language to which the name of Persian seems not appropriate."

In a subsequent part of his work he undertakes to show learnedly from various Rabbinical surmises and statements, from Kimchi and others, that the original Tuscans were but a set of emigrant Edomites. "The summary of these statements is," he says, "that a people speaking a Semitic idiom came by sea, and landed on the south-west coast of Italy; that they became powerful there, and proceeding northward took possession of Rome, which first attained to greatness under their dominion. It is impossible not to be struck with the close coincidence of this statement with the native Roman account, &c." (p. 198.) This extract occurs in a chapter entitled "The Origin and Prophetic Destiny of the Tuscans," to which sixty pages of learned nonsense are devoted; and to any one who wishes to walk up and down in the fog that the interpreters of prophecy have such special skill in spreading about them, here is an opportunity such as is seldom offered. In another chapter he resolves the Pelasgians into an Egyptian or Hamite race, as, in the chapter on the Tuscans, he also classifies them and the Romans and Corinthians under the same description. But enough of such philological drivel. The reader will forgive so many extracts, if he remembers that the object in quoting them is only to show the actual state of real philological science within the bounds of English authorship.

Garnett has written several articles of merit for the London Philological Society, which have been recently grouped together in a volume by his son. They are interesting; but relate chiefly to the Teutonic elements and aspects of our language.

Amidst such meagre demonstrations of English scholarship in the department of Indo-European Philology, it is pleasant to be able to add the name of one, in England though not of it, Max Müller, professor of European languages and literature at Oxford, who is at once an original investigator of its wonders, and able to set forth what others have done and to make the results of their labors available to the public. His leading work is entitled "The Languages of the Seat of War in the East with a Survey of the three Families of Languages, Semitic, Arian, and Turanian;" a second and much improved edition of which was published in 1855. It was prepared in answer to a formal request by an officer of the English Government in 1854, in connection with the siege of Sebastopol, "that he would prepare at once a treatise on the languages spoken in the East; their general character and structure, their alphabets, the classes of people by whom they were spoken, and the family to which they belong." His treatise, though brief, is one of great interest.

Chevalier Bunsen is himself but little of a philologist; but in his "Philosophy of History," he has devoted a large part of the first volume to treatises on the last results of philological research, by Max Müller, and Aufrecht, who has been for some years in Oxford. Bunsen is an earnest religious thinker, and has busied himself with the progress of theology, rather as a general scholar, than as one of special earnestness in this one direction. In the present low state of philological learning in England, he seems determined to obtain the best light that he can; and then to hold it up, high and bright, with all eagerness in the face of the age.*

* There is a group of a few celebrated English writers on language, grammar, etymology and words, that ought to be mentioned here, both by way of honor for their merit, and for the sake of being clearly discriminated as a class, from those spoken of in the text. They are Harris, Horne Tooke, Kemble, Bosworth, Richardson, Turner, Latham, and Trench. John Harris published in 1751 a book of much learning and talent, entitled, "Hermes," pertaining to matters of grammatical philosophy, which had great influence and estimation in its day, as its basis and bearings were classical. Horne Tooke, whose views were opposite to those of Harris, presented in his "Diversions of Purley," amid a good many mere speculations, whose only value was their ingenuity, some very important facts and principles, concerning the Teutonic features of English etymology. He never came for a moment, however, into the neighborhood of the idea of a scientific comparison of languages one with the other.

Kemble, Richardson, Bosworth and Turner, have all wrought and written well on the English, as a great Anglo-Saxon structure: the first two as general writers on the language and the last two as lexicographers. Latham has, in his latest edition of "The English language," both supplemented and supplanted most previous authors hitherto on the Teutonic features and philosophy of our language.

Rev. Richard C. Trench, Professor of King's College, London, has made himself more known in this country than any other one as a writer on "the study of words." Many of our common words he opens to view, and shows them to contain poetical, ethical and historical elements of great interest. His work is, however, as it was designed

HISTORY OF MODERN PHILOLOGY. 257

And what can we say of our own land, great in every thing but scholarship, but to be as great at some near day in this high element of power as in every other. Alas! one little upper chamber, how small! would hold the few elect spirits that have seen this new fire blazing on German altars, and snatched one spark from it to kindle the same glowing flame in their own hearts. Not only are very few works relating to general philology produced on our soil, but the number even of those imported from abroad is exceedingly scanty. We have in all the colleges of our country, only one professor of Sanskrit; and he, though a philologist of widely acknowledged eminence, finds but few pupils to avail themselves of his instructions.

In the outline above furnished of the steps by which philology has reached its present development, a sufficient view has been furnished, it is believed, of the literature that it has led in its train, to give the reader a true acquaintance with the men and the modes by which it has been advanced to its present position.

Behold now the most important of the different names that we have mentioned, grouped in classes according to their merit.

by him to be, entertaining rather than scientific: a book of suggestions and of a few mere outline-sketches, adapted to the popular reader, and not one of deep scholarly investigations of his own or of scholarly guidance unto others. He coasts only around about a few of the Anglo-Saxon, Norman and Latin elements of our language, and speaks of Latin in old style as "a compound of Grecian and un-Grecian derivatives."

258 HISTORY OF MODERN PHILOLOGY.

1. Bopp, Grimm, Pott, Diefenbach, Benary, Schleicher, The two Curtius, Kuhn, Diez, Mommsen, Aufrecht, and Weber.

2. Eichhoff, Ahrens, Giese, Hoefer, Heyse, Benfey, Donaldson.

3. Kaltschmidt, Rapp and Winning.

These writers may also be advantageously divided, for the reader's information, into different classes, according to the subjects that they have investigated.

I. LANGUAGE.

1st. The Indo-European languages generally : Schleicher (Sprachen Europa's) ; Max Müller (Survey of Languages, 2d edition); Heyse's System der Sprachwissenschaft, pp. 174–208 ; Eichhoff's Vergleichung der Sprachen, pp. 20–36.

2d. Specially,

(1.) The Græco-Italic : Schleicher (Sprachen, &c.) ; Mommsen (Römische Geschichte); E. Curtius (Griechische Gesch.) ; Aufrecht and Kirchhoff (Umbrische Sprachdenkmäler) ; Diez (Grammatik der Romanischen Sprachen).

(2.) The Lettic : Schleicher (Sprachen &c.).

(3.) The Gothic : Grimm (Deutsche Grammatik and Geschichte); Schleicher ; Diefenbach (Gothisches Wörterbuch).

(4.) Slavonic : Schafarik ; Schleicher ; Miklosich.

(5.) Celtic : Diefenbach (Celtica) ; Pictet ; Charles Meyer ; Zeuss (Grammatica Celtica); Ebel (Zeitschrift &c.) ; Prichard (Celtic Nations).

II. PHONETICS.

Benary; Hoefer; Grimm (Deutsche Grammatik and Geschichte); Bopp (Vergleich. Gramm.); Diez (Grammatik, &c.); Corssen (Lateinische Vokalismus); Heyse's System, &c.; Zeitschrift für vergleich. Sprachforschung; Arts. by Ebel, Benary, Kuhn & Förstemann.

III. THE PHILOSOPHY OF LANGUAGE.

Becker's various works on Grammar, &c.; Heyse's System der Sprachwissenschaft; Lersch's Sprachphilosophie; Humboldt's different essays on language; Bunsen's Philosophy of Universal History, vol. i.

IV. ETYMOLOGY.

Pott's Etymologische Forschungen, new edition.

Bopp (Vergleich. Gramm.); Schleicher (Litauische Grammatik); G. Curtius (Griechische Gramm., and especially Griechische Etymologie); Diez (Grammatik); Diez (Lexicon Etymologicum); Fritsch.

A beginner in the study of philology who desires, at the least outlay of money and time, to put himself as soon as possible into the possession of the main facts and principles of the science, will find the following few works admirably answer the purpose:

Schleicher's Sprachen Europa's.

Heyse's System der Sprachwissenschaft.

Diez' Grammatik der Romanischen Sprachen.

Max Müller's Survey of Languages.

In Germany by far the greatest attention has been paid from spontaneous impulse, to the claims of comparative philology; while in Russia the Government has as far exceeded all other governments, in its patronage of this delightful study, and of those who are devoted to it. This is one of the chief legacies left by the Empress Catherine, in her own zealous example, to her successors on the throne ; and in accepting it they have not forgotten to put it to good usury. The government publishes, at its own expense, the grammars, dictionaries and treatises, prepared by the best scholars ; and sustains travellers at its own expense, in making exploring tours for philological purposes in the East. Vienna, however, is the most prolific, of all single cities in the world, in oriental publications. In France, Prussia and Denmark also, much more zeal is shown in this captivating class of studies, than in either England or America. The Sanskrit has been indeed as long taught in England as in Germany, and even longer ; but not for classical and philological purposes : for commercial reasons rather, under the patronage of the East India Company, at the College of Haileybury.

But justice to the great dead, who distinguished themselves in classical philology, immediately before the dawn of comparative Indo-European philology, demands their distinct remembrance here ; and all the more, as some of their followers have endeavored, by voluntarily shutting their eyes to such light as their predecessors never saw but would have hailed with eagerness, to limit themselves and others to the mere paths which they trod, although with a far different spirit, and while moving in the van of their age instead of behind it.

Heyne was the first to awaken high interest in classical philology, as a special distinct study, in Germany, and was followed in his noble efforts by such men as Buttmann, Hermann and Passow : all men of splendid genius and scholarship, according to the highest ideals of their age. It is pleasant to pause at any time, and gaze at the dimensions of their scholarship, which rise before us like huge colossal structures, for their times, high and clear against the sky.

No one of them had finer tastes and larger powers than Dr. Philip Buttmann : a native philologist and a noble Greek scholar, unsurpassed alike in philosophical insight and scholarly enthusiasm by any student in any land. His Greek Grammar and his Lexilogus are his principal works, and exhibit the best possible qualities of linguistic investigation.

The advocates of mere classical philology now, are like an army that was once victorious, but has lost all its great leaders. Döderlein, one of the best representatives in Germany of the remnants of this school, still lives to look around him, with the loneliness of a man deserted by a generation that had no pride of its own to gratify in walking with him, and could not afford to gratify his pride in standing still and gazing with admiration upon him, while he walked majestically by himself. He has persistently refused to improve the light of the new philology, and has thereby exiled himself as a scholar from the generation with which he yet lives as a man. He has indeed furnished in his various works, in the mere isolated connections of Greek with Latin, a good deal of valuable material, which may be worked with care by other hands into a useful shape, by being re-adjusted and harmonized with the elements of a true and comprehensive etymology. His first great fault is the very fundamental conception of his whole plan, that of deriving the Latin immediately from the Greek, and his next great fault is his practical adoption of the Aristotelian system of squaring facts, with all possible ingenuity, to preconceived theories, instead of the Baconian system of first finding the facts and conforming his theory to them; so that he constantly bends whatever is opposed to his views in the Greek, by force, into his service. But surely and steadily the false light of a separate classical philology is fast waning away, under the brighter light of comparative philology. Classical philology, in its true form, and of its true dimensions, when built on the foundations of comparative philology, is a science of vast and beautiful proportions, in which as in a mansion of light the highest minds can tarry with joy and wonder; but, built on any separate, exclusive basis of its own, its dimensions are all contracted, and its uses are meagre and pitiful.

HISTORY OF MODERN PHILOLOGY. 263

In its philosophical aspects, comparative philology bears a most commanding mien. Its generalizations, like those of the great philosophies, are unbounded in their scope, covering the whole field of human language. It has, like Christianity, out of whose hand it has flown forth among the nations, and like the great elements of nature and of life, the mark of its divine origin, in its adaptation to all times and ages, all languages and words.

Comparative philology divides languages into two great classes, the old or primary, and the new or secondary. The primary are all arranged in a few family-groups, as the Indian, Græco-Latin, Lettic, Slavonic, Gothic and Celtic; while the secondary are the more recent languages derived from them, and usually with many admixtures. Constant commingling, and thereby constant renovation, is the law of Providence, in respect to tribes and races on the one hand, and correspondingly, by necessary result on the other, the law of language also; which is but a vast panorama, in word-scenery, of the winding stream of a nation's history. The established limitations to the working of any contrary law are remarkable. Commerce seems to be an absolute necessity to the world's progress, not only in business, but also in ideas and language, and even in blood. The secondary languages are classified according to their grammatical, instead of their lexical, resemblances. Thus, the English, though so largely Romanic in its constituent verbal elements, is yet, in its grammatical character, German. So, the New Persian, although full of Arabic words, is yet justly called Iranian and not Semitic, because of its inward Iranian structure.

The amount of investigation made in comparative philology is, when contrasted with none at all, very large; but, when contrasted with the whole area of all languages, it is yet small. The languages of the civilized world are those that have been most explored, and those only in their main outlines, rather than in all their vast fulness of details. Each year is adding new discoveries to this recent, though great science; and, though but partially developed, it is yet of gigantic proportions. The mighty intellects at work upon it, have made its foundations very large; and yet at the same time, they have carried up its walls already to an unexpected height of grandeur.

The principal results obtained by comparative philology are the following:

1st. To invest the study of language with new charms.

Language is now seen to be a vast store-house, full of treasures; and many new and wide avenues to research are open within it. The study of language is not only made a higher study than ever before, but also entirely different: a study worthy of the greatest efforts of the greatest minds: the study of its inward structure as an organic whole, and also of the origin, history, growth and elementary constitution of its separate words. The grammar and dictionary have now a new and high use : such an use as to an artistic eye, delighting in the logic of inward mutual adaptations, a steam engine has, as a piece of wondrous mechanism, compared with its uses to the unthinking traveller, for the mere object of locomotion. To the ignorant reader a dictionary seems but a vast mass of word-lumber; but to a mind that knows the inward essences of things, it is an immense museum of the most interesting antiquities and curiosities. Here are historical memorials without number, and the coins of thought and love, that have passed current in myriad hands from one generation to another.

And how is the silent past of language made, under the reviving touch of philology, all vocal of itself again. As from a vast seed-plot, once covered by many generations of plants and trees, but now long barren, from want of the necessary outward conditions of growth : there has been from every language, on which the light and heat of comparative philology have been poured, a wondrous, universal outburst of its ancient, inward, long-concealed vitality. The monuments left by any nation, are indeed very scanty relics of the whole round orb of its active life; but no monuments have been left in any part of the world, so determinate of their character, so full of their spirit, and so enduring in continuance, as hose of language. Language is in itself an impressible, elastic, ever yielding medium of social intercourse; but under the action of time its elements rapidly harden into fixed forms : retaining the impress of every thing stamped upon them, as, in the clear light of geology, we still find treasured in the rock forever the footprints of birds that walked centuries ago, on the yielding sands of the ancient world, and even the patter of rain-drops that poured their benediction upon the earth before man was here to receive it. In language, as in pure amber, the ideas, hopes, mistakes, experiences, follies, joys and sorrows of preceding generations are preserved, in clear, transparent beauty, for our constant appreciation and enlightenment. The study of language rises, under the light of true philology, like all high philosophy, into the very charms of poetry.

2d. To resolve many supposed grammatical irregularities, in different languages, into really regular forms.

Thus, for example, we learn that in Latin, the perfect tense has normally four different modes of formation, as 1st. By reduplication, which we find (1) in the first conjugation, as in steti and dedi, from sto and do; (2) in the second, as in momordi and spopondi, from mordeo and spondeo; (3) in the third, as in cecidi and tetendi, from cado and tendo; and each of these verbs is entirely regular in the formation of its perfect, as much as $\lambda \dot{\nu} \omega$ or $\gamma \varrho \acute{\alpha} \varphi \omega$ in their perfects $\lambda \acute{\varepsilon} \lambda \nu \varkappa \alpha$ and γέγραφα. 2d. By the addition of s, as in the Greek aorist, active and middle: the Latin perfect being in its use an aorist as well as a perfect. The perfect in s we find (1) in the second conjugation, as in arsi, auxi, haesi and risi, from ardeo, augeo, haereo and rideo; (2) in the third, as in scripsi and rexi, from scribo and rego; (3) in the fourth, as in hausi, sanxi, sensi, vinxi, from haurio, sancio, sentio, vincio; and these are all equally regular, although in our manuals of grammar all called irregular. 3d. By the aid of the auxiliary verb fui, sometimes hardened into vi, and sometimes softened into ui. Thus, (1) amavi is for amafui: the stem of amare being ama and not am, as erroneously stated in all school-manuals; (2) so monui is for monefui. (3) In the third conjugation we find this same auxiliary perfect, as in cupivi, lacessivi, petivi, quaesivi, trivi, from cupio, lacesso, peto, quaero, (for quaeso,) and tero. (4) In the fourth conjugation this is the prevailing form of the perfect, so that the mode of forming the perfect by the aid of auxiliaries, is not, as sometimes stated, a mere modern system of conjugation. In each, also, of the several conjugations, this style of perfect is as regular as in every other; and the perfect of petivi, from petere, is as normal as amavi from amare. 4th. By contracted forms of the preceding styles of the perfect: as (1) of reduplicated perfects in egi for e-agi, feci for fe-fici, veni for ve-veni, fugi for fufugi, legi for lelegi: (2) of perfects in s, as fidi (perf. of findo) for fidsi, and scidi (perf. of scindo) for scidsi. Here, indeed, we have irregularities, but of a very simple, intelligible kind. And so in Greek the analysis of forms in σσ is beautiful, as an euphonic symbol for γι, κι, χι, τι in various forms: as τάσσω for τάγιω, χαρίεσσα for χαρίεντια and ἥσσων for ἥκιων.

In a similar way supposed exceptions and irregularities in prosody are at once eclaircized by comparative etymology, as regular in fact although not in appearance.

3d. To show us that, of all the perishable things of this world, language is the least perishable. Here is a monument of national life, that not only outlives the nation itself, but also all its structures of art or enterprise. A language may be put to new uses and be borne to new climes; it may encounter, again and again, the shock of opposing arms, amid the terrors of invasion or of conquest; it may be beaten and bruised by the changes of time; and yet, while its surface is thus broken and worn, like that of a rock which fell ages ago from the bosom of some cliff into the arms of old Ocean, and which he has been ever since tossing about as a plaything, its substance itself remains unchanged. Its texture and color and hardness still indicate its first parentage and place.

4th. To show us, that the great law of analogy, pervading the whole outward creation, prevails also throughout the department of language: the law of perpetual unity in perpetual variety. All true ideas of perfection of form and of detail terminate in the conception of a grand unity. God himself may be defined as Infinite Fulness of all things great and good realized and impersonated in one, grand, glorious Being.

5th. To show us that each language, while specially endowed for its own wants and uses, has yet the divine stamp upon it of general utility, and of a large adaptation to relations and harmonies and benefits beyond itself.

Comparative philology combines all the languages, which it resolves, into a grand mutually-sustained harmony of dependence and service one to the other. It represents them, not, as each a separate musician playing among others a different melody in horrible discord; but rather, as standing up together like a band of brothers in full orchestra, with their different instruments, to join their notes together in one loud-swelling universal chorus.

6th. To pour new light on the history of nations. The migrations of nations into different zones and into scenes of a different aspect and influence, from time to time, have their history fully written, in their stature, figure, features and whole physical conformation: as every tree contains, in the shape of its boughs and stems and in the amount of its flowers and fruits, a record of every breath of wind, and of every drop of rain, and of every beam of light that ever have visited it. Our dull, coarse eyesight, which receives only the outermost disclosure that things around us make of themselves, is not able to traverse this multiform record of the past, in any thing; but yet every thing contains it. Each present object within our view, is the product of millions on millions of minute agencies, ever active in the past, interlacing each other with their influence, changing constantly from one form into another, and terminating in their present use and value, in the transient demonstration of themselves that they make at each moment to their casual beholder.

In the languages of the world, however, all its changes, even those too slight for the pen of history to sketch or its eye to see, are stamped, according to their precise value, beyond the danger of erasure. Time itself rolls the wheel of centuries, no matter how heavily, over the faithful record, but in vain. The history of each civilized nation has been often written and will be often written again; and so rapid is the progress of modern society, that each generation demands a new history for itself of all the leading nations of the world. So great have been the improvements made from time to time, that the model histories of preceding generations have come to be quite antiquated and to be valued now, rather for the special style of the philosophic or religious views expressed in them, or the high rhetorical beauty of their composition, than for their adequate representation of the people themselves whom they describe. Historic writing indeed has evinced as much growth, during the preceding century and the present alike, not only in public interest but also in its own triumphs of research and discovery, as any other department of human genius.

Ethnography cannot be written truly, except in the light of thorough philological inquiry. Much of our supposed knowledge of the earlier nations of the world and of the changes that passed over them, has been legendary: derived it is true from ancient sources, but of no better value for that reason than title-deeds which, although they have come down through a succession of men acting honestly in their transmission, were yet themselves at the outset invalid and worthless. A chain that has one imperfect link in it, is no stronger throughout than in the spot of its greatest weakness.

And, as the history of Nineveh has recently been disentombed out of the mounds of earth that had before concealed it from the eyes of the world, and the history of Egypt has been first opened in our day, with any fulness, from the records hidden within its own monuments; so, in the hitherto unexplored crypts and recesses of different languages, lie entombed the memorials of the world's slow marches and solemn changes; and, as the philologist has the high office of interpreting the voice of God, in the Holy Scriptures, to the world, so, is it his grand function to interpret man to himself, and to unroll at his feet the scroll of the past as it has actually been rolled up together in the gradual development of human life and action.

Philology supplies also to some extent the want of ante-historic records, and that too often with quite pictorial effect. Who would not delight to look within that shadowy dawn of humanity, on which no light from the hand of man has ever fallen, and to know well our race, in all the now unknown steps of its progress. But the first life both outwardly and inwardly of our original Arian ancestors, is painted to us clearly in word-colors* still fresh and strong of every varied hue.

---

* There is in Weber's Indische Skizzen a brief but lively picture, of the earliest unwritten history of the Indo-European family: drawn out of their words themselves, like the pictures made by geologists from the fossil records of the earth, of the flora and fauna of the world before man entered upon it. "Let us try he says (pp. 9—10), to present in a few touches a sketch of that primitive period. The common prevalence of most of the words for relationship, shows that family-life among our first ancestors, had a very definite position. The same expressions reappear, not only in reference to parents and children and brothers and sisters, but also to relatives in law as well as those by blood, in almost all the Indo-European tongues. The etymology of roots still living in the Sanskrit, teaches us that father, means a protector; mother, one who sets in order; brother a helper; sister the careful one; and daughter one who milks: in which we see the most simple patriarchal relations indicated. The prevailing use of domestic animals is shown, by the common names of the cow (the slow-marching) of the ox (the producing one) of the bull, the goat the sheep the sow (the prolific) the horse, &c. The dog (the swift) defended the herds: the wolf (tearing to pieces) and the bear (shining, from his fur) were their terror. The mouse (the thief) stole their provisions; the horse-fly buzzed about, the gnat stung, the snake crept. Goose, duck, dove, woodpecker, cuckoo, finch, chattered and sang, and the cock crowed. The light hare sprang before them, and the boar rooted in the

Their deepest thoughts and experiences lie spread out before us, in the inner sense of their speech, as in a full bright landscape. It is surely pleasant, to be able to look back in any way, and see them distinctly in the distant, dark, historic solitude of their first experiences of life, and find that they had the same human hearts

dirt. The house was firm, provided with doors. Wagons and boats served for their passage over fields and floods. The fields were tilled with the plough: barley and wheat furnished them meal and bread. Clothes, utensils and arms they had in abundance. Sword, spear, knife and arrow were all of brass. Intoxicating mead led the way to merry song, while large shells and reeds served for music. Conflict was a pleasure, and the sense of race was so strong that the word barbarian (stammering) was used indeed in that primeval time, to indicate other people of foreign speech. A subdued enemy was a slave. At the head of the many stood a ruler, defender or master, the leader in battle and the judge in peace. The country was mountainous and abounded in water. The forest furnished refreshing coolness: the oak was its principal ornament. The winter seems to have been severe; besides its name returns now still, that of the spring (clothing again). The sun was worshipped as the principle of life and praises were sung to the shining dawn of day: the moon served as the measure of time. The stars were regarded as ray-archers. The great bear whose Greek name ἄρκτος properly signifies only " the shining one " shone forth conspicuously among them. Thunder, lightning, storm, rain, cloud and wind sent terror and fear into the timid heart. The all-embracing Heaven whose Greek name οὐρανος reappears in the Vedic Varuna, was regarded as the father of all and the earth as the universal mother. The dark cloud-god, who plundered in his ravines the golden flock of the stars and sunbeams and the fertilizing rains of Heaven, was prostrated by the arrows of the god of lightning: his bands were torn in pieces and the plundered herd were set free. The mighty incomprehensible powers of Nature awakened in man, the sense of his weakness; and he bowed his head in recognition of the same, offered to them his sacrifices and his songs, and represented them to himself in gracious or in dire terrific forms, as he clothed them in his fancy with the physical that we have, with the same joys and fears and sorrows as our own. Thanks to Philology, for the clear telescopic view which it furnishes us, of the otherwise unsketched and invisible space, that stretches huge and dark beyond the misty outline of the first historic eras of our race.

aspects, that environed him. To this dawn of Time belong the representations also of a Manu, the first man and father, and of a great flood which devastated and devoured every thing, and from which he alone was saved. Both of these traditions we find also among the Semitic family; and they are to be regarded, among other lingual facts, as proof that the Semitic and Indo-European families were at a still earlier period united in one, from which state they afterwards separated, before however the two common languages had arrived at any grammatical precision of form."

III.

THE SCIENCE OF ETYMOLOGY.

III.

THE SCIENCE OF ETYMOLOGY.

THE very caption of this Article will astonish some and amuse others, who have been in the habit of regarding etymology as a mere mass of vagaries. That it has any such scope as to deserve the dignified name of a science, or any such interior frame-work of principles as to possess its essential nature, is quite beyond the general estimate of its character. In this country, indeed, and in England as also in France and everywhere but in Germany, both vernacular and classical etymology are in the same rude, unmethodized state of first and partial discovery, in which chemistry and geology existed half a century ago. What facts are seen and appreciated appear to most even of their admirers, but as isolated novelties and wonders, and have none of the charm or power of a splendid combination, of comprehensive and complicated affinities and relations.

Our modern languages are all derived from those of elder ages; and these are found when subjected to thorough analysis, to have been derived, in their turn, from those anterior to them; while on a wide and critical survey, all the tongues of the civilized world appear full of multitudinous correspondences and connections.

The object of this Essay will be realized, if the following topics connected with the science of etymology, are presented in sufficient outline :

    I. The general proportions and relations of the subject.
    II. The history of classical and vernacular etymology.
    III. The constituent elements of etymology as a science.
    IV. Its determinative principles and tests.
    V. Some of the advantages of the study of this science.

I. The general proportions and relations of the subject.

It has been often said, and truly, that the study of the Latin has a value in it in its mere relations to our language, sufficient to authorize for this reason without reference to many others also, the most zealous attention to its claims. But how can any deep scholarly insight into its relations to the English be gained, except in the light of a broad and complete classical etymology, which shall present the Latin truly in all its manifold connections, not only with succeeding languages, but also with those which were antecedent and contemporary? This ancient language must be seen in order to be rightly seen, while clothed in its own armor and bearing its own banners, not only leading other languages majestically in its train but also moving in solemn and sublime march along the highway of ages, with the great peoples and languages that anticipated and accompanied its glory and its doom. On account of the artistic treasures of the Greek language, and the fine, æsthetical influence of its higher literature upon those elect spirits who walk familiarly amid its Alpine wonders : an influence of which most American students of Greek, who are but dabblers in this tongue of the giants, have only heard by tradition, having never had a sensation of it themselves : it has come to be quite fashionable in the scholastic world, to speak of that noble language in terms quite disparaging, at the same time, to the Latin. And our classical students generally have fallen, under the influence of this sort of perpetuated pedantry, into an almost universal habit of placing the Latin in contemptuous contrast with the Greek. Few see even that it has any large connection with the Greek ; and few of those who have grasped that great fact comprehend, from the want of a wide philological view of the three classical languages in their mutual relations, the Sanskrit, Greek and Latin, what that connection is. But while its correspondences with the Greek cover a vast array of details, and many of them when disclosed become immediately apparent to the eye, many more become delightfully clear to one, who, by applying the chemic tests of phonology, knows how to reduce at once both simple and comparative forms to their original analytical elements. The Latin and the Greek are cognate languages, being of one common Pelasgic or Græco-Latin origin, and as such greatly illustrative of each other; while, placed together like associated mirrors, they reflect with strange exactness and fulness of effect the earlier Sanskrit, which is itself also a derived language, exhibiting not at all the ultimate origin of our present languages, but rather the farthest link backwards yet discovered in the chain of ascending relations and affinities. That chain of successive origination and derivation of all known languages runs backward from the centuries and countries of modern times, through one language and people after another more and more perfect in its texture as it rises, until it ends ultimately in that lost mother-tongue which Adam spoke in Eden; and which, as a matter of moral evidence, it is absolutely certain that he learned directly from God himself, since each man and generation succeeding him has learned to speak only from those who have preceded them. As in the material world man creates nothing, and only moulds and transforms substances and shapes already at hand, so, in the world of language he only re-casts and transmutes the materials furnished him by an earlier age. The same race bearing off the same original elements of speech in divided companies into different climates, amid diversified scenes and skies and modes of life, will as certainly change and conform them, though in-

THE SCIENCE OF ETYMOLOGY. 281

sensibly, to the new atmospheres of their new life each for itself; as that same race, departing into different zones, will erelong take on in each a different complexion, stature, and physiognomy, choose different food, employments, and dress, and adopt also different dwellings, institutions, and customs.*

Nothing is found in the realms of speech any more than in those of nature, "without father or mother." Here, as everywhere else, the maxim is true, "ex nihilo nihil fit." The languages, therefore, of the world, like the men who have spoken them, have all been bound together by a regular series of sequences, running link by link in luminous beauty from any and every language now spoken upon earth, to the first language in which listening angels heard Adam and Eve discourse to each other; and from that back to God himself, the great All-in-all, from whose own girdle the golden chain of human speech divine was dropped lovingly down to man, in order to bind him to himself and all nations in heavenly sympathy with each other.

As for the Latin, whose connection with the Greek and Sanskrit has thus suggested and required the farther and wider statement of the connection of all languages with each other, it has excellences and

* In Prichard's Natural History of Man, the curious reader will be interested to trace the different aspects and characteristics of the Jews, in different parts of the world, and even of Hindûstan alone, although everywhere living, in vaunted seclusion of blood from other people, as to their figure, countenance, color and whole physique.

advantages of its own; which, while they set the seal of its peculiar individuality upon it, demonstrate its capability to supply the varied wants of human speech to be broad and deep. It will be the quick, decided testimony of any one who has studied it for many years, having surveyed its dimensions on every side, having sounded all its depths and scaled its various heights, and scanned alike its inward treasures and its outward relations, that in respect to the history of its influence as much as to that of its origin, and in respect to its own iron-like stability and the stability, force and dignity which it has imparted to the different languages into whose bosom it has poured the current of its own living strength, it is full of wonders. Not only is no one study in the whole current of educational appliances equal to it, for all the purposes of mental and scholastic drill; but also, as a matter of actual fact, the great mass of all the linguistic culture, and of all the many rich results of the higher classical education of the whole civilized world, has been obtained from this source, in all ages. The Latin is thus distinctly dwelt upon at the outset and at length, because its position in the science of etymology is very high and altogether peculiar. And it is one of the first duties as well as one of the first instincts of an amateur of classical or vernacular etymology, to vindicate the Latin from the false ideas and estimates that prevail without thought concerning it in the community. The Latin is central in its position and bearings, between the first known languages and those now existing. In it they find their mutual bond of connection. No language upon earth has in it so much of what is old, at the same time with so much of what is new. But for the Latin and the Greek, the Sanskrit, that wonderful fossil language in whose extinct remains we find the types of all the subsequent Indo-European languages, would be well nigh devoid of interest to us; and but for the Latin, the modern languages would, all at least but the Gothic branch and that much more largely than most suppose, be tangled etymologically in a web of inextricable confusion. As, on Acro-Corinthus the classical scholar might stand and look down with swimming eyes upon the Saronic gulf to the eastward, where Athens still glitters in her beauty, and upon the Corinthian gulf to the westward, and see beyond its waters Parnassus, sacred to the Muses, with its snow-white crown, having the fountain of Castalia in its bosom and the oracle of Delphi at its feet: so, standing on the heights of the Latin language, as on a tall isthmus rising between two oceans, the far-off Past and the Present, we can look before us and see the waves of the elder ages as they bear on their bosom the wonders of India, Persia, and Greece, roll and break at our feet; or, turn and behold behind us the vast expanse of the future covered with the riches of all nations, retiring in the far-off horizon from the view, until sky and sea mingling together conceal it in their own indistinguishable confusion. Here is the high, true position for a complete survey of the facts of comparative etymology. From it, with a clear glass, the indistinct and mysterious forms of words are resolved in every direction into well-defined elements of vision. And as mountain ranges are precipitous on one side, while on the other, like weary camels, they couch down gradually into the vales below, so the farther side of the Latin, its archaic Sanskrit side, presents a bold, sharp outline from its summit to its base; while its hither Romanic side subsides in every variety of slope and sweep and angle and curve so gently into the modern languages of our times, that it is almost hard to say where it ceases to be Latin and where it begins to be something else.

But in no language is the area of etymological research so wide, and covered with such untold riches, as in our own language. He who would gather up the treasures of English etymology must make his garners large; for the harvest spreads over many fields and many centuries. Not only our own indigenous growths are in it, but exotics also from every clime and every age in measureless abundance. As in no nation there has been such a commingling of all affinities of blood, so also in no language has there been such a mixture of all etymologies as in the English; and as under the power of ancient Rome all nations soon became woven into one common web with her, of fortune and of fate, so, under the absorbing and assimilating energies of the English mind and tongue, the wealth of thought and of speech contributed by all nations has been incorporated into the greatness of our mother-tongue. The sentiments, experiences and utterances of every age and of every zone, belonging to the whole wide circumference of the earth and to the whole mountain-range of human development, from the lowest to the highest point, are in it and in the very forms in which, at the time, they burst spontaneously into view. Into the English, as into the bosom of a great central sea, all the streams of the past and present have poured and are still pouring their varied contents.

"Every language," says Richter, "is a dictionary of faded metaphors." Our languages in their present state, as known to the inner consciousness of those who use them, are but herbariums in which lie pressed and preserved, but unappreciated, the dry forms of words that once were green with life and beauty, and as now handled are but the relics of their former selves. As used by the ancients, to whom they were vernacular, the dead languages: as with very ironical propriety they are often called by those who thus speak of them, since in all their inner beauties as well as in all their outward scientific relations, they are so opaque and dead to them: were full, in whatever light they saw them, of ever-changing, opaline brilliancy. "Apples of gold in pictures of silver" were those dear old "words fitly spoken," to their interior sense; yea rather gems which had been dropped to their consciousness from a mother's hand into theirs, and which seemed in their very brightness to reflect forever that mother's smile. And to the student now who comprehends the power of words, to whom they are transparent, revealing all their inmost essence to his lingering gaze, their lost light returns again, and language is evermore living and lovely. Each lettered page is to him a mass of shining wonders, a tree of Eden, loaded with blossoms clustering upon blossoms, on boughs bending and waving with the precious weight. Language is to his eye one vast redundant flora, full of the glitter of leaves, the scent of flowers, and the lusciousness of celestial fruitage.

Each language, but most of all for our benefit our own language and those great languages, the Greek and Latin, with which it is so intimately connected, need to be elaborated, and to have all their inward treasures brought forth into clear view: in order that language, as such, the greatest of all the arts of life, may be truly comprehended by each succeeding generation of educated men, and employed by them according to all its deep, real capabilities, in the divine contact of mind with mind, and the still diviner labor of mind for mind. As the body is the temple of the soul and should be full, as it is, of strange adaptations to the wonderful sensibilities and energies of its immortal inhabitant; so, language is the temple of thought and love, the only exercises that ally earth to heaven, and man to God, and is full of all beauteous adaptations and uses which deserve to be searched and seen, as the divinely-constructed organ of communication between finite minds on the one hand, and also between mankind and the God that made them, on the other.

II. The history of classical and vernacular etymology.

This fully rendered, would involve a complete history of classical and comparative philology. But as the details of such a history have a special character of their own, and are presented in the preceding essay, it will be sufficient here to sketch its general philosophical outline. There have been three different stages in its development:

1. That of its popular empirical treatment,
2. That of its literary empirical treatment,
3. That of its true scientific treatment, under the exact laws of modern philology.

The etymological instinct is very common in all nations, among the thinking classes. It is as natural and pleasant for those who reason at all, to think about the origin and connection of words, as about relation and dependence, antecedents and consequents, cause and effect, in any other direction. There is full scope here for the play of all those faculties that demand adventure and enjoy invention. The ancients were quite addicted to this popular, random style of etymologizing, as is manifest in much of their mythology, their early traditional history,* and their poetical legends. Etymology in this period of its development leads of course but a vagrant life, and neither receives nor deserves

* Thus the names Romulus and Remus from ῥώμη strength, (Cf. Roma) and Numa from νόμος, law, are but beautiful etymological hieroglyphs, in legendary not exact history, of the first reign of physical force in Rome, and of the subsequent establishment of law and order, among the people. So also the story of the she-wolf suckling Romulus and Remus, from the name of the nurse Lupa; that of the low origin of Servius Tullius, from the resemblance of Servius to Servus; that of Brutus (brutus, stupid), reserving himself under a mask of pretended idiocy, for the crisis that was to come; that of Mutius Scaevola (from scaevus, left-handed), calmly burning off his right hand before Porsena, and that of Valerius Corvus, on whose helmet a crow lighted, and, flying in the face of the opposing Gaul, made him an easy prey to his sword, from corvus, a crow, with other stories like them originated merely in an etymological way. So also the conception of the one-eyed Cyclops, hideous and huge (from κύκλῳ, in a circle, and ὤψ, the eye), was born in the brain of some ancient etymologist, as was that of the Harpies (fem. pl. of ἅρπυιος, and meaning lit. the seizers), a name used originally to describe violent winds, blowing off the coast of the Ionian Sea, as their names also show, Podarge (swift-footed), Aello (whirler) and Ocypete (flying rapidly), daughters of Thaumas (wonder) and Electra (the lightning); and the details of the Greek theogony were of the same source, as of Uranus, Ge, Chronus, the Titans, &c. One of the best examples in modern times of this etymological way of writing history, that yet never actually transpired, occurs in those writers, and there are several of them, who have from Richard's title, Cœur de Lion, invented a story that he really slew a lion in single combat and so recorded a fable of their own devising, as a veritable reality. "The name," says Buckle (Hist. Civilization, England, vol. i. p. 218), "gave rise to the story; the story confirmed the name; and another fiction was added to that long series of falsehoods, of which history mainly consisted during the Middle Ages."

THE SCIENCE OF ETYMOLOGY. 289

much respect. It may be found in this form now in many a rural district, making its home at the house of the town-wit, the country-doctor or the village-pedagogue.* Nothing is aimed at in this style of etymologizing beyond the excitement of others' curiosity, or the show of a little learning or of a little wit; and it is subjectively but the indulgence of some momentary, frivolous or selfish impulse, out of which nothing great or good was ever born; while, objectively, it has no basis for its support, but mere shadowy empirical coincidences.

* In such a brain etymologies like the following will be spontaneously born, and held in high honor as its own children: catch from cat, ravenous from raven, rat from rapto, fudge from fugio. So similarly such empirics would be sure that Jove comes from Jehovah; German from germanus; dine (Fr. dîner, Lat. de-coenare) from δεἴπνειν; cover (Fr. couvrir, Lat. cooperire) from the Hebrew כָּפַר kaphar; and in German auge, the eye, from Gr. αὐγή, a word certainly very much like it by accident. The argument for each and all of these cases is one and the same, and it is this: why not? In some cases supposed etymologies have sufficed to alter the spelling of words, as in the word surname (supra-nomen, so called because originally written directly over the Christian name) which has been altered by many to sir-name; and so postumous (Lat. postumus) has been altered by a false theory to posthumous (as if derived from post+humus). In the phrases " you had better;" " you had rather," instances of the same sort occur, involving even a grammatical absurdity. The original forms " you would better" or " would rather" became shortened in common parlance into you'd better, or you'd rather, and then were afterwards, it seems, drawn out, by a foolish and utterly ungrammatical analysis of the contracted form into "had rather" and "had better;" which nearly every even educated man now says, in careful composition as well as in conversation, although this intrusive verb " had" can by no possibility be parsed by any one.

In the second phase of its existence, that of literary empiricism, its nature is no higher than in the first, but only its position. It no longer wanders about unwritten from mouth to mouth, but has a fixed habitation upon the lettered page. It has passed with favor or indulgence the ordeal of deliberate scrutiny, and been exalted on account of its supposed worthiness to an intended seat of high and permanent honor. Such etymologies, lexicographers and others glean sometimes with great care from standard authors; but they are all empirical in their own nature, and worthless. Science has foundations of its own which are divine, and its character can neither be made nor unmade by those who describe it. Truth is still truth, however it is overlooked, and error cannot be sanctified by being exalted into a high position, or by being worshipped by a crowd of false admirers. In this meagre, false, empirical state, classical etymology has wholly existed until of late, and in fact exists almost wholly now. Mere orthographical or orthoepical resemblances suffice among empirics, to introduce, without farther philological inquiry, any word into their magic circle of approved guesses and fancies. A radical difference of meaning in the case is as readily disposed of by them, as was any antithesis of fact and theory by the ancient philosophers; since they are utterly ignorant of that elementary doctrine of all true philology, that every word has a fundamental theme or base which determines absolutely its personal identity; and since like phrenologists they have a system of ideas, every one of which has a double polarity in it, by which it can be accommodated to any position or motion desired. The celebrated etymology of "lucus," a grove, " a *non* lucendo," from its not having any light, illustrates the ease with which such minds can weave positive and negative ideas together, into the meshes of their theories.

The first step taken in classical etymology was of this simple empirical kind. The second step forward in Latin etymology was taken so feebly, as to be rather the manifestation of a desire for progression, though in quite blind unconsciousness where or how to make it: that of introducing on a very limited scale some simple Greek correspondences, and in a very cautious manner and one not involving any idea of their mutual relation. From this advance was realized only the slender advantage of informing such minds, as had not before observed the wide and wonderful plexus of unities and analogies covering both languages, that they had had at some time a blended life and a strong, mutually penetrative influence on each other. The third step was one entirely false in its whole theory, and in all the results achieved under it: that of deriving the Latin immediately from the Greek. This was the prevailing conception of the relation of the two languages at the beginning of this century, among the best scholars.[*]

[*] Ludwig Ross, an extensive traveller in Greece and Asia Minor,

292   THE SCIENCE OF ETYMOLOGY.

As for lexicography it is in our best Latin, Greek, and English dictionaries, far behind the present advanced state of philology. The etymologies to be found, at this moment, in the leading classical dictionaries of this

but a far better observer of men than student of words, has undertaken in a formal treatise entitled, " Italiker und Gräken. Sprachen die Römer Sanskrit oder Griechisch," not only to revive the idea of the direct Greek origin of the Latin, but also to establish it as a fixed fact, upon an adequate scientific basis. He exhibits a large number, and this is all, of real correspondences between the two languages, which every Sanskrit philologer is equally eager to make good. Any amount of such resemblances does not however exclude an equal number, of even higher value (because so much more remote and, previously, so unanticipated) in the Sanskrit. Many that he quotes as existing between the Greek and Latin are ridiculous enough, as bellum and πολεμός : multus and πολύς: frons and φρήν: pars and μέρος: vates and μάντις: virago and virgo with μείραξ : juvenis and διογενής : litera and διφθέρα: famulus and θάλαμος : finis and θίς: verto and τρέπω : altus and αἰπύς : bonus and εὖς: pulcher and μελιχρός : caedo and παίω : quatio and κόπτω : κρίζω and rideo.

His chief outlay of feeling against the modern school of philologists, is directed against Mommsen, whom he represents as " almost the Oracle of the younger community (in Germany) whose crowned opinions are adopted, though unsubstantiated and undemonstrated, by thousands." He takes indeed his own key-note, from one of Mommsen's statements to this effect, that " the old opinion, that the Latin is but a mixed language composed of Greek and un-Greek elements, is now abandoned on all sides; and that, while some still regard it as a mixture of two nearly allied Italian dialects, one must needs ask in vain, for any philological or historical necessity for such a supposition." But he complains, "that so profound a philosopher, on the later political and juridical relations and circumstances of the Romans and their later language and literature, should have treated in a way of such unworthy trifling the ethnographic relations of the Latins and of the people of Middle and Southern Italy, as shows that he did not consider it worth the while, to make any earnest investigations on the subject." His country, are almost wholly those which are self-evident; while the small remainder is composed of mere guesses, derived from no philosophical principles, and suggesting none. Beyond this narrow range of etymological simplicities and novelties, the rest of the language stretches out before the lexicographer's eye, and under his influence before that of the student also, as a broad waste of unknown land. A true map, indeed, of the present state of classical etymology, as presented in our best dictionaries, would be as comical to one at all acquainted with Indo-European philology, as a Chinese map of the world to one versed in geography. It would be a map of every thing as it is not, and of nothing as it is. Freund represents the best development of Latin lexicography hitherto accessible to American scholars: Passow, as improved by Rost and others, that of Greek; and Webster, that of English. These all performed great labors and achieved great results; and their names will ever stand high on the list of man's benefactors. But on none of them had the splendid orb of modern philology risen in its strength. It was in 1833 that Bopp began to publish that great work, his Comparative Grammar, which in the department of language like Bacon's Novum Organon in that of physical science, lighted the

own position is that " over all Middle and Southern Italy only one great family-tongue prevailed, the Greek; and that Latins and Volscians, Sabines and Oscans, Messapians and Iapygians spoke only degenerate Greek, and that even in the Tuscan there are, at all events, Greek admixtures.

world on the way to a new era. And yet Freund, whose eyes actually beheld the rising dawn of comparative philology, the only one of the three lexicographers mentioned whose feet stood consciously upon the margin of the new order of linguistic researches and results, was in the midst of his long labors, at this very time, and, in January, 1834, wrote in his preface the following words: "The question of the origin of the Latin language is beginning to be far more involved than many are willing to believe. Germanism is opposing the Sanskrit with powerful weapons, and urges its claims to be the origin of Latin. The author therefore feels that he would be called overhasty, if he allowed the Sanskrit or the German element to have the predominance in his work." In the light of the present hour, how strange even to ridiculousness seems this language. It is by such strong high waymarks standing up in the past, that we can best realize how great progress has been made during the last quarter of a century, as in every thing else so also in the elements and processes of classical study. To dress, now, Latin lexicography in the etymology of Freund's day, when such a man as he thought that it was quite as likely as not that the Latin was but a child of the German that had been lost in other days, but was now found again, would be like undertaking to parade a full-grown man of our times, in the clothes of some petty underling that lived half a century ago. Our lexical Latin etymology wears, therefore, to one whose eye is open to the charms and claims of Indo-European philology, the most grotesque Lilliputian dimensions: casting the reproach of its dwarfishness and deformity upon the whole aspect of the lexicography into which it is introduced. In Freund's day Döderlein's star was in the ascendant, in etymology, who published his "Lateinische Synonyme and Etymologieen" in 1826. He derived the Latin immediately from the Greek, so far as he could either find or devise any similarity between them. And many and great were the tortuosities of his inventive genius in working its way through such a labyrinthine experiment. The Latin and the Greek are twin sisters, the Latin being the more antique in its features and bearing of the two, and having in its form and face and character much more resemblance to their elder sister, the Sanskrit, and so to the common parent of them all, than the Greek. Of what greater absurdity, therefore, could an etymologist be guilty, than that of undertaking to represent the Latin as the daughter of the Greek, its twin sister? With much labor in so false a direction, Döderlein has succeeded in building up, in his various works, a vast pile of learned and ingenious but false and worthless novelties and blunders; a remarkable specimen of a patient, vigorous, enthusiastic scholar, industriously misspending all his days. There has been great elaboration in the argument of his life, but it has been developed, throughout, from entirely wrong premises. Through Freund's deference to his false views, he has been permitted to perpetuate the blight of his errors, through this generation and perhaps through another, upon the scholarship of other lands than his own, where the light of better minds has sufficed to supersede forever the false glare of his philological misconceptions. To Freund* we must give, however, the credit of having uttered his deep sense of the want of a true etymology. He says, that "a scientific exhibition of the genealogy of words is needed, but hitherto [1833] has not been formed into a separate department of the general science of language, as it ought to be. In time there must and will, without doubt, be found a genealogy of words, which shall take its place as a science by the side of lexicography." But in the few correspondences of the Latin with the Greek which Freund ventured to indicate, how narrow was the prospect that he opened of their really wide and wonderful relations! And what an utter want of any system for its facts, and of any solution for its difficulties. In this period of well-nigh universal darkness in philology, but twenty-five years ago, the field of classical etymology was a favorite

* While Freund is so deficient in all true etymological relations, he is much to be commended for the simple, clear, critical and condensed character of most of his researches and statements in other respects, and yet his ideal was throughout above his attainments. His discrimination of words as ante-classical, classical and post-classical, is especially one of the highest benefits that could be conferred on young composers in Latin.

hunting ground for every sort of linguistic vagary, by all kinds of scholastic pretenders, who kept ever doubling again and again upon their own tracks, and ended all their toils only in making game of themselves to every intelligent beholder. Many, like Döderlein, derived the Latin from the Greek. Schwenck published in 1827 an Etymological Latin Dictionary in German, deriving the Latin from the Greek, for the most part; but sometimes also from the German. But, while its references to the Greek are somewhat copious, they have no scientific basis and are all empirical, and many of them far-fetched and false. Valpy also published in English a Latin Etymological Dictionary, in the same spirit and with the same faults as Schwenck. "It will be said," he says, "that there are numerous words which we cannot show to be taken from the Greek. Doubtless it is so, although the number of such words is constantly decreasing." For works based on such fundamentally wrong ideas, both of these dictionaries possess much scholarly merit.

Others, like Jäkel, in his "Germanische Ursprung Der Lateinischen Sprache" (in 1830), undertook, like one hunting for eggs among ashes, to find the origin of the Latin in the old Gothic; others still, like the great Gesenius, connected it, very largely, with the Hebrew. Nork, accordingly, prepared a Latin dictionary on this basis; and to one whose philological views are broad enough to enable him to appreciate the real quality of the book, it is full of all humorous elements. A brief quotation will show, at once, his position. He says [1827], "the relationship of the Hebrew with the Greek and Latin cannot be denied, for the following reasons, namely: because the Tuscans, like the Carthaginians, claimed derivation from the inhabitants of Tyre; and also the Hebrews, the neighbors of the Phœnicians, like the Greeks, had constructed their language out of Egyptian elements, while the Egyptians themselves, but colonists from Meroe, had been with the Ethiopians emigrants from India; and hence their agreement in language, culture, and philosophy. Hence it comes that almost all the names of the Greek and Tuscan gods can be deciphered only through the Hebrew (as Dido,* Hecate, Minerva, Venus, etc.). But also other words in those languages have rewarded the search for their origin, only when made in the Hebrew, as $\chi\alpha\lambda\varkappa\acute{o}\varsigma$, brass, from חָלַק (*chalak*) to divide; $\chi\varrho\upsilon\sigma\acute{o}\varsigma$, gold, from חָרַץ (*charats*),† to dig out, a name which, applying to every metal, came to be affixed, *par excellence*, to gold. So also the root of capio, to take, is found in כַּף (*caph*), the hand; as of cupio, to desire, in גוּף (*guph*), the body, and hence desire," etc. What a mass of misstatements and misconceptions! Is it any wonder, that such a book never saw a second edition, or that its author warned his readers to be

* Of what god is this the name?
† This verb means to cut into or on.

careful not to belong to a class who had sworn to any previous master? On principles like these one might derive any language from any other, and change the order of their sequence one to the other, ad libitum, forwards and backwards, backwards and forwards, upside down and downside up, and still always preserve, unimpaired, the same wonderful beauty of connection.

A new Latin Dictionary by Reinhold Klotz, Professor of Classical Philology at Leipsic, has just appeared (1858), which is in decided advance of Freund, in its critical and historical aspects, and in range of research, as well as in breadth and copiousness of details. In respect also to etymologies lying within the specific boundaries of the Latin language, that is, within the department of classical philology, as technically discriminated from the wider and richer field of comparative philology, with which however its connections are, after all, so vast and vital, he is also superior to Freund. But alas! the torch of Sanskrit discovery nowhere scatters its light here, and the eager philological student turns away, disappointed, from his pages. When will the day arrive when in our Latin school-lexicons we shall no more see the faces of Lobeck and Döderlein, Wachter and Scaliger, or Festus, Vossius and Varro, sitting in state to teach us as authorities the native origin and sense of words; but when in their places shall appear, in higher dignity and with purer light, the forms of Bopp and Pott and Grimm, Schleicher, Curtius, Aufrecht, Diefenbach, Ebel and Kuhn.

In Greek lexicography, Passow is of the greatest merit in every thing, but that inner presence of the true etymological element, which informs a dictionary with so much of its higher light and beauty. He lived and labored, as a lexicographer, earlier still than Freund; having published the first edition of his dictionary in different parts, between the years 1818 and 1824. The new edition of Passow by Rost and others was begun twenty years ago; and, though much enlarged and improved through this long course of years, was begun and has been finished without the introduction of that one savory element of philology, so necessary to the new and improved taste of the modern scholar. Pape's Greek lexicon, prepared more recently, comes under the same condemnation, in reference to its supply of any etymological stores for meeting the cravings of those desiring more philological knowledge. Kaltschmidt's comparative and etymological Greek dictionary, published in 1839, is an approximation in both spirit and form to what is wanted, but much below in quality. It is not, like the works of Grimm and Bopp and Pott and the leaders in the new philology, vast and profound, but is often fanciful and feeble, and therefore very generally unreliable; as unsatisfactory commonly in its conclusions as Benfey, of whom, in this relation, he constantly reminds an investigator; who, while being a fine Sanskrit scholar, is yet quite a visionary and indifferent etymologist. Eichhoff is Kaltschmidt's oracle ; and in so far as he follows Eichhoff he is always respectable, and in many cases valuable, as a leader ; but there is so much chaff mingled with the wheat in his lexicon, that, for a beginner in Greek philology, he is more dangerous than useful. His dictionary was probably, in its day, equal to the most advanced scholarship of the times ; and, if so, it serves to show in a striking manner, how much progress has been made in the short interval between. No adequate work, therefore, has yet appeared in Latin or Greek lexicography, in the department of etymology. The light, in which our present generation of classical students is walking, is : like that of the fixed stars, which are so far from us that the beams which we are now receiving from them, actually left the orbs themselves whole centuries ago : that, shed from the best scholarship that prevailed a quarter of a century since, instead of the light of the foremost minds which are leading the scholarship of our day. And the wonder is, that, while there is so much bright beautiful light on the mountain-tops of the classical world, it creeps down so slowly into the vast circumference of the vales below.

As for our own vernacular etymology, since our language is wholly secondary in its origin, and, so, mixed and modern in its structure, more copious materials and those for the most part of inherent value, have been gathered by Webster and preceding lexicographers, without the aid of comparative philology, than could be done in any other language. But, while in certain directions and on certain sides of the language, much labor has been well bestowed in making collections of classical and Teutonic correspondences, as well as of those in the various Romanic languages, with English words, here all the effort bestowed or designed to be has ceased. The facts established, or supposed to be established, have not been afterwards selected and arranged and compacted together, within the bonds of any true comprehensive scientific system. No phonetic principles have been developed, serving to ascertain or eclaircise all that large and best class of etymological facts, which are a little removed from immediate discovery, and so constitute, when found, the satisfying reward of successful scientific research. It is therefore but a mere chaos of etymologies that English lexicography yet furnishes; a jumble of true things and false, more like the extended ruins of some huge edifice, than like a structure built with jealous care, to stand high and strong in its appointed place. Under the princely tread of the new philology, multitudes of before valued resemblances in English etymology are at once trampled down, as mere stubble. Much of such a romantic style of etymologizing, as that with which Horne Tooke amused himself and his readers, in his "Diversions of Purley," disappears at once in the light of modern scholarship, as would mere elegant frost-work before a bright sun. The etymological treasures which Webster gathered together, with such scholarly industry and delight, excite our admiration at the breadth of his research and the luminous accuracy of his judgment, within the bounds of the narrow classical scholarship of his day. But the fountains of his learning were not drawn, since they could not be at first, from the heights of comparative philology. The salt of the Indo-European element is not in them, and they cannot retain their virtue. Nothing can make amends for this fatal deficiency but their perfect renovation. It was in 1828, five years before Bopp began to scatter the light of his great discoveries over the study of the various languages of the civilized world, that Webster published his large dictionary; and, when in 1840 he issued a new and last edition improved by himself, the additions designed to be made, as stated by him, did not embrace at all the results of the new philology. "The improvements," he says, "consist chiefly in the addition of several thousand words to the vocabulary, the division of words into syllables, and the correction of definitions in several of the sciences; as well as the introduction of many phrases from foreign languages, and of many foreign terms used in books of music." And what of all the wonderful researches and results of the last quarter of a century, serving to revolutionize all lexicography, all classical study, and the whole science of language? Watchman on the towers of American philology, what of the night? We wait for an answer after twelve years have come and gone, and only echo answers, *what!* The Semitic element, to which, according to the fashion of the times, he gave in 1828 such false prominence in the department of etymology, still retains its authority or rather its place unimpaired in 1840. And neither at first nor at last was any order of relation indicated or conceived to exist between the different correspondences of words, which are strung together as carelessly as were ever beads by a child upon a string. Some recent hand has undertaken to introduce the Sanskrit, somehow,* into this unmethod-

* As a specimen of the utterly unphilological aspect of the Sanskrit additions made to Webster's dictionary, witness the following facts, taken at random and only as samples of multitudes of the same sort. The Sanskrit equivalent is placed sometimes, between the Latin and Armenian (*navy*); sometimes between the Russian and Hebrew (to *bear*); and at other times, between the Persian and Malay (*name*), and between the Hindû and Persian (*new*); the Swedish and Latin (*stand*); the Swedish and Persian (*state*); the Irish and Greek (*brow*); the Greek and Zend (*mead*); the Persian and Russian (*mother*); the Russian and Persian (*no*); the Armenian and Persian (*seven*); the Greek and Hebrew (*six*), and between the Danish and Welsh (*luck*), and so on *ad infinitum*. The Sanskrit, besides being thus thrown in as a makeweight, among a mere disjointed mass of other etymologies, is introduced only in a very partial, meagre way, compared with its real claims; and it is always placed last or among the last, instead of first, and here as before in all sorts of laughable combinations; as, after the Irish and Slavonic (*night*); the Hebrew and Arabic (*mix*); the Danish and Russian (*nail*), etc. Could a more perfect wizard's potion be prepared with which to steep the thoughts of a young student of English etymology in "utter forgetfulness" of his work and of its

ized group of etymologies, but not in a way to throw any light upon them, or to draw them together around any common point of crystallization, or even of central preparation for it. The new comer from India, instead of being treated as a prince royal in his own lawful dominions, is here dishonored actually although not designedly, in the position assigned to him, as if a mere bantling, that must be taken care of in some way, and so is left by the way-side to be taken care of by others. There is no science or organific law prevailing in the series of connections and citations exhibited, nor can there be at any time, without an entire reorganization of the materials now employed, as well as their very great enlargement. The structure, therefore, which Webster built so industriously, must ere long be inevitably razed to the ground, as entirely inadequate to the more exact and vast scholarship of succeeding generations; or, be so built over and around with higher and better forms of lexical research, as to disappear itself wholly from the view. The scholarship of our country, now so destitute perchance of any strong traces of such

benefits? How does it remind one of the song of the three witches about the caldron in Macbeth:

> " Black spirits and white
> Red spirits and gray,
> Mingle, mingle, mingle,
> You that mingle may."

Webster is not, and cannot be, accepted as a standard by our best scholars in orthography, orthoepy or etymology, but only in definitions, in which he is certainly the foremost of all English lexicographers.

a fact, will soon become so lofty in its type, so broad in its demands, and so irradiated with the highest light of the age, as to require a style of lexicography that shall embrace in it a full view of all the vast array of scientific results developed by comparative philology. All honor to the man who shall arise in some future age, a man of exalted genius and splendid learning, to do this work! He will be born; and we record our hearty salutations to him in advance, across the stream of time which separates his day from ours. Let the motto of our American scholars be, both now and then, those sublime words of the great Passow in closing his labors in lexicography : " vorwärts! aufwärts "! forwards! upwards!

The only lexicography that has yet appeared in any language constructed after the true model and built without stint of means, according to the highest knowledge of the age, throughout every department of its wide-spread details, is the great national German Dictionary that the brothers Grimm (Jacob and William) are now laboriously preparing, and of which they have recently published the first part of the third volume (1859), extending through a portion of the letter E. In it is concentrated all the light contained in the history, literature, and constitution of the language itself, to which is superadded all the light which any and every other language, when searched through all its depths, can be made to contribute to its fulness, along the whole chain of Indo-European languages. The views and the spirit with which the Grimms undertake their noble work, will be seen by a brief quotation from the introduction. " Etymology," they say (page 47), " is the salt* or spice of a dictionary, without the addition of which the eating of it would still remain tasteless. The German language hangs by a chain which unites it with most of the European languages, and then leads back into Asia and directly to the Sanskrit, Zend, and Persian. From this proceeds a fulness of phenomena and relations, sometimes combined and sometimes separated from each other, as distinct peculiarities of different languages. Not a few links indeed of the great chain have fallen out and disappeared, so that many breaks in it must be skipped over. Every language possesses also in it an inward recuperative force, which gradually heals again any injury done, in sundering its connections. But this it can accomplish only by various compensations and special appliances, which afterwards come to be numbered among its individual peculiarities; and hence comes the necessity of recognizing the limits where its own specialties cease, and where it enters again under the prevailing law of the other languages with which it is allied."

Surely this is a new voice in the realms of lexicography: the voice of one of earth's greatest men,

* "Etymologie is das Salz, oder die Würze des Wörterbuchs, ohne deren Zuthat seine Speise noch ungeschmack bliebe," etc.

coming to cast down the fabrics of the past; not to rejoice over their ruin, but to gather their materials carefully together in order to build them anew, with other elements of greater strength and beauty, into an edifice of grander proportions, and adequate to the wants of the highest minds of the age.

Hail to the new era of linguistic exploration and discovery! The age of empiricism is forever gone in etymology, except to those still remaining in the darkness of the past generation, and even they can see that the mountain-heights above them are gilded with an unwonted brightness. Comparative etymology, like the solar spectrum, presents in separate order, and in all the harmony of their mutual connection, the different rays that combine to form what seems the single and simple light of each distinct language. That the Sanskrit, in both its orthoepical and grammatical structure, is most intimately related to all the languages of Europe, ancient and modern, is a discovery that constitutes one of the chief wonders of the nineteenth century. It is one of the results of the conquest of India: a tribute first brought back by English scholarship from that far-off, fabulous land of gems and spices, to its mother country and the world; but yet rather announced, than revealed in all its strange fulness of evidence, by the English. It was reserved for the strong, penetrative, analytic, persevering German mind, to explore and develop the untold riches of this new discovery. And what honor have they shed upon their age, Bopp and Pott and Grimm, and a host of others like them; for they form now not so much "a school" as an army: similar for honor, as adventurers upon these new seas and coasts of the science of language, to that won by Columbus and the great navigators who succeeded him, in discovering new countries and continents, and sailing around the world.

The absence of the Indo-European element in Greek, Latin, English, or any other etymology, makes it like a system of chemistry, in which oxygen, that universal agent in all heat and moisture, all growth and decay, and all the processes of life and of death, should be utterly wanting; or one of geology, in which no reference to stratification should occur, and to the agency of fire and water, separate and combined, in building up the stage of this world as it is; or a piece of music, without any clef; or a structure, erected according to no order or plan, and but the vast and shapeless agglomeration of the elements of an edifice, but itself no edifice at all. The Semitic languages have spread over no such field of development, as the Indo-European. The Indo-European languages are susceptible, to an almost unlimited extent, of changes made by the combination, composition, and attraction of their elements into ever-new forms and uses. They have a wonderfully mobile, elastic, and impressible nature, like those human constitutions of a high organization, that respond so sensitively to every influence, however gentle or occasional, that moves upon the delicate framework of their being. A royal family indeed is the Indo-European family of languages! Each of its members is, in the eye of art, "a study" by itself. As they pass, in stately review, before the mind: the Indian, the Græco-Latin, the Lettic, the Slavonic, the Gothic, and the Celtic families: each, with its splendid retinue of associated languages, whose heart does not dilate with admiration at the pageant? They are all sons of one ancient mother, and yet they have taken on such different complexions, in their different climates, and acquired such a different stature, as they have lived on the mountains or the plains; and such a softness or rigidity of muscular development, as they have toiled or lived in ease; and spoken so variously, in figures or with plain speech, as they have maintained an out-door or an in-door life: that they have been supposed, and have supposed themselves, to bear no relationship to each other, and nave gloried in wars, as races, one against the other, as if they were natural enemies and not brethren. And now, after four thousand years, they are found under the light of that sublime inductive philosophy, which has opened so many other wonders to modern eyes, to be all most intimately allied with each other; and that, by the use of a key to this new and strange discovery, that had lain hidden, for thousands of years, from view, in India.

Etymology is an inductive science, and rests upon the same strong foundations, in this respect, as any of the natural sciences. And very minute and wide and full have been the inductions made, and the comparisons instituted. The evidence of its facts is found by one who examines it, to be so various and so duplicated and reduplicated upon itself, as to rise everywhere, in high and golden piles around him, towards heaven. They will bear the closest scrutiny, however often repeated. Each time that they are sifted, they only appear more clear and bright, and the force of the most searching logic brought to bear upon them only serves, like acid upon gold, not to destroy but to beautify still more their claims. No wonder if, under the former empirical treatment of classical etymology, the more self-poised and stable scholars of the day, like those thoughtful ancients called $ἄθεοι$, not atheists, who rejected the contemptible mythology of their times, should discard the etymology, falsely so called, that was offered them, as having in it neither science nor sense. But mockery, now, of the science of etymology, or even indifference to its claims, will only rebound on him who indulges it, as a proof of the shallowness of his knowledge and the narrowness of his ideas.

III. The constituent elements of etymology as a science.

It has been shown that neither classical nor vernacular etymology have risen, by themselves, to the dignity of a science. They have had only an empirical development, when not under the light of comparative philology. And it is only, when grafted on the root of comparative Indo-European etymology, that they possess, either of them, any true life or value. The proper discussion of this part of the subject demands, at least, a brief presentation.

1st. Of the elements of comparative etymology.

2d. Of the principles that prevail, in respect to the specific etymology of any individual language, under its influence.

1st. The constituent elements of comparative etymology are threefold:

(1.) Comparative phonology,

(2.) Comparative lexicography,

(3.) Comparative grammar.

It is not meant that, historically, these different elements actually developed themselves in this order; but that, in reference to their mutual connection, this is the true philosophic order of their arrangement.

(1.) Comparative phonology.

It will not be manifest at first, probably, to every reader what this word may mean, and yet it has a very definite and important meaning. Phonology or phonetics is, literally, the science of sound, that is, the science of the mutations and transformations of consonants and vowels, in passing from one language to another. In Sanskrit, words merely joined together in

THE SCIENCE OF ETYMOLOGY. 313

simple sequence have an influence upon each other, such as to cause great euphonic mutations of their consonantal elements. This style of changes is called Sandhi (conjunction); and by its laws the juxtaposition of consonants of different orders, is forbidden; while the laws of composition themselves, whether in respect to the inward or outward blending of the elements which are combined are called samasa (coalition). Bopp was the first to exhibit a wide array of facts upon the subject of comparative phonology, which, however, being so intent on ends lying farther beyond, he did not bind into any system or science. It was Jacob Grimm, as splendid a scholar as any country or age has ever produced, who first, by a large and wonderful induction of kindred forms in Sanskrit, Greek and Latin, Gothic and High German, developed the law of actual correspondences in these languages, since called Grimm's law; according to which, a given letter in one of them is regularly transformed into a given letter in each of the others. Succeeding investigators in other languages, as the Celtic, Slavonic, Zend, and old Persian, have lengthened out the scale of comparison into them, and established a general scientific schedule of mutual equivalents, throughout the whole range of the Indo-European languages. Going forth to new researches, with such a scale of phonetic correspondences, not made of artificial materials, but found imbedded in these languages themselves like the diatonic scale in the very organs of the voice, philologists have been able, not only to verify abundantly, over and over again, the truth of the scale itself, but also by its aid to extend the area of their discoveries in every direction. Like the natural sciences, the science of philology is in a state of constant and rapid growth. It has already mammoth proportions, and yet what it is to be is but partially shadowed forth, in what it now is.

Comparative phonology is therefore the science of the transformations, substitutions and correspondences of sounds, in different languages; a science which had lain concealed in these languages for thousands of years, like a bird in a brake, which no foot had ever entered before: a beautiful many-voiced bird, now flying abroad everywhere, before the eyes of its admirers, in the horizon of letters.

The less a language has departed from its archaic forms, so much the more easily and certainly can the internal affiliations of its words, one with another, be traced. In the progress of ages, even in the same language, and much more as words traverse the domain of different latitudes and languages, do great changes in their primitive radical form occur. For, as the same words are put to different uses in the mouths of men, having different wants, experiences, and developments, even in the same age, and among the same people, and under the same culture; so, much more, do the shapes and sounds of words run through a wide range of variations, amid all the diversities of climate, employment, and character experienced over wide and varying tracts of the earth. The influence of climate on national physiognomy, stature, complexion, vigor, and every personal characteristic, is very apparent and has received formal recognition in history, geography and the natural history of man ; but its influence on the organs of speech, so as to make certain sounds difficult to one race or tribe, that to other races in other climates are easy and natural, has been little appreciated or considered. As the elements of man's primitive language have come in contact with all these various currents of influence in different nations and epochs, they have undergone great changes, in every direction. In the modern Romanic languages, the Spanish, Italian, and French particularly, the greatness of these changes in forms, once fixed in the Latin as if having a constitution of iron, is strikingly apparent within a period covered by the recent memory of men. No languages differ more in their phonetic elements from each other than these, although being of one immediate common origin.

By the careful analytic study of their variations, as also by that of the agreements and differences of the several dialects of Greece, one, who is just beginning to have some insight into just phonetic solutions of the problems of comparative etymology, may be greatly enlightened and aided.* In them, accordingly, as geologists can often witness in changes now going on in the world the true energy, direction, and mode of ancient agencies; we can see the real philosophy exemplified in actual view, of the various phonetic developments of the ancient languages.

When Cadmus brought the Phœnician alphabet of sixteen letters to Greece, he found some sounds prevailing there which his syllabarium did not contain, as the aspirates ϑ, φ, χ, the double consonants ζ, ξ, ψ, and the long vowels η and ω. The digamma F, which was at first used as the equivalent of the Phœnician Vau, was, in the Hellenic period, entirely dropped from

* The different forms of many of the same Christian names, and the different pronunciation of the same form to the eye, in several of the modern languages, illustrate well the greatness of phonetic changes in recent times. Remember that J is pronounced in Spanish as H and in German as Y.

Greek or Latin.	Italian.	Spanish.	French.	German.	English.
Ἰάκωβος	Giacomo	Iago and Santiago (St. James)	Jacques	Jacob	Jacobus, Jacob, James, Jack
Ἰωάννης, Ἰωάννα	Giovanni, Giovanna	Juan, Juana	Jean, Jeanne	Hans, Hannchen, Johanna	John, Jane, Joanna
Gulielmus	Gulielmo	Guillermo	Guillaume	Wilhelm	William
Carolus	Carlo, Carlotta, Carolina	Carlos, Carlota, Carolina	Charles, Charlotte, Carolina	Karl, Charlotte, Karolina	Carlos, Charles, Charlotte, Caroline
Edvardus	Odoardo	Eduardo	Edouard	Eduard	Edward
Josephus	Giuseppe	José	Joseph	Joseph	Joseph

the Greek language, as not euphonious to the ear; while in the Latin it was retained, in the letter v, with much favor. The breathing h was a great favorite in Greece, and often substituted for an original s; while in Rome, contrarily, h was little and s* was much fancied. In German, s is disliked in its common hissing sound, and accordingly is changed to z between two vowels in pronunciation, and in orthography it is often softened, by adding an aspirate, into sch. The guttural ch of that language, and of the Greek, Scotch, and Irish languages, is rejected by us and the French; while both the Latin and the French reject our w, and we are entirely destitute of the sweet soft u sound, found in French, German, and Greek. So, the Lithuanians have no aspirates. The letter r has a roll in it, as used by some nations, which is almost drumlike, compared with its liquid and indeed almost unmeaning pronunciation in English. Some races, like the Poles, delight in sibilants; others, like the Germans, in gutturals; some, like the Greeks, in aspirates; some, like the French and Portuguese, in nasals; and others, like the Italians and the Servians, in vowels and liquids. How differently is also the same letter pronounced in different languages. Our j is in German y and in

* The same fact characterizes the English in that class of words which we call Latin-English; while in French, though often occurring to the eye, it is generally rejected at the end of words and syllables in pronunciation, and often thrown entirely out of view, as is indicated by the circumflex accent in such a case.

318   THE SCIENCE OF ETYMOLOGY.

Spanish h. Our v is the German f and our w their v; ch is pronounced very differently by different nations.

Many correspondences of words, therefore, which a classical novice would reject at once, as not meeting the demands of his eye or his ear, are yet beautifully certified to be true by the wonder-working power of pho-

Sanskrit.	Greek.	Latin.	Italian.
janu, the knee*	γόνυ	genu / geniculum	ginocchio
vinsati, twenty	εἴκοσι / Doric εἴκατι for Ϝείκατι	viginti	venti
śatam, a hundred	ἑκατόν= / ἐν κατον	centum	cénto
yuj, to bind / yuga, a pair	ζευγνύναι / ζυγόν	jungere / jugum	giungere / giogo
dvar, a door	θύρα	foris / foras, out of doors	fuora
aśvas, a horse	ἵππος, Æolic ἵκκος	equus / equestris	equestre
hard, hrid, and hridaya, the heart	κῆρ and καρδία	cor(d)	cuore / coraggio
śvan, a dog † / gen. śunos	κύων / gen. κυνός	canis	cane
plâvayâ, to wash	λούειν	lavare	lavare
mahat, great, for maghat	μέγας / fem. μεγάλη	magnus / mactus / magis / magister	magno / maestro
mahiyas, greater	μείζων	major	maggiore
ashtâu, eight	ὄκτω	octo	otto

* These correspondences are selected from a list of some five thousand or more prepared with care by the author, in manuscript.
† Irish cu.

nology: the charm of the discovery being sometimes found in one language on an extended scale of comparison, and sometimes in another. It will interest the reader to examine the following brief schedule of a few correspondences,* such as are established by it, in great numbers, to be true.

Spanish.	French.	German.	English.
hinojo	genou	knie	knee
veinte	vingt	zwanzig	twenty
	cent		{ cent { (lit. a hundredth)
yugo	{ joindre { joug	} joch	{ join { yoke
fuera	hors	thür	door
ecuestre	ecuyer		{ equestrian { esquire
corazon	⎧ cœur ⎨ ⎩ courage	hertz	⎧ heart ⎪ core ⎨ cordial ⎩ courage
	chien	hund	{ hound { canine
lavar	laver	{ laben? { lauen	} lave
magno mas maestro	maint mais maître	⎧ manch ⎪ michel ⎨ macht ⎪ mehr ⎩ meister	⎧ mickle ⎪ might ⎪ more ⎨ master } ⎪ mister } ⎪ major }
mayor	maire	meier	⎩ mayor }
ocho	huit	acht	eight

* Even through the French, as any one may see, English and Latin words that, placed together, have little if any resemblance to each other, are yet found to be in origin and sense the same.

Sanskrit.	Greek.	Latin.	Italian.
dantas, a tooth	ὄδους, gen. ὄδοντος	dens	dente
vésas, and vaisas, a house	οἶκος for Ϝοῖκος	vicus	vico
akshas, the eye	ὄκος	oculus	occhio
panchan, five *	πέντε	quinque	cinque
pra	προ	pro	
tvam, thou	σύ	tu	tu
chatur, and chatvaras, four	τέσσαρες	quatuor, quadra, quartus	quattro, quadro, quarto, quadrone

Latin.	French.	English.
bellus, beautiful, fine	beau, beauté	beauty
bonus	bon, bonté	boon, bounty
cadere, to fall, part. cadens	chance	chance
caput, the head	chef, achever	chief, achieve
captivus a captive	chetif	caitiff
co-operire	couvrir	cover, cope
collocare	coucher	couch
computare	compter	count
crispus, wrinkled	crêpe	crape
debere, to owe	devoir, part. du	devoirs, due, duty
decipere, to deceive	duper (a)	dupe
dies, diurnus	jour	journal, journey, ad*journ*, journeyman
domina	dame, demoiselle	dame, dam, damsel

* Lithuanian penki.

(a) So de le becomes du and ducere, duire, to suit.

THE SCIENCE OF ETYMOLOGY.

Spanish.	French.	German.	English.
diente	dent	zahn	tooth
villa	ville		—wich villa / —ville / village
ojo	œil, pl. yeux	auge	eye
cinco	cinq	fünf *	five
por	pour	vor / für	fore / be*fore* / for / *fore*head
tu	tu	du	thou
cuatro	quatre	quart	quart / quarter / quadroon / square / squadron
esquadra	escadre	quartier	
esquadron	escadron		

Latin.	French.	English.
nocere	nuire	
noxa	nuisance	nuisance
	noise	noise
pagus	pays	pagan
paganus	paysan	peasant
pipire to pipe, to peep,	pigeon	pip / peep / pipe / pigeon
pipio (n) a young piping bird		
sedere, to sit	sieger	siege / besiege
senior, elder	sieur	sir
silva	sauvage	savage
silvaticus		
solidus	sold	solder
solidum	soldat	sôda / soldier
tegula, a tile	tuile	tile
vesper, the evening	ouest (*a*)	west
videre	voir / part. vu / voyager	vision / view / voyage / sur*vey* / —vide / —vise / visit

* Gothic fimf.
(*a*) Cf. Swedish vester.

Sanskrit.	Greek.	Latin.	Italian.
kas, who	τίς Æolic κίς	quis quisque quisque-unus aliquis-unus	che, and chi ciascuno alcuno
svapnas, a dream	ὕπνος	somnus (for sopnus) somnium	sognio sognare
upari, above	ὑπέρ	super	sur
bhrajj, to fry	φρύγειν	frigere	friggere
hyas, yesterday	χθές	heri, for hesi hesternus	ieri
hansas, a goose	χήν	ganta anser (for hanser)	
garhan, an enclosure	χόρτος	hortos cohors	coorte giardino
chut, to pour forth	χεῖν, fut. χεύσειν χύτος poured forth	gutta, a drop	goccia
śrat, credit	χρᾶν to loan or lend	credere (=srat + dâ Sansk. verb, to give)	credere

2. Comparative lexicography.

The component parts of lexicography are various, such as etymology, exegesis, synonymes, the statistics of words, and dialectic peculiarities. The exegetical element, which concerns itself with the meanings of words, is indeed the principal element of lexicography, both in respect to the amount of space that it must necessarily occupy, and in respect to the supply which it affords for the wants of the greatest number who use a dictionary. But in what close connection with it stands the element of etymology! It gives a pictorial

THE SCIENCE OF ETYMOLOGY. 323

Spanish.	French.	German.	English.
que		wer	who
quien	chaque		
alguno	chacun		
	aucun		
sueño	sommeil		somnific
	songer		
sobre	sur	{ über ober	{ super- over upper up
	frire		fry
ayer	hier		
		gestern	*yester*day
ganso	jars	gans	{ gander goose
{ huerto jardin	cour jardin	garten *	{ garden court cohort
gota grotera	goutte	{ giessen guss vergessen, to pour away geist	{ gush gust for*g*et gutter ghost
			{ credit creed

charm to the dictionary, and adds as much zest to the details of the lexicon as experiments in chemistry would to a collection of chemicals. And as the true etymology of a word establishes its original meaning, from which all its other meanings ramify, the etymological element forms the basis on which the exegetical element must logically rest. Any attempt, therefore, to separate it from lexicography is unnatural and absurd.

No lexicography is of any adequate form or dimensions, that is not comparative. Words hang in clusters;

* Gothic gards.

324 THE SCIENCE OF ETYMOLOGY.

and, as well might one attempt to show the strength or beauty of a vine, by single grapes growing upon it, as to exhibit the scope or the charms of lexicography in separate, disconnected words.

Wonders have been accomplished during the past twenty-five years, in gathering together large collections of materials for a true lexicography, in each one of the Indo-European languages; and the precious pile is growing larger and larger every day. And, as in ancient Egypt multitudes were busy in various parts of the land, for many years, in hewing out and transporting the blocks of stone which were to form their mighty pyramids; so now, in different lands, are many hands at work in many mines to quarry and prepare the materials, which shall serve to complete and to beautify the vast and splendid structure of comparative philology. The results already obtained lie scattered through many books, in diverse forms and connections. The lexicographers of each language have as open a field for their researches, and as unlimited opportunities for pursuing them, as geologists in every country have for theirs. Like the elements of nature, the benefits of all such discoveries are open to all, and may be used without stint or damage by all. The students of another age, standing under the scholarship of the future, rising over them in its colossal proportions and its temple-like beauty, will behold a field of research and pleasure spreading out before them in classical study, compared with which ours, in its best condition, will seem but an almost barren waste.

3. Comparative grammar.

It is common to limit the application of etymology to lexicography, and in its narrow sense this is right; but, on a broad view, comparative grammar also must be included, as derived forms are almost all of them, those at least of a simple uncomposite structure, of a grammatical origin.

One of the chief peculiarities of the new philology is, that it rests the comparison of languages so much on their grammatical correspondences. Not only the forms of declension and conjugation are found, under the lens of true analytic and phonological investigation, to be identical in all the Indo-European languages, but also all the various parts of speech down to the merest particles of these languages, and their very prefixes, suffixes and terminations. A given radical may be selected, in both its simple and its composite forms, and its nominal, adjective, adverbial and verbal derivatives may be compared in different languages, form with form and kind with kind; and everywhere, both generally and particularly, in great things and little, the most intimate union and communion will be found to exist between them.

Under the light of comparative grammar, the lexicographer's sense of the common origin and unity of our different languages, is heightened to perfect abso-

326 THE SCIENCE OF ETYMOLOGY.

luteness. He feels the self-reliance of complete vision. Our different languages, he sees, are but so many different dresses of the same essential, radical word, like the figures with which children amuse themselves, made to slip in and out of a dozen various styles of dress, with such ever changing effect that the same theme may be taken and robed in the flexion-forms of each several language, and transformed at will into Sanskrit, Greek, Latin, Gothic or Slavonic.

It may be well to detail some of the criteria by which the relative antiquity of different languages, and so of different words, may be determined.

(1) In reference to their phonetic constitution: the relative prevalence of the three original vowels, a, i, u, in their forms generally, and also their relative preservation of their original unmutilated and unmodified themes, as ascertained by careful analysis and the laws of analogy, both in the same language and also in other languages viewed in connection with it. These facts, an eye in the habit of tracing correspondences scientifically comes to have a trained sense for perceiving; as, in works of taste or matters of composition, a practised mind possesses, in its own cultivated judgment, a touchstone for discriminating at once the true from the false.

(2) In reference to their syllabication: the simpler and closer the consonantal drapery of each separate vowel, the older, as a general fact, is the family of

languages. In other words : the younger sisters of the great Indo-European family are much fonder of consonantal ornamentation, than were the elder; as is quite manifest in the Gothic and Slavic languages, compared with the Sanskrit and Græco-Italic ; and in the later, compared with the earlier dialects of the Greek itself. Such variations originate in different climatic influences, different occupations, and different degrees of intellectual culture. In the history of each separate family of languages by itself, the tendency is quite regular in derived branches to greater simplicity of consonantal structure, especially in terminal syllables.

(3) In reference to roots : the simpler they are in vocal substance, and the more distinct and full their own individual character, the nearer are they to their primal state.

(4) In reference to word-forms generally : the more distinct the analytic elements of their structure: the less of mere arbitrary symbolism, and the more of clear open significance that they possess, the older is the form ; and, where such forms abound, the older is the language. Symbols early part with all their inward life and heat. Time rapidly formalizes, stereotypes and petrifies, not only the outward institutions, but even the hereditary ideas of men.

II. The principles that prevail in respect to the specific etymology of any individual language, under the influence of comparative etymology.

328 THE SCIENCE OF ETYMOLOGY.

They are these:

1. The originals of words in the given language, and their meaning, must be furnished, whether in the language or out of it.

The radical element, stem, theme or base, as it is variously called, should be set forth distinctly by itself, and in compound forms each component part should be separately exhibited. The stem contains all that belongs to the word, as such. Every thing else connected with it is but some incidental affection, and belongs to the department of the pathology of words.

2. Comparative forms in other kindred languages must be given, serving to illustrate more fully its place in the great family to which it belongs.

In all lexicography, whether vernacular or classical, the history of each word should, so far as possible, be exhibited on the following scale of equivalents, and in the order here stated: the Sanskrit, Zend, and Old Persian, Celtic, Latin, Greek, Lettic, Gothic, and Slavonic.* In the etymology of the modern languages, full parallelisms also should be run between the different Romanic tongues, and in the order, for etymological value, of the Italian, Wallachian, Spanish, Portuguese, French, and English. A line or two of such etymological equivalents, standing side by side in mute array with any word, so significant are these symbols while

* The order, in which they are here placed, is that determined by their relative historical and geographical position combined.

THE SCIENCE OF ETYMOLOGY. 329

brief like those of chemistry, contains in itself a volume of history to the philologist. It is only also, by the comparisons of words in different languages, that the normal or abnormal peculiarities of any given language can become at all apparent.

In introductory chapters, phonetic principles should be fully discussed and illustrated, by which the various changes of words derived from the same root may be comprehended and appreciated.

3. Derived forms in the same language must be carefully presented.

Even derived forms have, most of them, analogies in the various Indo-European languages; and a thorough, comprehensive system of etymology and lexicography demands that such equivalents should also be exhibited. In all those derivatives, of whatever class or style, in each language, which have no analogies in other languages, we can best discover the distinctive genius of the specific language in which they occur; and these are of great value to us, by way of revealing the inward principles to our view of its own separate home growth. They are its peculiar characteristics and the marks of its own individuality.

4. The whole interior logical etymology of each language, in its separate words, must be carefully traced by the lexicographer himself, and as carefully set forth in full detail.

The sphere of secondary and derived meanings is

one in which a deep-searching mind can work with great effect : employing all its powers of comparison, discrimination, judgment, reasoning, memory, invention and research, in the fullest possible manner. Words are even more arborescent in the variations of their sense than of their form; rising up from their elementary signification into every possible modification of it, by light and shade, in largeness and littleness and strength and beauty, of which it is susceptible. The pleasure of tracing them is like that of an anatomist in dissecting and exhibiting the delicate net-work of nerves and veins and vessels in the body, or of a mechanician in comprehending and explaining the mysteries enfolded in a telescope or a steam engine, or of an amateur of nature, who is able to see and to say what effect each part and point of a charming landscape contributes to the varied whole. Greatness, as paradoxical as it may seem, best shows itself in little things : greatness of character, greatness of intellect, whether in forecast or in the adaptation of means to ends in view, and greatness of scholarship. As our dictionaries are now used by both scholars and teachers, they are made to answer merely the purposes of a commentary. Only the specific meaning of the word in the given connection is sought for; and that is determined, not by any process of judgment going forth from the radical etymological sense of the word, through its various ramifications, to the proper point of destination, but by merely searching after the quotation of the passage in which it occurs, or of a kindred one under some one of its senses; and, if such a quotation be found, its authority is commonly held to be as conclusive, as would be that of an infallible fiat. Whether the day will ever come, in these modern times of haste, in which classical school-lexicons shall be prepared, on the plan of a thorough philological and logical development of each word, from its ultimate root to its topmost branch, in both its form and sense, without note or comment; and in which the student shall be required to select his own meaning in each case without aid, and to be able to give his reason out of the very word itself as well as out of the context, for so rendering it: is quite uncertain, if not altogether improbable. But if ever the time comes, when such facilities are provided and used with enthusiasm and perseverance, there will be a body and substance in the style of mental discipline secured, far beyond any thing yet obtained in the whole round of scholastic appliances.

IV. The determinative principles and tests of etymology.

By these are meant certain fixed laws of evidence and judgment, by which any supposed or alleged facts are to be ruled in or out of this science, which is, as has been said, a strictly inductive science. The relations of cause and effect, therefore, or of antecedence and sequence, are to be traced here as they would be on any other field of investigation, and we must walk in the light of analogy.

1. The determinative principles and tests of comparative etymology.

2. Those pertaining to specific etymology in any and every language.

1. Those of comparative etymology are the following:

(1) Correspondence in the fundamental base or root.* A real difference of base is of course destructive of all etymological identity. The base or theme of a word is its whole substance and essence.

(2) Minute mutual resemblances, through a wide range of derivatives, and in all the details of prefix and suffix forms. Each new correspondence in the derivatives of different languages adds much weight, like the argument from multiplied undesigned coincidences in the Bible, in favor of the integrity of its writers, to the force of that probable evidence by which, in this science we are to determine all its facts and features.

(3) Euphonic laws of definite, ascertained scope and power.

These often avail to overrule and overthrow all conclusions derived from sight or sound, for or against

---

* Rapp says tersely, in the beginning of his Comparative Grammar: "a root is the skeleton of a word, the residuum of a logical operation, the result of grammar, but not its genetic origin," (p. 31), and again, "grammar must never lose from view that logic is its highest and absolute sovereign," p. 33.

THE SCIENCE OF ETYMOLOGY. 333

a given etymology. They are laws which are openly revealed to us in the language itself; laws which it observed in its own constant manifestation and growth, and by observing preserved as such in its own keeping, for its own sure interpretation forever.

(4) Certain specific axioms.

(a) One fact outweighs any and all theories to the contrary.

(b) No theory is adequate which does not embrace and explain all known facts.

(c) Of two varying theories equally supported in other respects, that should always have the preference which is the most simple.

(d) No etymology can be rightly rejected on general principles and modes of reasoning, for adopting which in receiving other etymologies one would be condemned. One may be as much of an empiric in his mode of rejecting an etymology, as he could possibly judge another to be in receiving it.

2. The authoritative principles pertaining to specific etymology in any given language.

(1) The genius of the language itself.

The genius of a language in respect to its etymology is determined by its general analogies, as discovered by a wide and thorough comparison of its derivatives and secondary forms, just as, by resemblances of structure and cleavage and essential characteristics, minerals are classified. Each language has a spirit, a mien and a gait of its own ; and, as we know a man's handwriting with whom we are familiar, or his style of composition, so as to recognise them readily without his name; so, to him who knows a language as his own, under the motion of whose thoughts and feelings its words move, like his limbs, as if a part of his inward self, that language has a familiar, cherished look in all its aspects. The true etymologist in any language does not stand outside of it, and take his observations of its dimensions and of its structure as a stranger to it, with ideals and formulas of criticism and comparison formed out of its atmosphere. His point of view, on the contrary, is within the bright azure sphere of the language itself; where he looks around upon every thing beautiful and true, with a deep, glad home-sense, in sympathy with all that he beholds. Possessed of such feelings and standing at such a point of observation, a true scholarly critic will soon become able to determine at once, by a sort of instinctive interior sense, the real or counterfeit value of many minor and yet significant points of etymology. The place thus allowed for disciplined philosophic insight is narrow and confined ; but it really has a function and a sphere for its exercise, and they should be pointed out. Perfect scholarship would seem when at work, both to him employing it and to those witnessing its manifestations, like perfect spontaneity in its decisions.

(2) Simplicity and naturalness of derivation, in respect to both form and sense.

Truth is always simple in its nature, as is also the mind in its spirit and tastes that seeks to discover and appropriate it to itself. And every science, as a fragment of the great orb of universal truth, is simple always in its elements and proportions.

(3) Archaic forms, having a determinate influence.

In the early state of a language, its original forms are least impaired. Connections that then existed between words are often covered up afterwards, by the growth of centuries. Thus, in the light obtained in such a way, we find that bonus in Latin was originally duonus (from duo), implying in its very origin, as all goodness does in fact, the existence of two parties, the giver and receiver.* So bellum was at first duellum, as also bis represents dvis, like the Greek $\delta i\varsigma$ for $\delta F i\varsigma$; and thus bis (for dvis) and viginti (for dviginti) twenty, stand together before the eye even, in close mutual connection : facts these, which, if only surmised without such evidence, would have been treated with ridicule.

(4) Double forms.

These occur in Greek abundantly in Homer. There is often a third form also exhibited, the second being in such a case medial between it and the one which

---

The creation of a receptive intelligent universe, was a necessity to the heart of God, who could not in fact, in the absence of any objects of His goodness, ever exercise that goodness itself.

was primitive, as in Dor. κώρα, Ionic κούρη, Attic κόρη. So also we find in Homer ὀφέλλω for ὀφείλω for original ὀφέλιω. Compare likewise Æol. αὔως (from Sansk. ush to burn) Dor. ἀώς, Ion. ἠώς, Attic ἕως, the morning; with which also compare ἥλιος (from same root) Homeric ἠέλιος, Dor. ἀέλιος, which original form was probably as Curtius suggests, αὐσέλιος. So the double forms of the A & O declensions, as κλισιάων and κλισιῶν, ανθρώποιο and ανθρώπου lay clear parallelisms with the results of recent Sanskrit research. In such forms also as μίσγεαι, and Attic μίσγῃ for μίσγεσαι, and πόλιος and πόληος, Attic πόλεως and σόος (for σάος), Comp. σαώτερος, and both Homeric and Attic σῶς, we see other illustrations of this class of words. Such different stages in forms are as interesting to a philologist, as specimens of the influence of time upon language; as to the geologist are the different orders of rocks, primary, secondary, and tertiary, in helping him to determine the mode, and the length of time, in which this world was fitted up for its present inhabitants.

(5) Dialectic changes and differences.

The Greek is the only specific language whose dialects are at the same time numerous, and each in marked advance beyond its predecessor; while all are mutually illustrative, in the fullest and strongest philological relations, of each other.

It is thus quite apparent, that a thoroughly accomplished etymologist must needs be a man of very comprehensive learning as well as of large intellectual capacities; and these brought under the power of long and intense discipline.

The supposition or dictum of an ancient himself, as of Cicero, many of whose etymologies are preserved to us in his essays, or of Varro, whom Cicero greatly admired, has no authority as such concerning the origin or elements of a word. An ancient was just as likely as a modern, under the influence of fancy or haste, to go astray; and, in the classical age of Latin or Greek, an author was as far removed from the *primas rerum origines*, so far as his power to give any *testimony* respecting them is concerned, as we are. His opinion is but a mere opinion, and no evidence. Varro's etymologies, which are not so simple as to be undeserving of any special notice, as of dux from duco, are, very many of them, like that of pater from patefacio; canis a dog, from *canere* (signa) to give warning; and vitis a vine, from vinum wine (itself from vis strength). So Priscian derives verbum from verberare (sc. aer) and litera (as if for legitera) from lego.

V. Some of the advantages of the study of etymology.

The word etymology ($\dot{\varepsilon}\tau \nu \mu o \lambda o \gamma \acute{\iota} \alpha$), is derived from $\check{\varepsilon}\tau \nu \mu o \varsigma$, true or real, and $\lambda \acute{o} \gamma o \varsigma$, speech. The Latin synonym, *veriloquium*, expresses the same elementary idea. So that a person is etymologically ignorant of language, who does not, like one seeing sands of gold through a limpid stream, behold within its forms, as if transparent, its etymological elements and treasures.

Among the advantages of studying etymology may be mentioned the following:

1. The high pleasure derived from it.

No study is more fascinating. "Diversions," the investigators into the origin of words, call their labors, and etymology itself they describe as "fossil poetry." It is indeed this, and more. It is fossil poetry, philosophy and history combined. In the treasured words of the past the very spirits of elder days look out upon us, as from so many crystalline spheres, with friendly recognition. We see in them the light of their eyes; we feel in them the warmth of their hearts. They are relics, they are tokens, and almost break into life again at our touch.

The etymologist unites in himself the characteristics of the traveller, roaming through strange and far-off climes; the philosopher, prying into the causes and sequences of things; the antiquary, filling his cabinet with ancient curiosities and wonders; the historiographer, gathering up the records of by-gone men and ages; and the artist, studying the beautiful designs in word-architecture, furnished him by various nations and especially by that greatest of all nations in all forms of art, the Greeks, whose language is the most perfect specimen of organism, for power and for beauty, to be found in the world of speech. Shall then the traveller, the philosopher, the antiquary, the historian and the artist, find high gratification, each in his exalted employment, and not he who unites all their occupations in one and all their pleasures in his own?

The pursuit of knowledge is always pleasant; and the mind engaged in it, walks, runs, flies in its course, as if born for any and every element; every limb instinct with motion, and every nerve vital and vivid with its impulse. The more rich the landscape is in details, and the more infinite its fulness before the ravished eye, the greater the pleasure in the survey, and the greater the consciousness of power in being able to appreciate and interpret such a wide array of beauties and wonders unto others.

Every language is polyhedral in its structure, and while for substance it is all of the same material, each side of it has a different face and different adornments from every other. He therefore who walks around about the whole castellated and turreted structure of the Latin, scanning thoroughly all its own inner beauty of height and breadth and multiform composition, and surveying, without, each wondrous side of the varied whole, its Sanskrit side and its Greek, Celtic, Gothic and Slavonic sides, one after the other, gratifies that natural love of curiosity, which is so strong an impulse to travel, research and effort in other things, and which nowhere finds a purer gratification, than in the realms of science and of letters.

As also it is one of the highest exercises of the mind, to adapt means to ends, the act of doing which we call skill in matters physical and intellectual, and wisdom in those which are moral; so it is one of the highest intellectual pleasures to trace adaptations, connections, sequences and harmonies, scientific and historical, and to find ourselves on a path of discovery in which they are perpetually coming into view, when and where we least expected them. It is specially pleasant to find analogies, mutually explaining objects before regarded as unrelated and isolated, and connecting together things widely separated and of a diverse aspect from each other. The formation of comparisons is one of the chief exercises and pleasures of the imagination. It is in this employment, that the poetic faculty in our nature, the natural fountain of youth in the heart, bursts forth in all its strength of life and joy. So much indeed are the faculties of invention and comparison stimulated into action in this study, that the tendency is ever present, to fly off from the centre of a real logical stability into the ideal and the fanciful, except in one of thoroughly scholastic habits; which indeed, as a centripetal force, balancing the opposite centrifugal tendency, serve to keep such a mind, though moving onward with delighted energy, yet true to its proper orbit of revolution.

2. Its great promotion of the higher mental discipline. Human language is the highest of all objective realms of art among men. The highest absolute realm of art on earth, as in heaven, is subjective; in the culture and perfection of character, in every thing lovely and heroic, manly and godly, according to the pure and perfect ideal presented to us, in the abstract, in the Bible, and, in the concrete, in the beautiful and sublime life of Jesus Christ. The Greeks deemed architecture, as the word shows in its very etymology, "the principal art" of life. But the art of speech transcends, in all its uses and relations, not only that of housebuilding, but also every other art that can be named among all the outward employments of men. A dead language is full of all monumental remembrances of the people who spoke it. Their swords and their shields are in it; their faces hang pictured on its walls; and their very voices ring still through its recesses. And in a living language you may see, as in a vast panorama, the whole varied busy activity and experience of a nation's present condition. Language has not merely, for height, and breadth, and organic structure as the dome of thought, all the sublime capacities of architecture; or, for severe chiselled dignity of form, all the majesty of sculpture; or, for wondrous power of imagery, all the exquisite beauty of painting; or, for sweetness and ravishment, the magic charms of music; it contains the mysteries and energies of all these exalted arts in one.

In it also, as a garner, are gathered together all the rich harvests of human genius, from every field which human thought or effort has essayed to reap. It is the archives of all man's history, migratory, civil, political, statutory, literary, scientific, experimental and personal. Surely on an area of action so wide and so varied, there must be scope enough for every kind of mental exercise and inquiry; and prizes, of every possible variety of value, must await the grasp of him who earnestly seeks for them.

And in no way, as a matter of general experience and of general testimony, can all the higher faculties of the mind be so well trained to lofty, vigorous, sustained action, as by the study of language; its analytic, philosophic, artistic, study. Classical discipline is, accordingly, the palæstra in which, throughout Christendom, the rising generation is everywhere prepared, and for ages has been, to wrestle manfully with the difficulties of after-life in whatever profession or calling. From Latin and Greek fountains, the living waters have been drawn, from which the intellectual thirst of great minds in all nations has been slaked. Those ancient languages, so often called dead, have ever had a very living use. But if the mental discipline of the civilized world has been secured thus far, to such a high degree, from the very imperfect study of language as hitherto pursued, how much more would be obtained by a deeper, broader, truer style of familiarization with its structure and spirit: so deep, and broad, and true as to seem to the mind swimming buoyantly in its depths, to be its very native element. By the study of etymology, in particular, habits of wide research, of patient comparison, of logical deduction, and of critical review are pre-eminently cultivated: all among the highest elements of mental energy and success. Who can speak too strongly of their necessity and value? or, of that insight into the living beauty of language which makes its words seem, whether standing quietly on the shore of our own thoughts, or coming and going on errands of truth and love to others, to be so many white-winged messengers, radiant themselves with the light that they bear before them?

And as the student finds in this path of study the sweet perpetually mingled with the useful, and, like one searching for gems in regions where they abound, obtains at every step a rich reward of his efforts, he feels perpetually freshened to new toil; and each new effort prepares the desire and the way for a greater. So that the spirit of study, instead of being as at first a matter of mere conscientious or manly resolve, rises rapidly into enthusiasm, spontaneity, and instinct. For there is all the excitement in such a style of classical study of pleasing travel and, more, of earnest scientific exploration and even of rare adventure. This, it may well be assumed, is the only world in which mental effort is a labor and, at times, a weariness; and the nearer that we approach the point of making real toil at the same time real joy, the nearer do we bring earth to heaven and the mortal to the immortal.

3. Its peculiar value in preparing the mind for the work of communication and communion with other minds. The chief end of knowledge and education is never personal. Their true uses are not to be found in centralization but in distribution; in participating with others, as God finds his infinite joy in doing, all one's full resources. The greatest possible benefaction to all our fellow-men: this is the true end and aim of all mental and moral culture. Language, therefore, as the divinely-constructed vehicle for communicating thought and feeling between human beings, deserves, in all its forms and details, the most complete mastery. Shut up within one's self, thought stagnates and knowledge decays. The subjective is developed by the objective; and the objective by the subjective. The creation is a great duality. Every thing exists in pairs: males and females, vegetables and animals, matter and spirit, fire and water, land and ocean, the sky and sea, light and shade, birth and death, time and space, substance and shadow, the present and future, the world without and the world within, the finite and the infinite. When man most addresses himself, yea, rather, most abandons himself to all that is without him, he becomes most conscious of all that is within him; and, when he enters into the pavilion of other minds, to shed the light of

his love upon them, or to draw the light of their spirits into his own, he knows, he feels, with what a spark of the Divinity his nature has been lighted from on high. His whole inward being unfolds at once its native splendor to his own deeply-awakened consciousness.

The genius and the power of language are best comprehended, as its words are contemplated, not so much in their separate individual character, or in their syntactical combinations, as in their formative, derivative and mutually correspondent aspects. The very processes in which they originally crystallized into their present forms, are almost enacted over again, in the laboratory of etymology. Etymology is, indeed, the chemistry of language. But not only is the genius of language, universal language or word-architecture, best comprehended by the study of etymology; skill also in the use of words, so as to be able to employ them with beautiful aptness in themselves, and with delicacy, harmony and richness of effect in combination one with the other, is thus acquired. There is as wide a difference in the use of words by different writers, as of paints by poor artists and great; and as wide a difference in the effect upon the understanding and the sensibilities of their readers. And so also, in spoken words, there is as great a variety of utterance, as in the whole array of musical instruments, from the most obscure nonsense or empty bombast or wearisome platitudes, up to the deep, pure eloquence of a heart overflowing with thought and love, on the bosom of which every hearer floats with joy, as on a sea of light and rapture.

And he who masters etymology, and to whom words take on again their original aspects of life and beauty, will become conscious, even in the use of our language, which is but a grand composite of the best parts of many other languages, of the primeval pleasure that men enjoyed who used words when in themselves they were fresh and new. They will be musical to his ears, as are the chimes of sweet bells when heard far off upon the sea, to those who themselves founded them, and dissolved their hearts in song with the melting metal, as its fiery streams ran into the strong mould. And since each human spirit throws its own light on all surrounding objects, and does but see them as they are reflected in it to its eye, a heart, that finds joy in the very utterance of its thoughts and feelings, will be sure, like one whose nature revels in the sweet concords of music, to carol forth perpetually the pent-up melodies that are ever sounding to his inner ear, in the voiceless depths of his own being, and to excite in other hearts, while doing so, the same rapture that burns with divine brightness in his own. Celestial pleasures are but labors of delight: efforts so true, so high, so joyous, that they become perpetual pastime; and he who imbues, by set purpose at first, and spontaneously afterwards, his own toils on earth with deep inward gladness, gives wings to his feet in climbing towards the holy and sublime, and charms those who behold him into an instinctive imitation of his happy, soaring flight on high.

INDEX AND MAPS.

INDEX.

A

Ablaut, in German, 147.
Achæmenidian Kings, 47.
Acro-Corinthus, 283.
Adelung, 200.
Æolic Dialect, 50, 51, 55, 62, 233.
African Languages, 18, 103.
Agglutinative Languages, 16-18.
Agriculture, 51.
Ahrens, 233.
Alaric, 65.
Albanian, 65-67, 99.
Allahabad, 203.
Alphabets, 27, 40, 48, 68, 119.
Americanisms, 141-4.
Anglo-Saxon, 133-144.
Arabic, 20, 21-22, 47, 88, 104.
Aramæan, 20,
Archaic Forms, 335.
Arian, 30-1.
Armenian, 48, 198.
Arnautic, 66.
Aryavarta, 30.
Asiatic Society, 200, 205.
Aspiration, 63, 76, 317.
Attic Dialect, 50, 67.
Aufrecht, 241.
Augustine, 21.
Auxiliary Verbs, 146.
Avesta Zend, 45.
Axioms (in Etymology), 333.

B

Babel, 198.
Babylon, 23.
Baltic Sea, 114.
Barth the Traveller, 103.
Basque Language, 102, 106, 110.
Bechuana Languages, 18.
Belgium, 111, 144.
Benary, 230-2, 247.
Benfey, 241.
Benloew, 223.
Berbers, 104.
Berlin Academy of Sciences, 199.
Bhagavad Gita, 204.
Boethius, 108.
Bopp, 212, 219-225, 240, 293, 303.
Brahma, 33, 39.
Brahmanas, 34-5.
Brahmins, 37, 203.
Brittany, 110, 155.
Buckle, 69, 288.
Budaeus, 196.
Buddhism, 38, 42.
Bulgarians, 99, 118; their Language, 123.
Bunsen, 28, 151, 174, 255.
Burnouf, 227, 249.
Buttmann, 214, 261.
Byzantium, 67, 93, 105.
Byzantine--Greek, 67, 101.

C

Cadmus, 316.
Cæsar, 109, 117.
Camoens, 106.
Carthaginians, 21, 101, 103, 298.
Caste, 42.
Castilian Dialect, 102; poetry, 105.
Castren, 17, 214.
Catharine II., 199, 260.
Caucasian Languages, 16, 17.
Celts, 66, 71, 101, 109, 134.
Celtiberians, 101.
Celtic, 28, 151, 161.
Charlemagne, 89, 93.
Chinese Language, 14, 15, 17, 168, 200.
Christian Names, 316.
Christianity, 69.
Cicero, 337.
Cid, Epic of, 105.
Classical Discipline, 342.
Climatology, 68, 80-81, 162.
Colebrooke, 33, 203, 205, 248.
Columbus, 309.
Congo Languages, 18.
Consonantal System, 22.
Corvus Valerius, 208.
Croesus, 56.
Cyclops, 288.
Cyril St., 119.
Cyrillic Alphabet, 99, 119, 123.
Cyrus, 56, 59.
Curtius, Ernst, 239.
Curtius, George, 236.

INDEX.

D

Dacia, 100, 130.
Danes, 130; their Language, 132.
David, 104.
Derived Forms, 329.
Deutsch, 53, 146.
Devanagari Alphabet, 36, 37, 40, 208.
Development-theory, 16, 167–173.
Dialects, 36, 41, 50, 66, 76, 85, 87–8, 98, 336.
Diefenbach, 156, 234, 236.
Diez, 92, 95, 96, 237, 246, 259.
Digamma, 62, 316.
Diversions of Etymology, 5, 230, 338, 343, 346.
Döderlein, 49, 261, 295, 297, 299.
Donaldson, 14, 59, 71, 121, 249–252.
Doric Dialect, 50, 55, 233.
Druids, 153.
Dual Number, 77.
Düntzer, 234, 247.
Dutch Language, 144.

E

East India Company, 203, 260.
Edda, 132.
Edomites, 254,
Education, 35.
Egyptian, 23; Old do., 152.
Eichhoff, 39, 228–30.
Emigrations, 47, 71, 74, 91.
Empiricism, 45, 49, 222, 238, 287–290.
English, 134–144.
Erasmus, 196.
Ethnography, 199, 269–272.
Etruscan. (See Tuscan), 70–74.
Etymology: Greek love for it, 125; Critical and Uncritical Methods, 238, 259; Science of it, &c., 277–347; History of it, 278–311.
Etymologies: Particular ones, 33, 48, 73, 110, 146, 217, 317–322, 335.—False ones, 288–9.
Eugubine Tables, 78.
Euphony, 317, 332–3.

F

Ferdousi, the poet, 47.
Flemish Language, 144.
Franks, 89, 109.
French Language, 108–113, 144.
French People, 109.
Freund, 293–297.
Frisic, 144, 213.
Fritsch, 247.

G

Gabelentz, 17.
Gadhelic and Gaelic, 157.
Gallic, 110–111.
Garnett, 255.
Gascony, 110.
Genesis, 162.
Germans, 53, 86-7, 150.
German Language, generally, 21, 104, 137, 149; its Influence on Latin, 89–95.
German, High, 145–151; Old do., 89, 147.
German Mind, 308.

Gesenius, 21.
Giese, 62, 230.
Glago-litic Alphabet, 124.
Goths, 90.
Gothic Language, 65, 130, 151.
Græcia Magna, 60.
Græco-Italic race, 48–112.
Grammar, 19, 194; Comparative, 325.
Grammarians, 39, 40.
Grammatical Correspondence, 19, 73.
Grammatical Irregularities Solved, 266–268.
Greek, Ancient, 48–70.
Greek, Modern, 64.
Grimm, 147, 215; his Scale, 216, 240, 313; his Dictionary, 307; his Scholarship, 313.
Guna, 231.
Gutturals, 317.
Gypsy Language, 43–45, 53, 226.

H

Halhed, 203–4.
Hamilton, 206.
Harris, 256.
Harrison, 134.
Hastings, Warrren, 203.
Heathenism, 68–70.
Hebrew, 20, 22, 26, 104, 138, 197.
Heliand, 145.
Hellas, 53.
Hellenes, 53; Hellenic Greek, 58–64, 75.
Heroism of a Student's life, 209.
Heyne, 261.
Heyse, 242, 259.
Hibernia, 101, 158.
Hieronymus, 119.
Hoefer, 232.
Home-growth of Greeks, 36, 54–63.
Home-growth of Romans, 74.
Homer, 33, 49, 61–62, 67.
Huc, 35.
Humboldt, William, 102, 226.

I

Iapygian, 70–1.
Iberians, 101.
Icelanders, 114; their Language, 132.
Iliad, 46, 62, 147.
Illyrian, 65.
India: its Climatology, 68–70.
Indische Bibliothek, 210.
Indische Skizzen, 243.
Indische Studien, 243.
Inflection, 16.
Inscriptions, 37, 45–7, 70.
Inventiveness of men small, 164–178.
Ionic Dialect, 50.
Iran, 30, 45, 48, 158.
Iranian, 45–48.
Irish, 157–8.
Italian, 87, 95.
Italic race, 50, 70–112.

J

Jäkel, 297.
Jones, Sir Wm., 151, 200, 203–4, 248.
Judaism and its influence, 26, 43, 59, 86,

INDEX. 353

K

Kaltschmidt, 234.
Kemble, 256.
Klotz, 299.
Koshas, 205.
Kuhn, A., 241, 243.
Kymric Languages, 154, 156, 157.

L

Language: Divine Origin of, 16, 164-178; Impressibility of, 85, 98; History of, 258; Philosophy of, 259; its Imperishableness, 268; its Capacities, 341; Pleasure of studying it philologically, 264-6.
Languages: (1.) Monosyllabic, 15-6, 226; (2.) Agglutinative, 15; (3.) Inflected, 18-200, 226; Dead, 19, 144.
Latham, 256.
Latin: its Characteristics, 82-5; its History, 83-97; Specimens of its different phases, 83, 84, 94; its relations to other languages, 281-4; its relations to the English, 278.
Latium: its Climatology, 79-82.
Lautlehre (phonetics), 218.
Lautverschiebung, 94, 96, 147.
Lechish, 127.
Liebnitz, 199.
Lepsius, 40.
Lettic, 113.
Lettish, 116-117.
Lexicography, specific: History of, 292-311; Comparative do., 322-325.
Lithuanian, 113-116, 317.
Livingstone, 54.
Lobeck, 299.
Locative Case, 77.
Lombards, 89.
Lord's Prayer, 200.
Low-German, 132-145.
Lusiad, 106.
Luther, 147, 196.
Lyrics, 33, 104.

M

Macbeth, 305.
Macpherson, 153.
Mahâbâratah, 39, 204.
Maltese, 23.
Mantras, 34-35.
Manx, 158.
Materialism, 162. See Climatology.
Mechanical Study, 211.
Meyer, Charles, 157.
Middle Ages, 85-90.
Middle Latin, 85-95.
Mohammedism, 24, 47.
Mommsen, 77, 239, 292.
Monosyllabism, 14-15, 168-174.
Moors, 103-104.
Müller, Max, 173-5, 256, 259.
Muretus, 197.

N

Nature: its power over man, 46. See Climatology, Materialism, &c.
Niebelungen, 147.

Niebuhr, 14, 60.
Nork, 198.
Normans, 134.
Norse Languages, 132-133.
North American Languages, 15.
Norwegian, 132.

O

Objectivity, 32.
Orthoepy, 140-142.
Orthography, 140-142.
Oscan, 51, 75-76.
Ossetian, 48.
Ossian, 152.
Ostrogoths, 89, 131.

Pali Language, 41-42.
Pânini, the Grammarian, 39.
Parkhurst's Dictionary, 198.
Passow, 293, 300-301, 306.
Pazend, 47.
Pehlevi, 47.
Pelasgian, 36, 58-64, 73.
Persia, 25.
Persian, 45-6, 88; its influence on Hellenic Greek, 58-60, 201.
Peter the Great, 119.
Philology: its condition here, 8; a delightful study, 5; its influence on Ethnography, 57; its History, 194-280; Classical Philology, 262.
Philosophy, Schools of, 34.
Phœnicia, 20, 25, 26, 27, 298.
Phonetics, 38, 98, 106, 115, 117, 259. Comparative Phonology, 312-322, 326.
Phonography, 244.
Pictet, 101, 157.
Poland and the Poles, 122, 127-8, 317.
Polysyllabism, 15.
Pompey, 117.
Popery, 34, 80, 121.
Portuguese, 87, 105-107.
Pott, 255.
Pråkrit, 37, 41-42.
Pråtisåkhyas, 38.
Prepositions, 16, 18, 63.
Prichard, 28, 67, 151, 248-9, 281.
Priests, 34, 87.
Prosody: rules of, explained, 67.
Provence, 107. Provençal Dialect, 107-8.
Prussian, Old, 116.
Puranas, 38.
Purley, Diversions of, 256, 302,
Pushtu, 47.

R

Rapp, 244, 332.
Râmâyana, 39.
Rask, 17, 212, 215, 249.
Rawlinson, 23.
Remus, 288.
Reuchlin, 196.
Reynouard, 108.
Richter, 285.
Rome: its situation, 79-83.
Romaic Language, 67.
Romanic Languages, 87-112, 284.

Romance, 47, 108.
Roman Influence, 82
Romulus, 288.
Roots, 327, 328, 332.
Rosen, 249.
Ross, Ludwig, 292.
Ruskin, 109.
Russian, 120, 128.

S

Salmasius, 197.
Sandhi, 159.
Sanskrit, 31–43; its Literature, 202, 229.
Sappho, 104.
Sassanides, 47.
Saxon, 145.
Scaliger, 197, 299.
Schlegel, Augustus, 105, 210–2, 224.
Schlegel, Frederic, 206–9, 240.
Schleicher, 67, 124, 234, 242, 259.
Scholarship (German, 219, 313), 334.
Schwenck, 49, 297.
Scriptures, Indian, 33.
Semitic Languages, 19, 20–27, 43, 309.
Servians, 125.
Sibilants, 76, 118.
Shakspeare, 135–6.
Siksha, 38.
Slavonic Languages, 117–131.
Solomon, 25, 33, 38.
Spanish, 87, 100.
State-Languages, 20.
Subjectivity, 32.
Swedish, 132.
Syllabication, 316, 326.

T

Tabular Views, 181-90.
Tatar Languages, 16, 17.
Teutonic Grammar, Grimm's, 215, 240.
Tooke, Horne, 256, 302.
Trajan, 100.
Trench, 256.
Troubadours, 107–8.
Turànian Languages, 16, 17, 43.
Turkish, 17.
Tuscans, 33, 254, 298.

U

Ulphilas' Translation, 59, 215.
Umbrians, 75–79.
Umbro-Samnite Dialects, 76.
Unity of the Race, 162.
Upanishads, 35.

V

Valpy, 49.
Vandals, 101–105.
Varro, 299, 337.
Vater, 200.
Vêdas, 33 39, 202.
Vienna, 260.
Vindhya, 30.
Visigoths, 90, 92, 131.
Vossius, 299.
Vriddhi, 233.

W

Wachter, 299.
Wallachian, 87, 99–100, 112.
Weber, 243; Sketch by, 272.
Webster, Noah, 198, 293, 302–306.
Weil, Henri, 223.
Welsh, 58–59, 157, 159–161.
Whitney, Prof., 38, 224.
Wilkins, Charles, 203, 248.
Wilkins, I., 204.
Wilson, H. H., 205–6, 248.
Winning, 252–255.

Y

Yajnyas, 3.

Z

Zeitschrift fur Vergleich, &c., 240
Zend, 39, 45–46, 213.
Zeuss, 236.
Zoroaster, 31, 46.

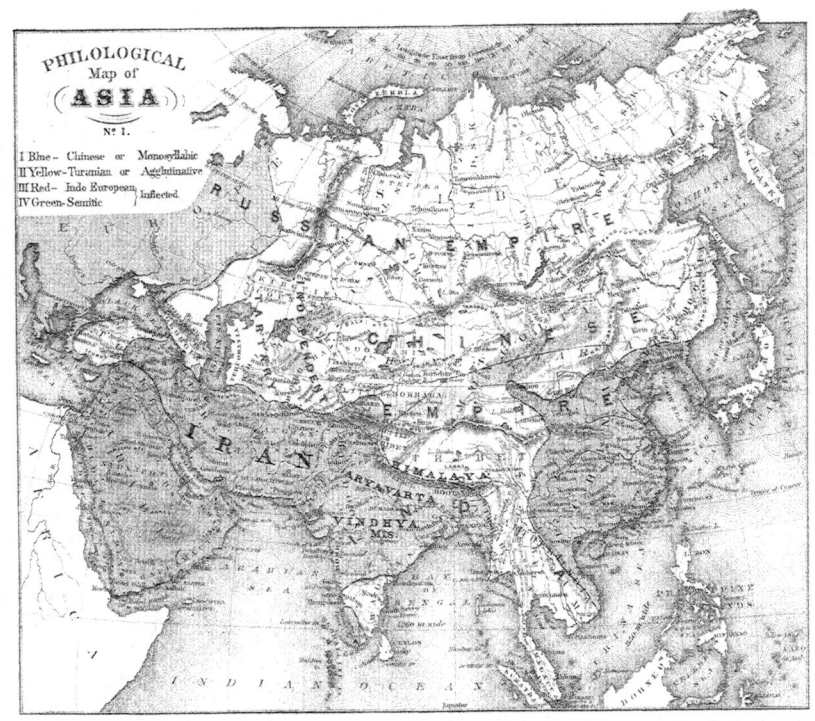

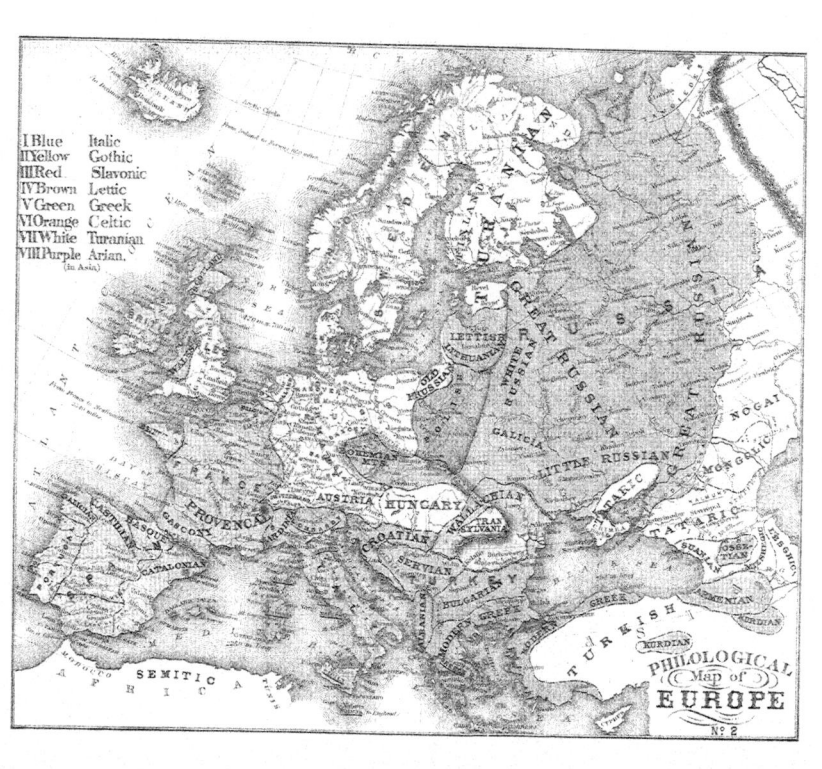

For the sake of facilitating in every way possible the study of Philology in this country, the author has taken pains to obtain a list of prices of the principal authors referred to, from the two firms of booksellers, from which he has obtained his own supply of books, and whose promptness no less than their integrity he is happy, from long experience, to commend. B. Westermann & Co., No. 440 Broadway, New York, will furnish the following books, unbound, at the prices named.

Bopp's Vergleichende Grammatik, 3 vols.	$10 50
Bopp's Vokalismus	1 38
Bopp's Accentuations System	1 75
Bopp's Grammatik Der Sanskrita-Sprache	2 25
Bopp's Glossarium Sanskritum	6 00
Rapp's Vergleich. Grammatik, 3 vols.	5 00
Grimm's Teutonische Grammatik, 5 vols.	17 38
Grimm's Geschichte Der Deutsch. Sprache	3 50
Diefenbach's Gothisches Wörterbuch, 2 vols.	8 00
Diefenbach's Celtica	6 00
Mommsen's Römische Geschichte	3 88
Schleicher's Linguist. Untersuchungen	2 50
Schleicher's Litauische Grammatik	1 75
Heyse's System der Sprachwissenschaft	2 25
Diez's Grammatik der Roman Sprachen	6 63
Diez's Lexicon Etymologicum	3 50
Pott's Etymologische Forschungen. 1st vol.	4 38
Aufrecht's Umbrisch. Sprachdenkmäler.	8 38
Kuhn's Beitrage zur Sprachforschung. Per vol.	3 50
Gesenii Monumenta	10 50
Gloss. Med. Latin, (Du Fresne, Du Cange, &c.).	18 00
Giese's Æolischer Dialekt. 2 parts	2 00
Eichhoff's Vergleich. der Sprachen	2 75
Humboldt's Verschiedenheit der Sprachen	3 50

Lersch's Sprachphilosophie	$3 50
Curtius' Griechische Schulgrammatik	63
Curtius' Griechische Etymologie. Vol. I.	2 38
Benary's Römische Lautlehre	1 00
Hoefer's Beiträge zur Etymologie	2 25
Düntzer's Lehre, &c.	1 25
Corssen's Aussprach, Vokalismus, &c., des Lateinischen	4 50
Zeitschrift der Vergleich, Sprachforschung, (bi-monthly). Per year	3 00
Max Müller's Survey of Languages	1 50
Garnett's Philological Essays	1 85

Of D. Appleton & Co., 348 Broadway, New York.

Niebuhr's Rome, 3 vols.	$10 00
Niebuhr's Ancient History, 3 vols.	5 50
Brown's History of Greek Classical Literature	1 75
Brown's History of Roman Classical Literature	1 75
Donaldson's New Cratylus	5 50
Donaldson's Varronianus	3 50
Bunsen's Philosophy of Universal History, 2 vols.	9 00
Bopp, translated by Eastwick, 3 vols.	16 00
Winning's Comparative Philology	3 00
Monier Williams' Sanskrit Grammar	4 00
Prichard's Natural History of Man, 2 vols.	10 00
Prichard's Eastern Origin Celtic Nations	4 50
F. Schlegel's Æsthetical Works	1 25

THE END.

Printed in Dunstable, United Kingdom